A Study of the Turning Point of China's Debt

Xiaohuang Zhu • Song Lin • Lin Wang
Wenqi Wu • Quanli Qin

A Study of the Turning Point of China's Debt

Springer

Xiaohuang Zhu
CITIC Group
Beijing, China

Lin Wang
Risk Management Division
China Construction Bank
Beijing, China

Quanli Qin
RenMin University of China
Beijing, China

Song Lin
Central University of Finance and Economics
Beijing, China

Wenqi Wu
China Asset Management Company
Beijing, China

ISBN 978-981-13-1324-0 ISBN 978-981-13-1325-7 (eBook)
https://doi.org/10.1007/978-981-13-1325-7

Library of Congress Control Number: 2018948363

Printed on acid-free paper

This Springer imprint is published by the registered company Springer Nature Singapore Pte Ltd.
The registered company address is: 152 Beach Road, #21-01/04 Gateway East, Singapore 189721, Singapore

Preface

Debt is an organic component of the macroeconomy. A country or region cannot run smoothly without a reasonable amount of debt; however, excessive debt can significantly weigh down the macroeconomy. China's ballooning debt in recent years has raised concerns at home and abroad. Institutions and scholars hold divided opinions – with some even predicting that China's excessive debt could trigger an economic crisis.

The 2015 Central Economic Work Conference emphasized "de-leveraging" as one of the government's five major tasks. The Expert Opinion column of the *People's Daily* in 2016 diagnosed a high leverage ratio as the "original sin" and the "culprit of high financial risks"; it prescribed "de-leveraging according to the requirements of supply-side structural reform" as the cure. Meanwhile, the State Council recently released the *Emergency Response Contingency Plan for Local Government Debt Risks*, working to establish a tiered response mechanism for local debt risks. The plan specified four types of government debt risk events based on their nature, reach, and damage: grade IV (moderate), grade III (moderately severe), grade II (severe), and grade I (major). This policy was introduced to call for market-oriented, law-based measures to defuse government debt risks, to identify the bottom line in risk prevention, to establish a mechanism for early warning and tiered responses, to strengthen the accountability for risk events, and to ensure that no regional or systemic threats arise. It seems safe to say that China stands poised to tackle its debt dilemma.

Nevertheless, there are still many difficult questions to answer about debt issues and economic development, such as the following: How should the current size of China's debt be measured? Is the current volume of China's debt within a reasonable range? What is the debt situation in different social sectors? In what sectors should China begin de-leveraging? These fundamental questions require profound, clear, scientific, and quantitative elaboration.

This book explores new methods for measuring China's total debt. Quantitative analysis is used to study the relationship between debt volume and economic growth. This examination suggests that China's total debt level has surpassed the turning point; this means its influence on GDP has become negative. The book further probes into the relationship between government debt, debt in the banking sector and economic growth. The research indicates that for the central government, debt is still positively related to economic growth; but for local government, debt has exceeded the turning point and has been a drag on the economy for many years. Meanwhile, debt in China's banking sector is now on the verge of exceeding its notable turning point and may begin to take a toll on GDP growth. In addition to debt in the macroeconomy, the book also analyzes the leverage in various industries. The analysis reveals that debt in the chemical fiber manufacturing industry might have come to its turning point in 2014 when PTA capacity peaked, while debt in the petrochemical industry might have crossed its turning point in 2011. As for the industrial chain of the real estate industry, debt within the coal industry reached its turning point in 2011, with steel industry reaching its turning point the following year and the nonferrous metals industry and real estate industry reaching their turning points in 2013. Meanwhile, the debt of the building materials industry has yet to reach its turning point. Another finding of this research is that the turning point in the industrial chain of the real estate industry is "contagious" from upstream industries to downstream – an order opposite to that of the business cycle. The analysis of the real economy and the virtual economy in this book suggests that since 2009, the ratio between the two in China has gone beyond a reasonable range, which means that the virtual economy has ballooned and deviated from the real economy.

This book is aimed at satisfying the actual needs of China's economic and social development. Further, it offers quantitative models and research conclusions concerning debt analysis. The research results can fully serve the supply-side structural reform and facilitate the adjustment and optimization of the economic structure.

Beijing, China

Xiaohuang Zhu
Song Lin
Lin Wang
Wenqi Wu
Quanli Qin

Contents

About the Author

About the lead author

Professor Xiaohuang Zhu was born on July 2, 1956, in Cili County, Hunan Province. He obtained his doctorate in international economy from Lingnan College of Sun Yat-sen University in 2006.

Zhu previously worked in China Construction Bank as the executive director and then as deputy president/chief risk officer. In August 2012, he was appointed as the deputy general manager of CITIC Ltd. and president of CITIC Bank. In May 2014, Zhu became chairman of the supervisory board of the CITIC Group Corporation. He is a part-time professor at Renmin University of China, Wuhan University, Shenzhen University, and Hunan University. As a senior economist, Zhu is entitled to the State Council Special Allowance. He also serves as the vice chairman of China Behavior Law Association and chairman of its Branching Financial and Legal Behavior Research Society. Professor Zhu has published a variety of monographs and collections of works including *The New Study of Economic Law*, *Random Collections of Past Days*, *Lingnan Notes*, *Risk Management of Commercial Banks*, *Be Away from Iceberg*, *Weaving Net While Standing at Riverside*, *Value Banks*, and *Faith in Wealth*.

Chapter 1
Debt and Economic Growth

It is a universal rule that quantitative accumulation will ultimately lead to qualitative transformation and, during this process, there is an turning point where the former ends and the latter starts. The point can demonstrate how things' natures change at the junction between two phases. In view of mankind's current cognitive capabilities, such a turning point can be deduced from adequate data through mathematic, metrological and modelling methods, based on which we can assess theories concerning the past and the future. This is a modern technique applicable to all scientific studies, including those of the social sciences. Present day economic studies can pinpoint the turning points of many economic phenomena in their evolutionary processes, providing some guidance on policies and strategies.

1.1 Theoretical Basis of Debt Studies

1.1.1 Classical Economic Growth Models

Debt studies are essentially aimed at exploring the relationship between debt and economic growth. In economic theories, that is the focus of economic growth theories and models.

In general terms, economic growth theories concentrate on the economic aggregates in a specific region or country and, using the methodology of equilibrium analysis, establish a particular economic model and discuss the conditions required for a stable equilibrium among various factors in the long-term development process. Under this condition, the economic aggregates of a region or country will grow with certain characteristics. According to economic growth theories, the 'economic aggregates' of a region or country usually refers to the sum of all goods and services produced in a given period by that region or country as an individual economy. In some cases, economic growth theories also look at real output per capita, calculated using the total population of a region or country.

X. Zhu et al., *A Study of the Turning Point of China's Debt*,
https://doi.org/10.1007/978-981-13-1325-7_1

Sources of economic growth, namely those factors that might impact economic growth, are at the heart of economic growth theories. In macroeconomic theories, scholars often study the impact of various factors on economic growth and the equilibrium among factors using the production function. The Harrod–Domar model, proposed in the 1930s, is the earliest model of economic growth.

The Harrod–Domar model is based on Keynesian economics and assumes that there is only one type of product in a society, which is not only a capital good, but also a consumer good; at the same time, there is only one sector and one production technology. To produce the aforementioned goods, this model also assumes that only two production factors exist: labour and capital. The two factors are used in a fixed proportion to produce goods and cannot be substituted for one another. Additionally, the model introduces the factors of time and capital, thus making Keynesian theories dynamic in the long run.

At its core, the Harrod–Domar model seeks to explain the conditions for steady economic growth, causes of economic fluctuations and how the economy can be regulated to achieve long-term balanced growth. According to its assumptions, to achieve the steady growth of a society's economy, the expected investment demand of investors must be equal to the supply of savings in the same period: in this way, savings can be translated into investments so as to achieve equality between the two and, thus, to promote steady economic growth. Subject to many restrictions, this model assumes that there are constant returns to scale and does not allow for a society's technological progress. Hence, it became the target of fierce criticism from neoclassical economists who proposed the Solow growth model to replace it in the 1950s.

The Solow growth model is also called 'the neoclassical growth model' and 'the exogenous growth model'. This model uses Cobb–Douglas' production function to describe the production process of a whole society. It, like the Harrod–Domar model, assumes that a society's savings can all be translated into investments. Nevertheless, it holds that investment and capital, as two factors of production, can be substituted for each other and that the marginal return of investment is diminishing; additionally, it identifies the significance of technology in the production function.

As the results of the Solow growth model indicate, capital is not the only major determinant of the long-term growth rate of economic aggregates; the increase of labour and technological progress also play a critical role in economic growth. In view of the labour factor, in addition to an increase of workforce, its overall quality – especially its increasing technology-related capabilities – is conducive to economic development. Yet, the Solow growth model has a clear limit, for it ignores the investment function. In reality, capital and labour cannot be completely substituted for each other. The model can thus ignore the important role played by entrepreneurs in integrating these two factors.

1.1.2 The New Institutional Economics and Economic Growth

In contrast to the Solow growth model, the new institutional economics holds that, apart from capital, labour and technology, the institutional environment of a country is also a key factor in promoting economic growth. First, institutions can determine transaction costs in the market and thus determine the capability of a producer to obtain investment, a labour force and technology. In this way, they can have an impact on the rate of economic growth. Second, institutions also determine the incentive structures of organizations and workforces, and thus impact the potential technological innovations of economic organizations, thereby either promoting or hindering economic growth.

First, the new institutional economics argues that lower transaction costs can be the fundamental guarantee ensuring that the market functions well. With relatively low transaction costs, both parties to a transaction can have a clearer understanding of market supply and demand, and transactions can be settled in a more explicit and smoother manner. When coordinating capital, labour and technology for economic activities, producers are able to achieve an economic output at a lower cost. Meanwhile, a highly specialized system and detailed division of labour can develop across the economy, which will improve the economy's output efficiency. In the new institutional economics, transaction costs are determined by various factors, including institutional frameworks, policy and legal systems, and the social and cultural environment of a country. Governments play a critical role in the institutional environment, as most institutions are made and implemented by them. Hence, governments must be able to create an institutional framework that can proactively and effectively decrease transaction costs and make transaction rules more formalized and transparent.

Second, progress in technology, the most important factor in the Solow growth model, is closely tied to the institutional environment. In general, technological development is prompted by three factors. The first factor is the creativity of human beings. Humans essentially make technological progress possible. Technological research and development and innovations can involve a long and costly process. Hence, if a society does not have a sound institutional environment that can encourage people to undertake research activities, it will be difficult for organizations and individuals to be actively engaged in technological development. The second factor is a well-functioning capital market. Technological innovations require a constant inflow of capital, and funds from individuals or organizations can hardly satisfy their financial needs for long-term development. In that scenario, an effective capital market can draw funds from different sources so as to provide financial support for promising technological innovations. Third, effective market competition is also important for technological development. It can serve as an essential approach for evaluating the market value of technologies developed by individuals and organizations, and only those surviving market competition can boast of a promising future. Therefore, it can be concluded that the three factors above are all closely related to the institutional environment of a country. A sound institutional framework can sufficiently encourage technological progress and innovation, thereby nourishing economic growth.

1.1.3 The Population Problem in Economic Growth

The importance of increases in workforce, emphasized in the Solow growth model, has been challenged by the macroeconomic activities of various countries, primarily due to the weakening demographic dividend.

The demographic dividend is evaluated based on the distribution of a country's labour force. If the working-age population is a large share of the total in a country, a decent number of workers are available for production in that society, and people will not need to pay high child-care and pension costs. This will facilitate economic activities and growth. The demographic dividend can also provide strong support for the role of labour in the Solow growth model. In existing studies, scholars in China and abroad have established various models with different measures, and their results all indicate that the demographic dividend can significantly impact economic growth. The research on China's economic activities has in particular demonstrated the importance of the demographic dividend. However, due to differences in indicators and measures, the impact of the demographic dividend on economic growth may vary to some extent. According to existing studies, the huge growth in the size of a workforce, driven by the demographic dividend, can impact economic growth in three ways. First, the increasing supply of labour can help to achieve economies of scale, thus improving overall output in the economy. Second, it can also promote an increase in the savings ratio and investment rate, thereby accelerating economic growth. Third, as the life expectancy of the workforce increases, people's perceptions of human capital investment change, which then creates more opportunities for using technological inventions, improving the quality of labour and boosting economic growth. Overall, therefore, existing studies have acknowledged that the demographic dividend has been an important driver of rapid economic development in China and East Asia in recent years.

However, in view of the reality in China, the positive impact of the demographic dividend is constantly diminishing. Both economic growth and population theories show that the demographic dividend in a country is not a sustainable factor for that country's development. The overall aging of the workforce also means the end of the demographic dividend. China has implemented a family planning policy since the 1980s, leading to a constant decrease in the birth rate. Although the two-child policy has been in effect in recent years, a change in the birth rate is still a long way off. At present, the aging trend in China is accelerating. Hence, in the long run, the workforce may account for a smaller share of the total, and the demographic dividend assisting China's economic growth will be constantly weakened. The labour-driven growth model will therefore be significantly transformed.

1.2 Debt and Economic Growth

Debt plays an important role in economic growth, which has been especially evident since 1980s, when debt-driven economic growth took hold in many Western countries and the United States in particular through financialization, during which time economic growth was accompanied by a rising fiscal deficit, corporate debt, consumer credit and international trade deficit.

The fundamental feature of debt-driven growth is that it allows major social sectors to invest and consume first and to accumulate and profit later through borrowing money. During this process, debt serves as advanced capital supporting the operation of social sectors, after which lenders repay their debt, creating a virtuous cycle of economic activities. A debt-driven economy, in which the cost of borrowing money is reduced, provides social sectors with easier access to capital, facilitating social investment and consumption. When coming from other sectors, such advanced capital means that those sectors idle resources are full utilized; when drawn from future income, it indicates the continuity of social sectors' accumulation and reproduction processes.

Despite its merits, a debt-driven economy risks bringing dire consequences once the economy becomes over-dependent on debt and the debt build-up exceeds a normal range. The greatly reduced cost of investment and financing in a debt-driven economy encourages investment efforts across social sectors, including some sunset sectors with bleak prospects, resulting in overheated investment or even financial bubbles. For example, in theory, central and local governments can boost domestic demand and thus economic growth through infrastructure investment while keeping debt in a reasonable range through macro-control. Yet, academically and practically speaking, it is not 'the more the merrier' with central and local government debt, which begs the question of what the parameters of debt management should be: where should the boundaries on debt be set to maximize its productive force while keeping its counter-productive force in check?

Continuous debt expansion may prompt financial institutions, an important capital intermediary in the social economy, to venture into risky speculation, making the already fragile debt chain even more so. Once the debt chain fractures, a financial crisis becomes unavoidable. This is exactly what happened in 2008 with the 'sub-prime crisis' in the United States.

Thus far, the text has provided a general account of the relationship between debt and economic growth. The following will break down the impact of debt on economic growth from the perspective of different debtors.

1. **Central government debt**

This section mainly focuses on treasury bonds issued by central governments, which are an important source of state income. By issuing treasure bonds, the central government can pool together superfluous savings on the credit market and reinvest it to improve infrastructure, the social security system and people's livelihoods, thus meeting the demands of economic growth.

Compared with other fiscal instruments, treasury bonds have advantages, especially in times of economic recession. During a recession, the actual national income is lower than the potential national income and the government's budget deficit is very high. If the government choses to increase state revenue and reduce the deficit through higher tax rates, people will have less money in their pockets and bank accounts; hence, there will be less social capital for investment, which will ultimately aggravate the economic recession. However, if the government chose to turn public savings into investment by issuing treasury bonds, it can close the gap in the fiscal deficit while spurring economic growth.

Despite treasury bonds' merits, the amount issued should also be kept within a reasonable range. Excessive treasure bonds, on one hand, can negatively influence the long-term actual interest rate and social investment and, on the other hand, worsen fiscal imbalances or trigger a bank or currency crisis. Increasing debt and issuing currency as a way of repaying government debt are equally detrimental to the economy.

2. **Local government debt**

Local government debt is good for economic growth in two ways: Pooling together the capital necessary for local economic regulation is an important tool of macro-control for regional governments. This is especially true in places where the local government is financially inadequate and local financial institutions are not mature enough. Second, issuing debt enables regional governments to provide better public products and services, as money raised through issuing debt is usually spent on local infrastructure construction and public product production, thus boosting local development and improving living conditions.

But, like central government debt, local government debt also has its limits, which are determined by government revenue. A local government that issues more debt than it can repay will put itself under huge pressure, struggling to meet deadlines through strenuous efforts and finally getting stuck in a vicious circle of debt. Once a government fails to cough up enough of a payment on the due day, its expenditure will soon be compromised, preventing it from operating on-going projects and even from performing necessary functions. Furthermore, a debt crisis at the local level will eventually put more pressure on the central government, which usually foots the bill for local governments.

3. **Corporate debt**

Companies, as a major part of the modern economy and society, create value and satisfy market demand. Corporate debt, which mainly supports corporate operations and management, can be divided into three categories: long-term debt that serves long-term capital needs, short-term debt that makes up for temporary capital shortages and payables arising from daily operations. A company's long-term debt mainly supports its production and investment activities under its long-term strategy, including equipment purchasing, technology introduction, new product development and mergers and acquisitions. Short-term debt is a makeshift solution allowing companies to bridge over a temporary lack of funds, such as to smooth hitches in capital turnover or to cover an impromptu purchase. Operating payables are closely linked with a company's daily operations, such as regular purchases, stock management and salary payments. Debt is a basic financing instrument for companies, and a reasonable amount of debt is necessary for the development of both companies and the national economy.

With that being said, companies cannot afford to build their debt load too high. If companies borrow money faster than they can earn it, their debt will pile up, consuming corporate capital that could otherwise be spent on research and development and mergers and acquisitions, thus undermining their innovation, transformation and upgrading efforts. And, when such a case is prevalent throughout an industry, the entire industry's ability to innovate and upgrade will stagnate. Besides, high corporate debt, mostly banks loans, will increase banks' financial risks and reduce the efficiency of regional resource allocation.

4. **Debt in the financial sector**

This section focuses on the banking sector. As the financial intermediary for the entire society and economy, banks usually have abundant capital, good credit and many financial products, making their sound operations crucial to the stability of both the financial system and the national economy as a whole. Therefore, debt in the banking sector has an important influence on economic growth.

Debt service constitutes the cornerstone of the banking sector, which is the credit intermediary of the entire society. The size and stability of a bank's debt determines the size and stability of its assets and intermediate business. Therefore, commercial banks usually make debt structure the priority of risk management. A reasonable debt structure can facilitate assets and intermediate business, providing great potential for a banks' overall development. Excessive debt, an unreasonable debt structure or an unbalanced ratio between long-term and short-term debt will hinder assets and intermediate business having less mobility, thus putting a brake on the development of commercial banks or even jeopardizing the stability of the national economy and society.

5. **Household debt**

Household debt is defined as the amount of money that all adults in a household owe financial institutions, which is an important factor in household consumption. As the current capital market in China is not mature enough to offer the public adequate financial products for investment and consumption, debt is an important choice for people to conduct inter-temporal consumption and improve their livelihoods.

Household debt has clear microscopic consequences. Within their range of repaying ability, individuals can complement their income with some debt to purchase expensive products and improve their life quality; yet, too much debt will put mounting pressure on families' living standards. Household debt has clear macroscopic consequences too. Rapid growth of household debt will encourage irrational consumption among middle- and even low-income families, disturbing normal consumption structures and industry development. Too much household debt also implies higher risks for the financial system. Higher debt often comes with a higher default rate, leaving commercial banks to take the brunt of bad loans. Therefore, household debt has a significant influence on social stability, financial security and the entire macroeconomy.

6. **Foreign debt**

Foreign debt is money borrowed by a country from foreign citizens, companies or governments. With deepening globalization and increasing capital account mobility, reasonably increasing foreign debt is conducive to economic development, especially for developing countries with low foreign debt, in the following ways: first, foreign debt can serve as a substitute for domestic debt, reducing the effect on domestic interest rates and the cost of financing, thus avoiding the potential negative impact on economic growth caused by massive debt; second, medium- and long-term foreign debt is usually invested in infrastructure construction, which facilitates economic development. Moreover, foreign debt often has spillover effects for technology and innovation, boosting research and development and organizational and institutional innovation, as well as employment and occupational training.

Yet, excessive foreign debt or unbalanced foreign debt structure, like too much commercial debt or medium- to long-term debt, will heighten risks and stem economic growth.

1.3 Theoretic Meaning of Turning Point of Debt

1.3.1 Economic Meaning of the Turning Point

'Turning point' has different definitions in mathematics and economics. In mathematics, turning point means a point on a curve where the curve changes from being concave (concave downward) to convex (concave upward), or vice versa; while in economics, turning point refers to changes in a trend or situation (a turning point) instead of a change of sign in second derivative (from being above 0 to below 0 or vice versa).

Two of the more important turning points in economics are the Lewis turning point and the turning point of the Kuznets curve. The Lewis turning point often occurs in developing countries having a dual economic structure, where rural labour lives on subsistence wages due to a labour surplus and low agricultural productivity. And, since the industrial sector pays higher salaries than does the agricultural industry, it is able to attract a continuous flow of rural labour without having to raise salaries too much. At this stage, the curve of labour supply and demand is flat. Later, massive migration of rural labour will force agricultural productivity to improve and result in a labour shortage in rural areas, eventually driving up rural salaries. Therefore, the Lewis turning point refers to the point when surplus labour changes from being infinite to being limited and salaries start to rise from a stationary level.

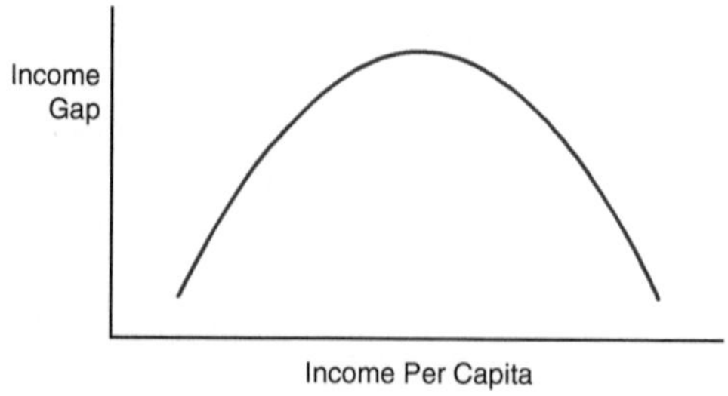

Fig. 1.1 Kuznets curve

The Kuznets curve describes the relationship between economic growth and income distribution, as well as the environmental problems of a country with an inverted U-shaped curve. With income distribution, as an economy grows, income inequality first increases to a high point before it declines, suggesting that when an economy grows to a fairly high level, its focus will shift from efficiency to equality. The same rule applies to environmental pollution, which rises as an economy grows to a high point before descending. The high point in both cases is what we call the turning point of the Kuznets curve. Thus, the Kuznets curve for the environment represents the inverted U-shaped changes of environmental degradation (Fig. 1.1).

1.3.2 *Economic Meaning of the Turning Point of Debt*

In economics, the relationship between debt, one factor of production and economic growth follows the law of diminishing marginal utility.

1. **Short-term effect of debt**

The relationship between the short term input and output of debt follows the law of diminishing returns, which is also called the law of diminishing marginal productivity, meaning that in the production process, as we increase the input of a production factor while keeping the input of other factors unchanged, there is a decline in the marginal utility derived from each additional unit of that factor after it reaches a certain level.

The law of diminishing marginal utility is based on the condition that technology and the input of other production factors are kept constant. In terms of a specific industry or economy, when debt becomes part of its production funding, there will be a decline in the marginal utility derived from each additional unit of debt resources. In other words, although output will at first grow, with the second derivative of the equation being negative, the growth rate will start to slow down, finally reaching the limit and taking a downturn, and this is when the marginal utility of debt starts to decline (Fig. 1.2).

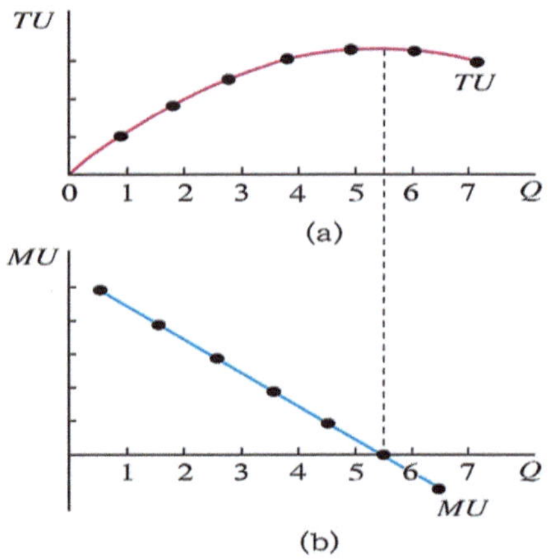

Fig. 1.2 Short-term effect of debt

2. **Long-term effect of debt**

In view of the long-term effect of production, debt as a factor of production will impact output in the way suggested by the law of decreasing returns to scale as long as the other conditions are kept constant. In economics, 'decreasing returns to scale' means the situation where output increases by less than the proportional change in factors of production. Western economists suggest that the change in enterprises' returns to scale might follow a pattern: When a small start-up enterprise begins to grow fast, it enters a period of increasing returns to scale; driven by profits, it may continue expanding its production after benefiting from a larger scale of production, and its returns will remain scale invariant at this stage. However, if it aggressively over-pursues market dominance and market share and thus keeps expanding its production, it is likely to enter a period of decreasing returns to scale.

Similarly, for an industry or a country, if the economy begins to take off after the initial stage, it will enter a period of increasing returns to scale; driven by profits and economic benefits, the economy may further increase the input of debt after realizing that this can promote economic growth and scale expansion, and its overall returns will be scale invariant. However, if it keeps over-pursuing economies of scale and continues increasing debt, it may enter a period of decreasing returns to scale (Fig. 1.3).

The law of diminishing returns (i.e. the law of diminishing marginal utility) states that, within a relatively short period, as a certain factor of production is increased while other factors are kept constant, there will be a decline in the number of products derived from each factor of production. The law can be expressed with the formula $Y = f(L)$, in which $f'' < 0$.

In the case of decreasing returns to scale, the overall output increases by less than the proportional change in the factors of production. In simple terms, it can be expressed with the Cobb–Douglas production function: Y = AK^aL^b. When $a + b < 1$, the function is exhibiting decreasing returns to scale.

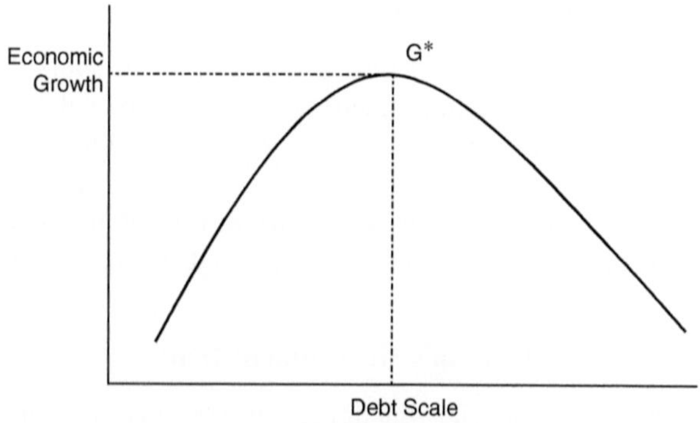

Fig. 1.3 Long-term effect of debt

If the output in an economy increases by less than the proportional change in factors of production (e.g. capital), when production is expanded, the situation can be referred to as 'diseconomies of scale'. During the process of economic development, all economies will pursue economies of scale and avoid diseconomies of scale. Hence, it is necessary to figure out how much capital investment (e.g. debt) can achieve the best economic benefits, explore the relations and matches among various economic scales, reveal the trend of the economic scale and structure and seek to design major principles and countermeasures for an optimal structure.

Therefore, the short-term and long-term effects of debt show that a threshold exists for the size of debt in the economy of a region or country. When the overall debt remains below the threshold, it can positively impact economic growth in both the short and long run. However, when the overall debt exceeds the threshold, the debt will exert negative impacts on economic growth. The threshold for the size of debt (i.e. the turning point of debt) is the focus of this study.

1.4 Research Framework

This study aims to identify the optimum debt scale for China as a whole, and with this ideological and methodological guidance, to explore the optimal boundary for deleveraging and reducing debt. Based on the laws of market economy development, in combination with the characteristics of China's economic development and with reference to the theoretical framework of the 'threshold theory', the authors analyse and summarize the general and regular characteristics of the development of China's economy and all types of debt. Furthermore, by constructing a scientific and reasonable statistical regression model, the authors attempt to identify the turning point of debt in terms of its influence on economic growth. The main contents of this book are as follows.

- **A Study of China's Debt**

The study of China's debt is the most important part of the book. In this section, the methods for defining and measuring China's debt, as well as the laws of debt growth during the past decade, are determined. On this basis, the authors develop an econometric model of debt and economic growth and calculate the debt turning point through quantitative analysis. The results of the study demonstrate the general features of China's debt, and general management suggestions are provided accordingly.

- **A Study of China's Government Debt**

With their special functions, governments play an important role in economic restructuring and development; therefore, government debt is also a highlight of economic study and analysis. With clear knowledge of China's debt on the whole, it becomes necessary to analyse the characteristics of government debt with quantitative methods and to explore whether a similar turning point exists. In recent years, the size of government debt has expanded rapidly, which makes this study all the more relevant.

- **A Study of China's Bank Debt**

The banking industry constitutes an important part of the financial industry; thus, it is also a pillar industry supporting the operation and growth China's macroeconomy. The authors focus on the banking industry, probing the debt development trend of China's financial industry, which has banks at its core. In light of similar research ideologies, a quantitative model of banks' debt size and economic growth is constructed, on the basis of which the authors attempt to identify the possible turning point. In addition the internal and external challenges confronting China's traditional financial service model with banks at its core are described in this book and relevant suggestions on its transformation are provided.

- **A Study of the Appropriate Proportion of the Virtual and Real Economy**

The serious imbalance between the virtual and real economy is an unavoidable problem that must be tackled in the operation of China's macroeconomy. Debt constitutes an important part of the virtual economy. This chapter first calculates China's total factor productivity and analyses its development trend and changing features. Then, it studies the proportion of China's virtual and real economy from the perspective of their contributions to improving total factor productivity, and it proposes an appropriate proportion that complies with market laws and can maintain sustainable and stable economic development.

- **A Study of Different Industries' Debt Leverages**

The debt sizes of different industries are also a research focus of this book. The authors conduct a descriptive analysis of the debt of several key industries, as well as a quantitative analysis of boundary effects of industry debt scale growth on economic growth (or industrial added value) to obtain the debt turning points of different industries and provide references for debt leverage analysis and decision-making.

- **A Study of the Debt Leverage of the Real Estate Industry**

Real estate is very important to China's economy and its people's livelihoods. Therefore, after analysing the debt leverages of several industries, the authors focus on the real estate industry and propose an econometric model for calculating the debt turning points of key real estate–related industries and the space for deleveraging. With a quantitative methodology, the authors compare important factors such as as the time when turning points will be reached and the space left for deleveraging. The conclusions of this chapter are targeted.

As mentioned earlier, based on the relationship between debt and economic growth, the economic meaning of turning points and the pressures that debt places on China's economy and people's lives, the authors hope to identify an appropriate range of debt sizes, in other words, to define the turning points in objective terms.

Among all kinds of economic growth elements, such as capital, labour, technology and growth mechanisms, this research focuses on debt, the only important economic factor in capital. As an impetus for economic growth, debt is actually a double-edged sword. The turning points of debt are critical to a market economy. Through an analysis of debt scale changes, the authors try to reveal the laws of economic growth. This is especially significant for developing countries that are relatively short of capital.

Chapter 2
A Study of China's Total Debt

Debt is a natural component of the macroeconomy, but its sound development cannot be achieved without proper debt leverage. In fact, the macroeconomy may be jeopardized when the total debt volume becomes too large. The current total debt of China is nearly twice its GDP, and non-governmental debt accounts for more than 80% of the total. Furthermore, during the last 5 years, the dependence of China's economic growth on debt has nearly doubled. All these factors imply that it's critical and urgent to study the size and scale of China's debt.

Previous studies have mainly concentrated on debt issues through analyzing the general operations of the macroeconomy, while those focusing on the quantitative relationship between debt and economic growth have been rare. In addition, many studies have focused only on the central government debt or local government debt, but have failed to assess the total debt volume and analyze the influences of debt on economic development. Using the available data, we specify the measurements for China's total debt and the debt of various entities within China, and we elaborate on their current situation and distribution characteristics. The curvilinear relationship between the total debt volume and economic growth is illustrated with a linear regression model.

The results of the data analysis in this book appear to prove the existence of the turning point of China's total debt: the increase of total debt directly boosts the growth of GDP; however, **as the total debt amounts to RMB 96.98 trillion (in 2003 prices) or RMB 134.12 trillion (in 2015 prices), the GDP is predicted to decline. Data shows that the current total debt of China has already exceeded the turning point**, which means that debt is now adversely influencing GDP. Therefore, it is urgent to promptly curb the total debt, improve economic structure and thus enhance the sound development of the economy.

X. Zhu et al., *A Study of the Turning Point of China's Debt*,
https://doi.org/10.1007/978-981-13-1325-7_2

2.1 The Definition and Characteristics of Total Debt

2.1.1 Total Debt

At present, it is difficult to obtain data about debt in China, and there is no first-hand data on total debt. Hence we attempted to measure the total debt in China from two alternative perspectives: the use of capital (debt 1) and the provision of capital (debt 2).

The use of capital perspective divides society into two parts: debt providers (mainly lending institutions such as banks and trusts) and debt users (a major measurement of debt). There is a mirror image relationship between debt providers and users, as the users' liabilities are the providers' claims. So from this perspective, we can determine the overall levels of financing based on total social financing (TSF). Debt financing – provided by financial institutions for non-financial institutions – is TSF minus direct financing, i.e. equity. However, this measurement fails to consider all elements and underestimates financing from other sources, such as non-governmental financing and peer-to-peer (P2P) financing. Nor does it include national liability (national debt and local government debt). Therefore, debt 1 can be calculated as:

$$\begin{aligned}\text{Total debt 1} = {} & \text{TSF} - \text{domestic stocks of non-financial enterprises} \\ & + \text{national debt} + \text{local government debt}\end{aligned}$$

The provision of capital perspective focuses on the aggregate debt of all debtors in an economy. Usually, organizations or individuals that raise financing by assuming debts include government agencies, enterprises and households. Government agencies can be subdivided into the central government and local governments. Enterprises can be classified into various industries: for example, a separate study can be conducted on financial institutions or auto businesses. Therefore, debt 2 can be calculated as:

$$\begin{aligned}\text{Total debt 2} = {} & \text{government debt} + \text{corporate debt} + \text{bank debt} \\ & + \text{household debt} + \text{foreign debt}\end{aligned}$$

As we can see, the first perspective defines total debt based on the function and role of capital in an economy. It demonstrates that debt serves as a foundation of the society. There have been sufficient, publicly available data concerning TSF, domestic stocks of non-financial enterprises, treasury bonds and local government debt, which makes debt research easier. Yet due to the complexity of the economy, this method can hardly cover all financing sources in the society, thus underestimating total debt.

The second perspective analyzes possible debt sources by defining various debtors in the society. It can explicitly present the debt volumes assumed by different debtors and provide information for the analysis of total debt structure. However, it draws on debtor data from diverse sources, making it difficult to distinguish between them. Moreover, the debts of different debtors may overlap: for example, the debts of financial institutions are, in a way, assets of non-financial enterprises and government agencies. Hence the perspective may overestimate the total debt. Meanwhile, since it is difficult to access data concerning government debt, and the debt data of various debtors differs in periods of availability, total debt 2 covers only a relatively short period of time, hence hampering empirical research.

There is a chance that the first perspective could underestimate total debt. Nevertheless, in view of the accessibility of data and the sustainability of follow-up research, in this book, total debt 1 is used as the principal measurement of China's total debt.

2.1.2 The Debt of Various Entities

This research included various types of debts such as those incurred by the government (including central and local government debt), corporations, households and foreigners. These are all effective components of the macroeconomy.

Central Government Debt The data were derived from statistical yearbooks published by the Ministry of Finance and figures released by the National Bureau of Statistics. In the research, central government debt refers to the balance of treasury bonds, classified by maturity. Bond issuances with a maturity above 1 year are counted by par value, and short-term discount bonds with a maturity of less than 1 year are counted by the actual amount raised. Treasury bonds are bonds issued by a country's central government to raise fiscal funds. They are debt obligations that the central government issues to investors, by which they promise to pay interest at stated periods and repay the principal in due time. They funds raised are used primarily for construction. By issuing treasury bonds, the central government can effectively pool a great deal of construction funds and accelerate economic growth.

Local Government Debt Some data on local government debt at various levels since 2007 is publicly available.

Corporate Debt The data were derived from the annual figures published by the National Bureau of Statistics. Corporate debt refers to debt assumed by enterprises that can be measured by currency and repaid with assets or labor. It includes both borrowings between enterprises and interest-bearing debt between enterprises and financial institutions (mainly banks and trusts). Due to its particularity, we conducted a separate analysis on the banking sector (and other sectors). We also briefly compared and analyzed debts of state-owned enterprises.

Household Debt The data were derived from the People's Bank of China, including – but not limited to – loans to residents.

Foreign Debt The data were derived from the National Bureau of Statistics. Foreign debt refers to borrowings from foreign countries by the Ministry of Finance

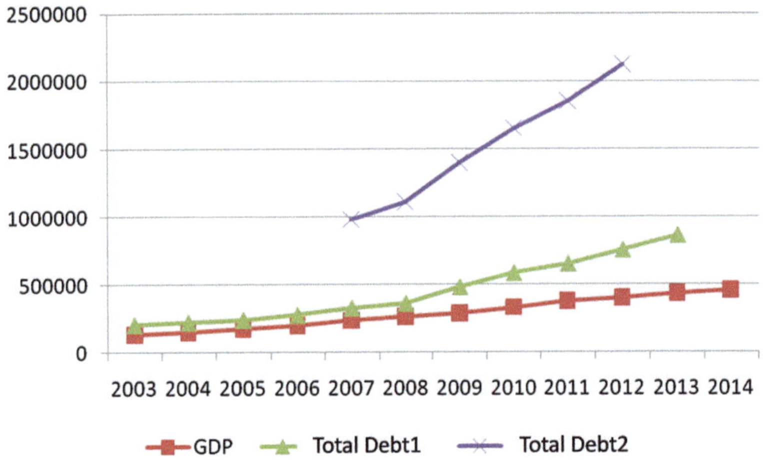

Fig. 2.1 China's total debt and GDP

on behalf of the central government. Backed by sovereign credit, it is also called sovereign foreign debt, and it includes loans from international financial organizations, loans from foreign governments and foreign currency denominated sovereign bonds issued overseas.

2.1.3 A Trend Analysis of Debt

Due to limitations on the availability of data, we took the total debt and the debt levels of various entities from 2003 to 2014 (inflation-adjusted figures, based on the 2003 price) in China for our trend analysis. From the data distribution, we identified the following characteristics and development trends regarding the total debt and the debt levels of various entities:

1. **The total debt continuously increased.**

In recent years, the total debt and the debt levels of various entities have continually increased. The total debt data calculated with method 1 indicated the lasting rise of the total debt in the society (Fig. 2.1). Compared with the 2003 level of RMB 20.37 trillion, the total debt increased to RMB 86.12 trillion in 2013 – almost twice the GDP of that year (RMB 43.36 trillion). In 2015, it rose to RMB 147.13 trillion, which was seven times that of 2003 and more than twice the GDP of the year of 2003 (RMB 67.67 trillion). The debt data calculated with method 2 – though covering a shorter time period – also revealed remarkable growth speed: the total debt rose from RMB 97.91 trillion in 2007 to RMB 212.5 trillion in 2012, at an average annual growth of 23.4%. The total debt in 2012 was nearly five times the GDP of the year of 2012 (RMB 40.41 trillion).

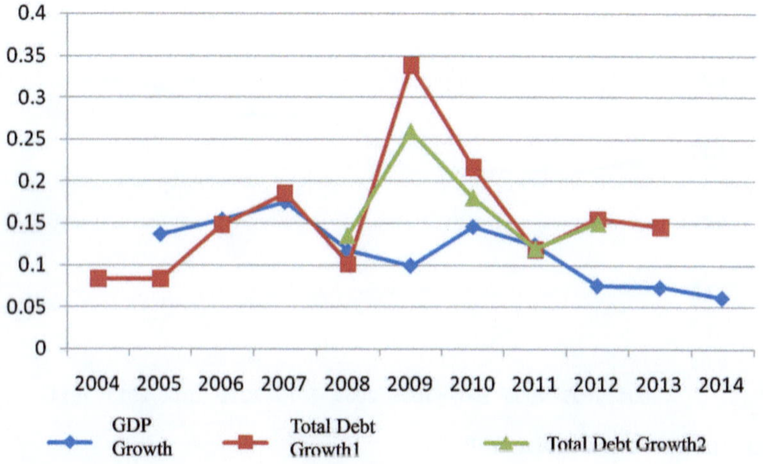

Fig. 2.2 The growth rate of China's total debt

Admittedly, as the latter simply added the debts of various entities, there may have been double counting that led to an overestimated result. Nonetheless, the above results show that the total debt in China reached a remarkably high level. The ratio of China's total debt to GDP was in line with data from McKinsey and Standard & Chartered.

2. **Debt growth peaked in 2009 and formed a difference from economic growth like a scissor.**

Comparing the growth of total debt with that of GDP during 2004 and 2014, we can observe that GDP growth generally declined in recent years, but not remarkably. In contrast, the total debt of the whole society – regardless of calculation method – declined sharply in 2008, which may be associated with the global financial crisis that year. In the following year, both growth figures rose quickly to the peak and then began to fall.

We can divide the whole 2003–2014 period into three stages according to the characteristics of total debt growth. Before 2008, total debt increased steadily, at a growth rate ranging from 10% to 20%; between 2008 and 2010, there was high volatility in total debt; the post-2010 period witnessed the rebound of debt size. Despite some fluctuation, China's total debt growth practically returned to its pre-2008 level (Fig. 2.2).

3. **Debt size was correlated with economic growth.**

We found a correlation between total debt and GDP, but the driving force of debt increasingly weakened. The data shows that the correlation coefficient between total debt and GDP was close to 1, which demonstrates a statistically significant correlation between debt and economic growth and illustrates the role of debt in boosting GDP.

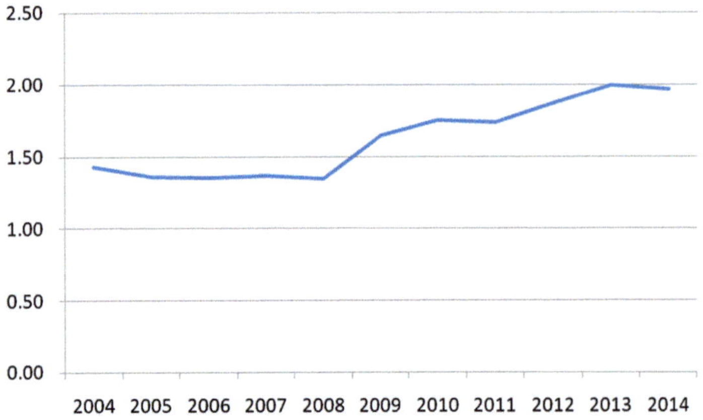

Fig. 2.3 The ratio of total debt to GDP

Fig. 2.4 The structure of debt by entity

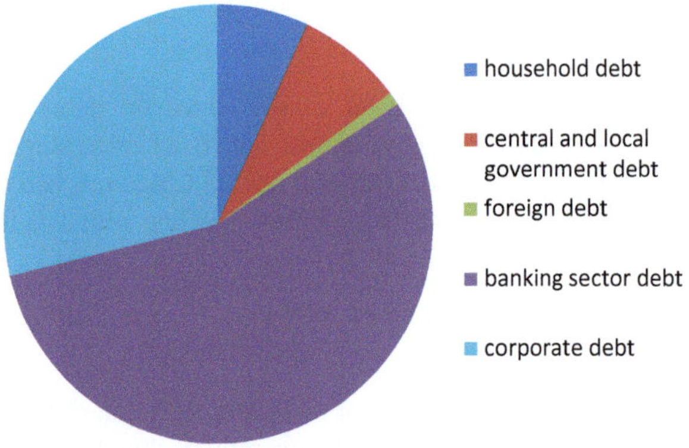

Having calculated the ratio of total debt to GDP, we found that while the debt of various entities and GDP grew continuously, the ratio of debt to GDP kept increasing. This means that as total debt increased, its stimulation effect on GDP weakened (Fig. 2.3).

4. **Debt of various entities also continually increased.**

Debt was unevenly distributed among various entities in China. For instance, in 2012, the banking sector represented the largest portion (around 56% of the total debt). It was followed by corporate debt which stood at 29%. The central and local government debt jointly accounted for 8%, household debt accounted for 7% and foreign debt was the lowest (less than 1%) (Fig. 2.4).

The volume of corporate debt was so large that it even exceeded that of GDP. It shared a roughly similar growth trend with GDP, and the support of corporate debt for GDP growth became increasingly weak (Fig. 2.5).

The size of household debt in China was close to that of government debt. However, as urban residents have been increasingly interested in purchasing assets

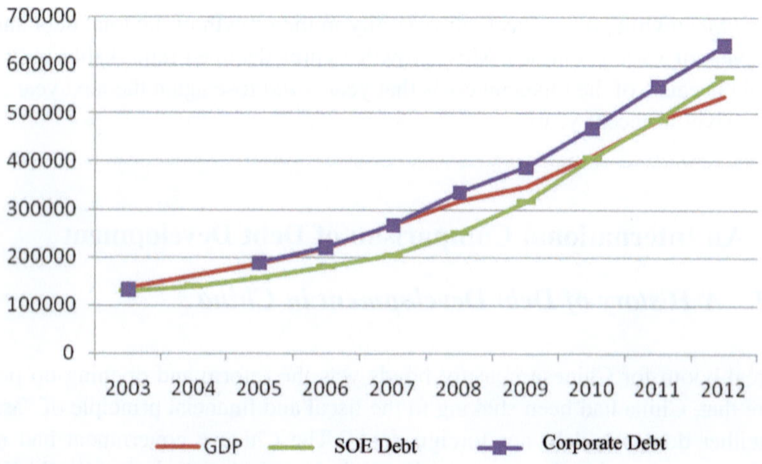

Fig. 2.5 Corporate debt and GDP

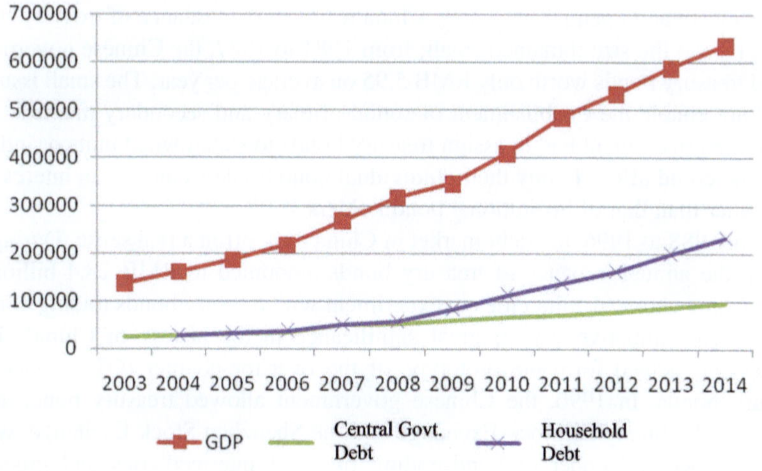

Fig. 2.6 Household debt and GDP

such as real estate and cars in recent years, the stimulation effect of household debt on economic growth has become a great concern in the society. The growth trend of household debt is very similar to that of total debt, and its role in GDP growth has been weakening (Fig. 2.6).

In sum, the total debt in China and the debt levels of various entities have been continuously increasing in recent years. In view of the absolute value of figures, the total debt calculated with our methods and indicators was RMB 86.12 trillion in 2013 – almost twice the GDP (RMB 43.36 trillion) for the year. To some extent, this matches with data from McKinsey and Standard and Chartered. However, in terms of the total debt structure, debt in China was not evenly distributed among various entities. Meanwhile, there was high volatility in the growth of the total debt and the debt levels of various entities. Most growth figures declined remarkably in 2008 – possibly because of the financial crisis that year – and rose again the next year to the highest level in recent years.

2.2 An International Comparison of Debt Development

2.2.1 A History of Debt Development in China

The real boom for Chinese treasury bonds was the reform and opening-up policy. Before that, China had been sticking to the fiscal and financial principle of "assuming neither domestic debt nor foreign debt." The Chinese government had never issued any treasury bonds except the People's Victory bonds during World War II and the economic construction bonds issued during the Great Leap Forward in the 1950s. Hence the debt market in the 1950s was dormant. Following the introduction of the reform and opening-up policy, China resumed the issuance of treasury bonds in 1981 – yet the size remained small: from 1981 to 1987, the Chinese government issued treasury bonds worth only RMB 5.95 on average per year. The small issuance could not enable the establishment of sound primary and secondary markets. As a result, the government had to assign treasury bonds to state-owned units or individuals who could afford to buy them. Individual bond holders enjoyed an interest rate 4% higher than that of institutional bond holders.

From 1988 to 1996, the debt market in China took off in a real sense. During the period, the annual issuance of treasury bonds amounted to RMB 28.4 billion. In 1988, China chose 61 pilot cities to experiment with treasury bonds trading consecutively. This initiative was of great significance in the history of China's bond market and helped form the prototype of the over-the-counter (OTC) market of treasury bonds. In 1990, the Chinese government allowed treasury bonds to be traded on the Shanghai Stock Exchange and the Shenzhen Stock Exchange, which then spawned a number of bond-trading financial intermediaries and gradually created the floor trading market for treasury bonds. In 1991, the Ministry of Finance began experiments with the voluntary placement of treasury bonds, symbolizing the initial establishment of China's treasury bond issuance market. In 1993, the Ministry of Finance began building a system of primary dealers of treasury bonds, and launched two innovative financial products: treasury bond futures and repurchases. In 1995, as the speculation of financial institutions in the treasury bond futures market amounted to a grave breach of relevant regulations, the Chinese government had to halt the trading of treasury bond futures in May. The next year saw a series of changes which got China's treasury bonds back on track: treasury bonds were now issued monthly; the variety of treasury bonds was significantly enriched; the issue-by-tender method was introduced in the issuance of treasury bonds and paper bonds were abandoned, leading to full-scale paperless issuance and higher issuance efficiency. The People's Bank of China (PBC) began purchasing treasury bonds, and

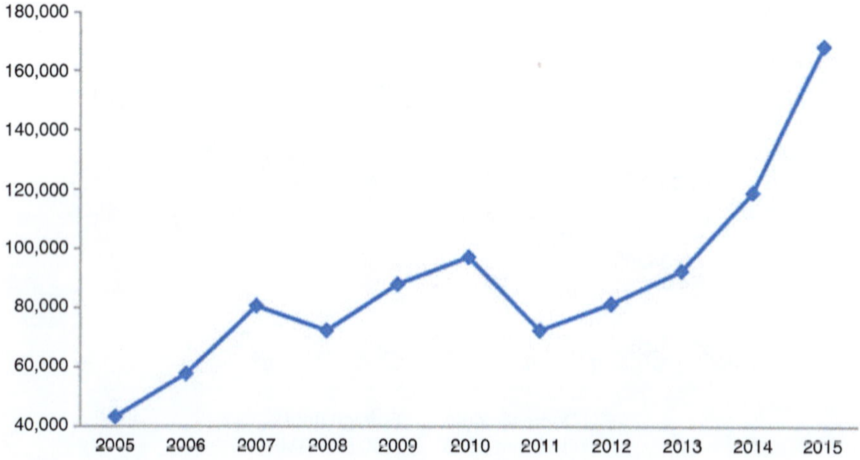

Fig. 2.7 Issuance trends in the bond market, 2005–2015 (Unit: RMB 100 million). (Source: China Central Depository & Clearing Co., Ltd. (CCDC) 2015)

treasury bonds were playing an increasingly important role as a financial instrument in the open market.

China's bond market entered its current stage of development in 1997. That year, the PBC mandated all commercial banks to move their repo and bond trading out of the stock exchanges and established the inter-bank bond market. In 2002, the Chinese government began formulating quarterly treasury bond issuance plans and developed an underwriting syndicate. In 2003, the Chinese government issued the *Administrative Rules on the Cross-Market Custody Transfer of Treasury Bonds*. Since then, China's treasury bond market has maintained a tripartite structure, i.e. the inter-bank bond market, the treasury bond market of Shanghai and the Shenzhen Stock Exchanges, and the OTC treasury bond market.

Figure 2.7 displays the total issuance of the bond market from 2005 to 2015. As shown, China's bond issuance steadily increased from 2005 to 2010; the only exception was the year of 2008, when the bond issuance declined slightly due to the economic crisis. In 2011, due to the macroeconomic adjustment, the PBC reduced the issuance of treasury bonds and its bills, and it encouraged the issuance of corporate debentures. This restructuring effort, for the most part, lowered the growth of the aggregate bond market in a short run. However, it still significantly facilitated the development of the bond market. For example, the bond issuance in China grew sharply over the 5 years after that. And in 2015, the total bond issuance in China grew 53.12% year-over-year to RMB 16.82 trillion, with the growth rate increasing by 16.7%. The issuance of local government bonds soared as well, mostly because the Ministry of Finance issued bonds to replace outstanding local government debts. Meanwhile, local government bonds were considered to be collateral under the central treasury cash management and some monetary policies, which made local governments more willing to use this financial instrument. At present,

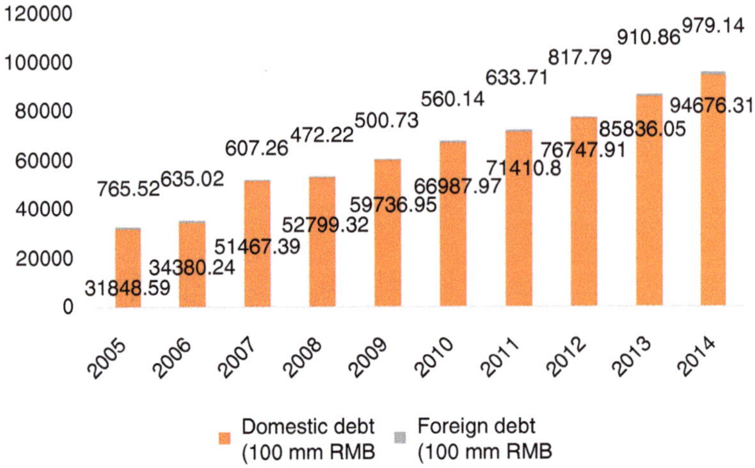

Fig. 2.8 Balance changes of China's central government debt. (Source: CCDC 2015)

local government debt has become the type with the largest issuance volume in China's bond market.

Meanwhile, China's sovereign debt has been steadily growing. As Fig. 2.8 shows, most owners of the central government debt were domestic entities or individuals, similar to the situation in Japan.

China's bond market, though developing rapidly, was still no match for the stock market in terms of overall size. In fact, the bond market remained at a primary stage in its development. Yet in the long run, the bond market has played an increasingly important role in China's financial market. In recent years, mainstream bonds in the market have not been sufficiently diversified, and policies are playing a strong guiding role. For example, the debt-converting bonds issued by the Ministry of Finance in 2015 instantly made local government bonds a mainstay in the bond market. In addition, China's treasury bond futures remained suspended, and corresponding bond derivatives were not in place on the market, which was not conducive to the development of the bond market.

2.2.2 A History of Debt Development in Japan

Japan is among the countries which use treasury bonds most frequently. After World War II, Japan resumed the issuance of treasury bonds in 1965, to rapidly restore its economic development and raise funds for national construction. At that time, the Japanese government issued only one type of treasury bond – the 7-year construction bond – which totaled JPY 200 billion. However, the Japanese economy was battered by the first oil shock in 1973. Hence, to finance the rising fiscal deficits, the Japanese government issued a new type of treasury bond termed "special deficit-financing bonds." Such bonds helped to properly address the deficit in Japan and later were sold in larger and larger amounts. Since 1983, the Japanese government authorized domestic banks and other financial institutions to engage in the OTC trading of bonds, so that financial institutions, established corporations and individuals were allowed to purchase treasury bonds. Therefore, these groups accounted for a larger proportion in the investment market. In 1985, all domestic financial institutions in Japan were authorized to issue treasury bonds, which significantly increased the number of participants in Japan's treasury bond market. During this period, individual investors became the principal purchasers of bonds.

As the Asian financial crisis broke out in 1997, the market demand for Japanese treasury bonds increased dramatically. As a result, the Japanese government had to reduce the interest rates on treasury bonds, to lower costs. Although the interest rates on the 10-year treasury bonds issued in 1998 were as low as 0.9%, the total issuance in that year alone amounted to JPY 1.2 billion. The excessive issuance of treasury bonds impaired the balance between supply and demand in the market and led to sharp declines in treasury bond prices. Meanwhile, the build-up of treasury bonds added to the repayment burdens of the Japanese government. Following the second oil crisis, the bursting of Japan's economic bubble and other economic events, the Japanese government had to handle its deficit by launching special deficit-financing bonds, which in turn increased the pressure of treasury bonds on the country. Over the course of the past 20 years, Japan's treasury bonds have been growing by JPY 40 trillion annually.

Figure 2.9 shows that treasury bond issuance in Japan got its first big boost in 1991. As the economic bubble in Japan burst, the Japanese government ran into huge

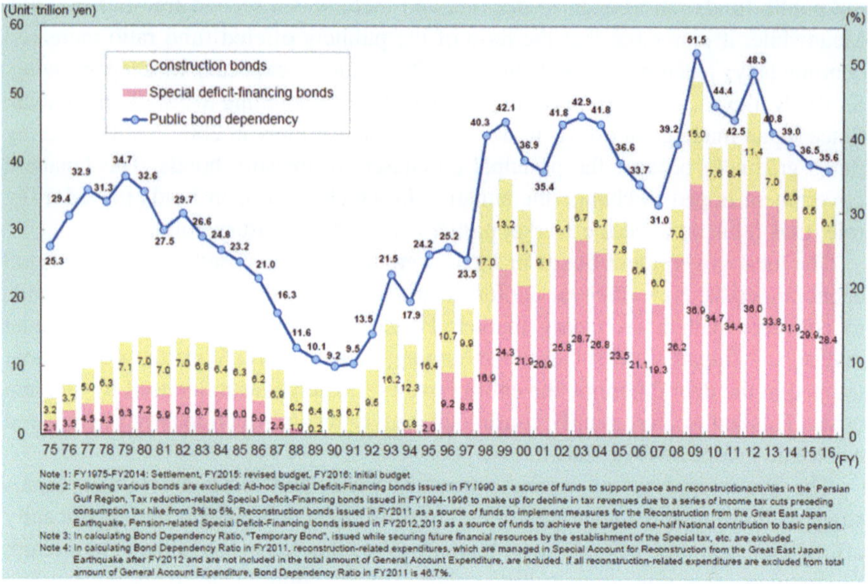

Fig. 2.9 Total volumes of treasury bonds, 1980–2016. (Source: Financial Bureau, Ministry of Finance, Japan (2016), *Debt Management Report 2016*, p. 170)

financial troubles, with its revenue falling by nearly JPY 15 trillion within a year. Meanwhile, Japan began spending massively on infrastructure development, lifting the infrastructure budget from an average of JPY 6 trillion before 1991 to JPY 16.2 trillion in 1993. During this period, the Japanese government issued many treasury bonds to fix its broken financial system. Since then, the total volume of Japanese treasury bonds has grown rapidly. The Asian financial crisis in 1997 frustrated Japan's economic growth and led to the second big boost for its treasury bonds. The volume of the special deficit-financing bonds increased sharply from JPY 8.5 trillion in 1997 to JPY 16.9 trillion in 1998; in the same years, the volume of the construction bonds also rose from JPY 9.9 trillion to JPY 17 trillion. The changes thus led to the dramatic increase in the total volume of Japan's debt and added to the debt loads of the Japanese government. The 2008, the economic crisis was an important factor triggering the third big boost for Japan's treasury bonds. As the recession further enlarged the fiscal gap, the Japanese government had to invest more in infrastructure development to ensure economic growth. As a result, the volume of its construction bonds issued rose to JPY 15 trillion in 2009, nearly doubling that of 2008 (JPY 7 trillion). The bond issue has become a major obstacle for Japan's economic development.

The development of local government bonds in Japan shared similar characteristics with that of Japanese treasury bonds. First, the local government bonds experienced a series of changes: it first increased rapidly, then leveled off, then gradually declined and, finally, took off again. The figure shows that the public funds ratio peaked in 1985, reaching 75.9% of the total. However, after the Japanese government authorized all domestic financial institutions to issue treasury bonds, the public funds ratio began to decline, and there was a second free-fall in 2002. Meanwhile, it is notable that the ratio of the publicly offered fund ratio increased continuously, reaching its peak in 2016. The ratio is expected to keep growing. Similarly, the fiscal loan funds ratio peaked in 1986, amounting to 58.7% of the total. Since Japan made great efforts to develop its real economy in 2002, public offering funds gradually became the principal purchasers of treasury bonds. The Japanese government hoped to change the situation in which fiscal loan funds played a big role; thus it encouraged the market participants to buy treasury bonds.

The local government bonds in Japan were intensely exposed to the unexpected economic crisis. Nevertheless, the funds structure of local government bonds tends to converge with a secondary market. Hence, we can conclude that individual investors in Japan were subject to mounting debt pressure. With the government trapped in the debt dilemma, the entire Japanese society was influenced by the debt crisis. This led to increasingly conservative investments which may have impaired economic prospects (Fig. 2.10).

The above analysis of Japanese treasury bonds and local government bonds suggests that Japan is under great pressure from fiscal debt, which has significantly affected its economic development. It is safe to say that Japan has failed in its attempt to stimulate economic growth by issuing a lot of bonds. Due to its outstanding treasury bonds and high bond dependency ratio, Japan is on the verge of a debt crisis. It is the low interest rates of treasury bonds that enable the Japanese government to

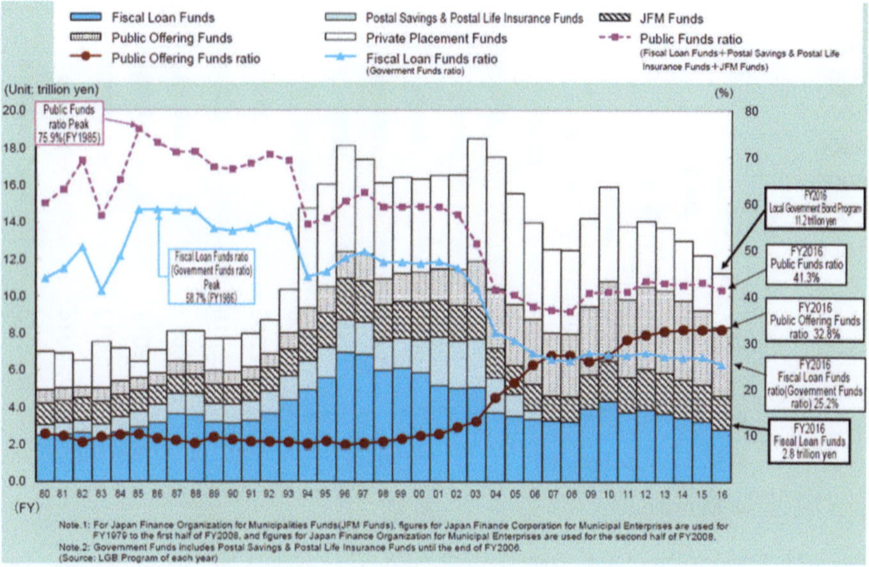

Fig. 2.10 Local government bonds outstanding and changes in the funds structure in Japan, 1980–2016. (Source: Financial Bureau, Ministry of Finance, Japan (2016), *Debt Management Report 2016*, p. 164)

service the debt, so that the country can maintain its current stability. Moreover, since Japanese treasury bonds are mostly held by domestic institutions and individual investors, they are less likely to be manipulated by overseas financial institutions. Hence the country has a relatively stable debt level. However, if the Japanese government wants to address its debt problem by facilitating economic development, it must find a way out – other than issuing more and more bonds.

2.2.3 A History of Debt Development in the U.S.

The U.S. first issued treasury bonds during the American Revolution (1775–1783). The government-issued war bonds were worth more than USD 190 million and were used to provide much-needed financial support for the Continental Army led by George Washington. Since then, the U.S. bond market had not been well advanced through the first half of the twentieth century.

As the oil crisis broke out in the 1970s, the U.S. economy was characterized by high inflation. In addition, following the collapse of the Bretton Woods system, the market interest rate in the U.S. increased sharply with dramatic fluctuations. To hedge risk and guarantee the liquidity of assets, investors began to purchase bonds. Meanwhile, with the globalization of interest rates and financial liberalization, enterprises and local governments began to issue their own bonds for short-term

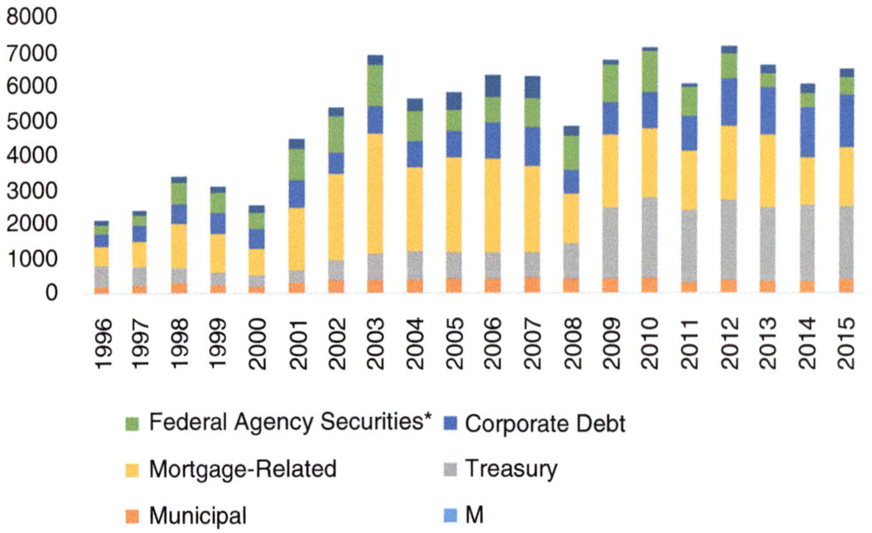

Fig. 2.11 Composition of U.S. bond issuance, 1996–2015 (unit: USD billion). (Source: The Securities Industry and Financial Markets Association (SIFMA) 2015, available at http://www.sifma.org/legal/)

financing, instead of borrowing from banks. All these changes facilitated the regularized development of the U.S. bond market.

From the 1980s to the present, the U.S. bond market entered a period of high growth. The annual growth rate of U.S. bonds from 1980 to 2012 was as high as 8.84%, well above the 5.55% growth rate of GDP. Meanwhile, with the strong support from the Federal Reserve ("the Fed"), the U.S. bond market has become one of the global financial markets with the widest range of products, providing a financing platform for the federal government, local governments and enterprises.

The bond market in the U.S. has the highest level of diversity of any bond market in the world. In 2000, the U.S. bond market became the biggest securities market in the world: the volume of outstanding bonds amounted to USD 1.73 trillion, exceeding the volume of outstanding stock for the first time which was USD 1.5 trillion. At the end of 2001, the volume of outstanding bonds in the U.S. market had reached USD 3.95 trillion, with as much as USD 0.96 trillion held by foreign governments and enterprises. This change signaled that the U.S. bond market truly became an international financial market.

Figure 2.11 displays the total volumes and composition of U.S. bond issuance from 1996 to 2015. Bond issuance volume in the U.S. increased significantly after its economic bubble burst in 2001. Further, the development of the real economy – including the property sector – sent mortgage-related bonds to their peak in 2002. The economic crisis in 2008 led to a noticeable gap of issuance volume in that year.

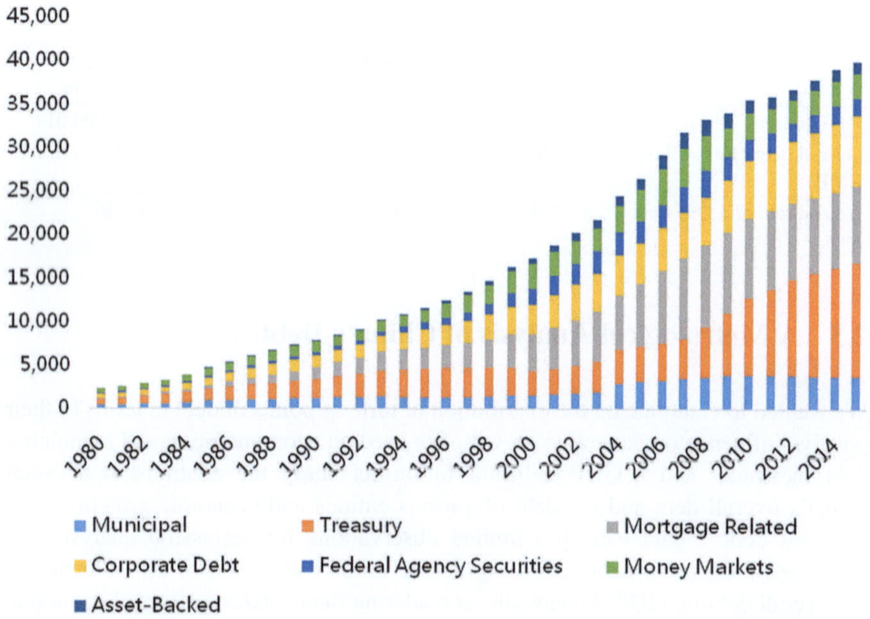

Fig. 2.12 U.S. bonds outstanding, 1980–2015 (unit: USD billion). (Source: The Securities Industry and Financial Markets Association (SIFMA) 2015, available at http://www.sifma.org/legal/)

Later, to stimulate economic recovery, the U.S. government rapidly increased its treasury bond issuance, which then reached a relatively stable level. Meanwhile, the issuance volume of corporate debt increased each year. Companies have gradually made debt financing a major way of financing and it is becoming increasingly important in the U.S. bond market.

Figure 2.12 shows the outstanding volumes of the U.S. bond market. Similar to bond issuance, the outstanding volumes of U.S. bonds grew steadily; meanwhile, the issuance and outstanding volumes of each category of bonds grew in tandem. However, the outstanding volumes of treasury bonds did not significantly increase after 2001, but rose remarkably after 2008. The total volume of bonds did not decline sharply in 2008, suggesting that the trend of the outstanding volume was different from that of the increment. The relatively smooth curve of outstanding volume shows that the U.S. had an accurate understanding of the bond market in the long term, as the market was unaffected by economic volatility. This suggests that the U.S. has a well-developed bond market with strong risk tolerance. Therefore, the duration of the whole bond market increased. Extended duration of bond portfolios could significantly ramp up the risk of a debt crisis. Consequently, since the U.S. is currently facing considerable risk of a debt crisis, there is growing concern for how to address this problem.

Table 2.1 Descriptive statistics (Unit: 100 million RMB)

	N	Minimum value	Maximum value	Mean value	Standard deviation
(100 million RMB)	12	154,681.809	459,917.926	303,403.130	105,900.014
Overall debt (100 million RMB)	12	203,699.600	903,267.965	488,226.228	256,636.421
Interest rate of a One-year loan	12	5.310	7.470	5.888	0.626

2.3 A Metrological Analysis of China's Debt

We wanted to elaborate on the distribution of turning points of debt in terms of their positive influence on economic growth. We used an econometric model containing debt indicators and a GDP indicator to further study the relationship between China's overall debt and the debt of various entities and economic growth. Since the total debt 2 data were too limited observations for regression analysis, we calculated the overall debt data using debt 1 in the calculation of the influence of the overall debt on GDP. Meanwhile, considering the hysteresis effect of economic activities, we used data from period t in the regression of data of period t+1.

We referred to Checherita-Westphal and Rother in studying the relationship between government debt and GDP and took the interest rate of a one-year loan as the control variable which in effect represented the cost of the use of funds.

The descriptive statistics of indicators used in the model are shown in Table 2.1. The data were based 2003 prices. The statistical distribution of indicators tallies with the characteristics of the debt of various entities analyzed in chapter one.

Debt growth rate and GDP growth rate were the major variables in the regression analysis. The econometric model was:

$$\begin{aligned}\text{GDP growth rate}_{t+1} &= C + b_1\text{debt growth rate}_t + b_2\text{debt growth rate}_t^{\,2} \\ &\quad + b_3\text{one-year loan interest rate}_t + e\end{aligned}$$

The model illustrates whether the current debt growth rate will affect the GDP growth rate of the next period. Regression results are shown in Table 2.2. The regression coefficients of regression were not statistically significant given that neither the debt growth rate nor its square demonstrated a significant influence on GDP growth rate. This implies that there was no obvious correlation between debt growth rate and GDP growth rate.

We then used the debt/GDP ratio and the GDP growth rate as the major variables for regression analysis using the following econometric model:

$$\begin{aligned}\text{GDP growth rate}_{t+1} &= C + b_1\text{debt/GDP ratio}_t + b_2\text{debt/GDP ratio}_t^{\,2} \\ &\quad + b_3\text{one-year loan interest rate}_t + e\end{aligned}$$

Table 2.2 Regression results of the debt growth rate

Model	Unstandardized coefficient		Standardized coefficient	t	Sig.
	B	Standard error			
(Constant)	14.594	13.874		1.052	0.328
Debt growth rate	14.396	85.605	0.302	0.168	0.871
Square of debt growth rate	−1.005	215.141	−0.008	−0.005	0.996
One-year loan IR	−0.933	2.801	−0.151	−0.333	0.749

F = 0.275
Adjusted $R^2 = -0.278$

Table 2.3 Regression results of the debt/GDP ratio

Model		Unstandardized coefficient		Standardized coefficient	t	Sig.
		B	Standard error			
1	(Constant)	−1.306	18.083		−.072	0.944
	Debt/GDP ratio	21.598	14.097	1.436	1.532	0.169
	Square of debt/GDP ratio	−4.189	1.747	−2.242	−2.398	0.048
	One-year loan IR	−0.876	1.097	−0.142	−0.798	0.451

F = 8.549*
Adjusted $R^2 = 0.786$
*Significantly correlated at 0.05 level (tow-tailed)

This model shows whether current debt/GDP ratio will affect the GDP growth of the next period. Regression results are shown in Table 2.3. The regression coefficient of the square of the debt/GDP ratio was statistically significant – which was in line with our assumption – but that of the debt/GDP ratio was not. Therefore, this model was not suitable.

Therefore, given the above analysis, we decided not to use growth rates or ratios as the major variables. Instead, the overall debt volume and GDP were the major variables in this econometric model:

$$GDP_{t+1} = C + b_1\text{overall debt}_t + b_2\text{overall debt}_t^{\ 2} + b_3\text{one-year loan interest rate}_t + e$$

The lack of data in the model made the unit root test and co-integration test unnecessary. As a result, this model was an exploratory model aimed at explaining the possible quantitative relationship between debt and GDP. A more normative and rigorous study will require further data collection and variable definition. In the meantime, in the regression results of the model, the existence of the turning point means that the marginal contribution of debt to GDP at that point was zero.

Results of the least squares regression are shown in Table 2.4.

Table 2.4 Regression results of the overall debt

Model		Unstandardized coefficient		Standardized coefficient	t	Sig.
		B	Standard error			
1	(Constant)	−30,771.842	40,350.496		−0.763	0.471
	Overall debt	0.931	0.106	2.037	8.767	0.000
	Square of overall debt	−0.00000048	0.000	−1.081	−4.671	0.002
	One-year loan IR	5888.476	6315.492	0.036	0.932	0.382

F = 231.035**
Adjusted $R^2 = 0.986$
*Significantly correlated at 0.01 level (tow-tailed)

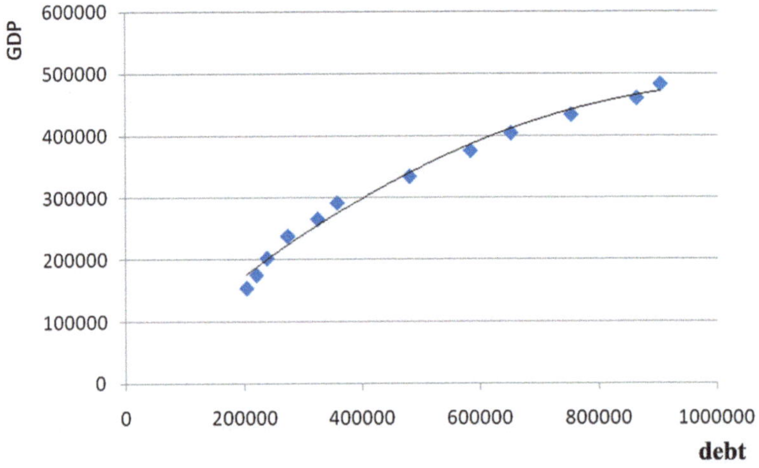

Fig. 2.13 The relationship between China's overall debt and GDP (Unit: 100 million RMB)

2.3.1 *An Analysis of the Turning Point of China's Overall Debt*

Table 2.4 illustrates the positive impact of China's overall debt on economic growth and possible existence of the turning point. A scatter plot of China's overall debt 1 and GDP shows the quadratic relation between debt and GDP (Fig.2.13).

One unit of increase in China's overall debt resulted in a 0.931 unit of increase in GDP, which is generally in compliance with the historical development of China's economic activities. At the same time, the squares of debt indicators were highly negatively correlated with GDP; this proves the existence of the turning point of debt. We can infer that the turning point of China's overall debt appears when the debt volume reaches 96.98 trillion RMB (the 2003 price) or RMB 134.12 trillion (the 2015 price).

In our statistics, China's overall debt reached 147.13 trillion RMB (price of the same year) in 2015.

This shows that the driving effect of China's overall debt on economic growth gradually weakening, and the marginal effect of the overall debt on total GDP turned negative. Rising overall debt exerted a more significant negative influence on GDP. The negative stimulation to GDP meant rapidly mounting fiscal pressure for the country, and this meant that the government needed to spend more revenue to pay down debt and interest charges. For other debt entities in the society, excessive debt pressure means that businesses rely too much on debt, which is harmful to their development. The European debt crisis exhibited a dragging effect on the economy far bigger than its stimulation effect. Thus the debt risk-assuming capacity of the macro economy will decrease quickly. Consequently, problems of any debt entity will be magnified by the market, resulting in a chain effect until the whole economy is unable to deal with the problems caused by debt pressure. In this sense, the current overall total debt has become the sword of Damocles hanging over China. Therefore, we are faced with an urgent issue to properly arrange the overall debt level and enhance the risk management and tolerance of debt entities.

2.4 A Metrological Analysis of the Debt of Various Entities

To further elaborate on the influence of the debt of various entities in China on economic growth, metrological analysis models of the debt of various entities and economic growth can be established. Certainly, due to data limitations, some conclusions might not be accurate enough. In addition, the analysis of the debt of various entities in this section involves corporate debt, household debt and foreign debt excluding government debt and banking sector debt (which we will discuss later).

2.4.1 *Corporate Debt*

Total corporate debt and total GDP were the major variables in our econometric model:

$$\begin{aligned} \text{GDP}_{t+1} = {} & C + b_1 \text{corporate debt}_t + b_2 \text{corporate debt}_t^{\,2} \\ & + b_3 \text{one-year loan interest rate}_t + e \end{aligned}$$

Results of the least squares regression are shown in Table 2.5.

Table 2.5 shows that corporate debt was significantly positively correlated with economic growth, while its square was significantly negatively correlated with economic growth. Thus we can infer that corporate debt had a positive influence on economic growth, and this influence had a turning point. The scatter plot of

Table 2.5 Regression results of corporate debt

Model		Unstandardized coefficient		Standardized coefficient		
		B	Standard error		t	Sig.
1	(Constant)	−11,627.645	23,524.959		−.494	0.647
	Corporate debt	1.250	0.115	1.680	10.883	0.000
	Square of corporate debt	−0.00000077	0.000	−0.690	−4.469	0.011
	One-year loan IR	3399.952	2237.885	0.030	1.519	0.203

F = 881.390**
Adjusted $R^2 = 0.997$
*Significantly correlated at 0.01 level (tow-tailed)

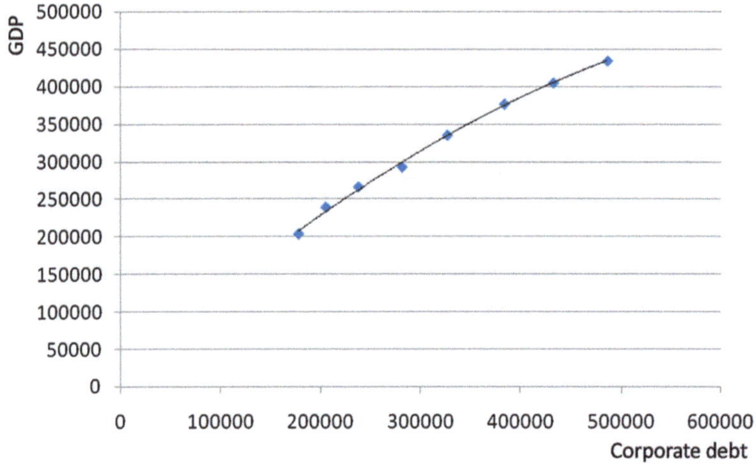

Fig. 2.14 The relationship between corporate debt and GDP

corporate debt and GDP is shown in Fig. 2.14. There is a quadratic relation between corporate debt and GDP. The results imply that corporate debt may reach its turning point at 81.17 trillion RMB (the 2003 price) or 113.89 trillion RMB (the 2015 price).

Corporate debt reached 64.19 trillion RMB (price of the same year) in 2012. If growing at the debt growth rate of 2012, it would have reached 98.21 trillion RMB in 2015 and 113.18 trillion RMB in 2016, which is fairly close to the calculated turning point of 113.89 trillion RMB (the 2015 price). This means that corporate debt had a positive correlation on economic growth. Further, the rise of corporate debt can still exert a positive influence on GDP, but the current size is very close to the turning point, leaving little room for future expansion.

Table 2.6 Regression results of household debt

Model		Unstandardized coefficient		Standardized coefficient	t	Sig.
		B	Standard error			
1	(Constant)	79,186.836	47,521.735		1.666	0.147
	Household debt	4.648	0.616	1.984	7.547	0.000
	Square of household debt	−0.00001435	0.000	−1.028	−3.914	0.008
	One-year loan IR	258.296	7433.128	0.002	0.035	0.973

F = 138.356**
Adjusted $R^2 = 0.979$
*Significantly correlated at 0.01 level (tow-tailed)

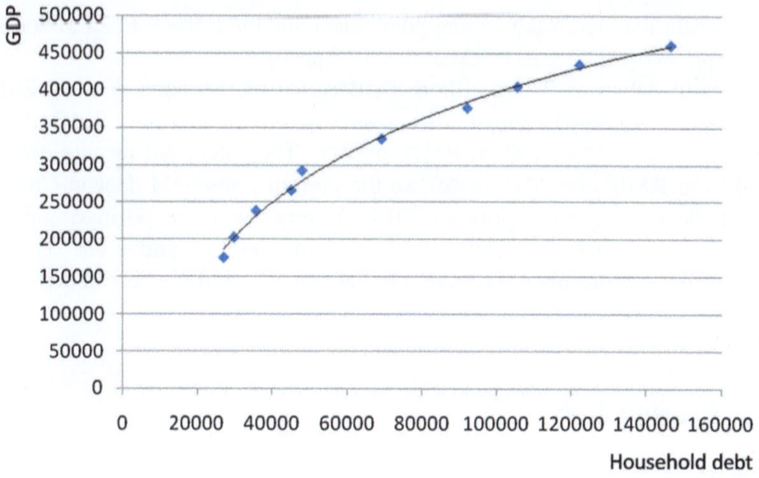

Fig. 2.15 The relationship between household debt and GDP

2.4.2 *Household Debt*

Household debt and GDP were the major variables in this econometric model:

$$GDP_{t+1} = C + b_1 \text{household debt}_t + b_2 \text{household debt}_t^2 + b_3 \text{one-year loan interest rate}_t + e$$

Results of the least squares regression are shown in Table 2.6.

The positive impact of household debt on economic growth and the possible existence of the turning point were verified. The influence of household debt on GDP was quite meaningful as one unit of increase in household debt resulted in 4.648 units of an increase in GDP. Moreover, the square of the debt indicator had a strong, negative correlation with GDP; this proves the existence of the turning point. The quadratic relation between household debt and GDP is shown as a scatter plot (Fig. 2.15). We can infer that

Table 2.7 Regression results of foreign debt

Model		Unstandardized coefficient		Standardized coefficient		
		B	Standard error		t	Sig.
1	(Constant)	−21,680.339	15,199.963		−1.426	0.168
	Foreign debt	26.186	4.831	1.230	5.421	0.000
	Square of foreign debt	−0.00053	0.001	−0.148	−0.775	0.447
	One-year Loan IR	2907.852	1384.164	0.163	2.101	0.048

F = 218.204**
Adjusted $R^2 = 0.964$
*Significantly correlated at 0.01 level (tow-tailed)

household debt may reach the turning point when volume reaches 16.20 trillion RMB (the 2003 price) or 22.72 trillion RMB (the 2015 price).

Household debt was 23.14 trillion RMB (price of the same year) in 2014. If growing at the debt growth rate of 2014, it would reach 26.98 trillion RMB (the 2015 price) in 2015 and 31.45 trillion RMB in 2016. The calculated turning point was 25.66 trillion RMB (the 2015 price), so the current household debt in China had exceeded the turning point prior to 2014. At this stage, the positive correlation between household debt and GDP was transforming into a negative one. Therefore, we need to be cautious about encouraging the expansion of household debt.

2.4.3 *Foreign Debt*

Total foreign debt and total GDP were the major variables in this econometric model:

$$GDP_{t+1} = C + b_1 \text{foreign debt}_t + b_2 \text{foreign debt}_t^{\,2} + b_3 \text{one-year loan interest rate}_t + e$$

Results of the least squares regression are shown in Table 2.7.

The total foreign debt volume was small, but it had a positive influence on economic growth, and there was possibly a turning point. Foreign debt was highly significantly correlated with GDP as one unit of increase in foreign debt led to a 26.186 unit of increase in GDP. Meanwhile, the square of the debt indicator was highly negatively correlated with GDP, which proves the existence of a turning point. The quadratic relation between foreign debt and GDP is shown as a scatter plot (Fig. 2.16). We can infer that foreign debt would reach the turning point when its volume reaches 2.47 trillion RMB (the 2003 price) or 3.47 trillion RMB (the 2015 price).

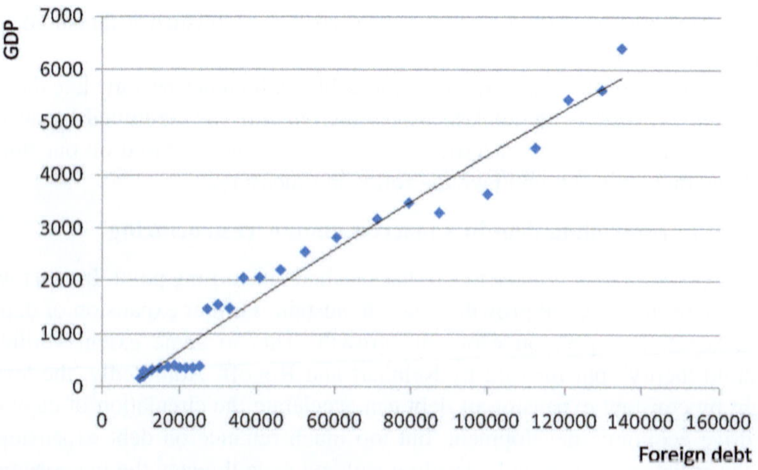

Fig. 2.16 The relationship between foreign debt and GDP

The volume of foreign debt was 0.90 trillion RMB (price of the same year) in 2014. If the growth rate of 2014 continued, it would reach 0.93 trillion RMB in 2015 and 0.96 trillion RMB in 2016. The calculated turning point was 3.47 trillion RMB (the 2015 price), and China's foreign debt was quite far from the turning point. This means that there was a turning point of foreign debt in terms of its influence on total GDP, but at the current stage, foreign debt is still positively correlated with GDP and has much room for expansion.

2.5 Summary and Suggestions

We adopted an econometric model containing debt indicators and variables for system control, to thoroughly study the relationship between China's overall debt and the debt of various entities. We also examined economic growth and explained the turning points of debt in terms of their influence on economic growth. Our empirical results were similar to those of a seminal paper published in *The American Economic Review* by American economists Reinhart and Rogoff in 2010. Using an international comparison of debt issues, the researchers found that when the government debt/GDP ratio exceeded 90%, the economic growth rate was reduced by 1%. Therefore, Reinhart and Rogoff in effect put forward the concept of the "threshold" of government debt.

The turning point analyzed here was similar to the debt threshold proposed by Reinhart and Rogoff. In other words, when debt size exceeds a certain turning point, the economic aggregate will take a downward turn. However, the turning point in our study involved China's overall debt, which extended the issue of government debt as studied by Reinhart and Rogoff. Our conclusion is that there was a turning point or threshold for China's overall debt, so we established a threshold theory based on the overall debt of a society.

As mentioned earlier, the current overall debt in China has become like the sword of Damocles. If there is no quick measure taken to curb the continued expansion of debt, there could be serious macroeconomic consequences. Based on our findings, we believe that China should take the following measures:

1. **Prioritize controlling debt in a macroeconomic restructuring**

China's overall debt is close to – or has reached –its turning point. In other words, credit or debt-driven GDP growth is hard to sustain. Further expansion of debt will exert a negative impact on economic growth. This to some extent verifies the "threshold theory" put forward by Reinhart and Rogoff. Admittedly, the leverage brought by constant expansion of debt can accelerate the circulation of capital and even drive economic development, but too much reliance on debt expansion will harm the structure of economic development and even threaten the macroeconomic security of the society. Given current overall debt in China, various debt entities have been adept in using debt leverage to acquire funds for development and have even turned to debt issuance once any financial problems arose. The abusive use of debt instruments has caused a drag on economic development. Therefore, adjusting debt size is a pressing task given that China's overall debt in approaching – or may have reached – its turning point.

Relevant authorities should take multiple measures to adjust the overall debt level in China to make it converge and stay at the optimum level in the long run. This means that China's overall debt size should correspond with economic growth and the growth rate of debt balance should be coordinated with the changing pace of macroeconomic figures. In the debt of various entities, government debt and corporate debt are situated at extremely high levels that have generated potential risky situations that might exert a negative impact on macroeconomic operations. Thus auditing and supervision of debt should be enhanced, and debt expansion should be curbed immediately. As for the incurred debt, the repayment pressure should be gradually relieved until the economic entities operate steadily.

Apart from helping businesses and government set up a reasonable debt management system by strengthening supervision, the public should be further educated about debt issues and the risk of debt leverage. Popularizing financial knowledge and raising awareness of how to effectively use debt can help the debt market develop in an ordered and rational fashion.

2. **Establish a sound financial supervision system and prioritize the control of total volume.**

Effective solutions to debt problems must be based on an efficient financial supervision system. At present, the overall debt level in China is so high that financial supervision must be made the top macroeconomic priority. It can be seen from a series of debt crises – from 2008 financial crisis in the U.S. to the European sovereign debt crisis – that if the government is not equipped with a sound financial supervision system, then any minor problem in the domestic financial system can be magnified quickly, which can affect macroeconomic development. Considering the on-going growth trend of China's overall debt, it seems urgent to build a financial supervision system.

In developing such a system, real-time supervision and early supervision should recognized as important principles. Relevant authorities should no longer only pay attention to debt problems at debt settlement intervals since at this stage, debt is already on the verge of explosion. An effective whole-society, real-time supervision system must assess the level and risk of the overall debt in the society at any given time. It also must oversee the debt level of all debt entities to prepare for debt issuance and repayment plans to urge all parties to reduce the expected risk in a timely manner. For example, local governments can accumulate some capital as a buffer when the debt pressure is low, to prepare for the debt repayment peak.

Certainly, the establishment of a supervision system is not only targeted at various entities such as governmental organizations and businesses. The supervision of senior executives in the financial sector also should be propped up. A crackdown on corruption is gaining momentum, but corruption is still frequently seen in the financial sector – including within the debt market – due to the temptation of high profits. So the supervision system for senior executives should be established while improving the supervision on debt entities to guard against a debt crisis caused by improper policies. Additionally, appropriate regulation targeted at senior executives can prevent local governments from pressing for bank loans with their power to reduce the possibility of a breakout of debt risk at its source. To stabilize the debt system, the remuneration of senior executives can be linked to the local debt risk level. To guard against moral hazard, a mechanism of lifelong accountability can be introduced to help reduce the power of senior executives regarding debt risk to ward off moral hazard.

3. **Improve the fiscal decentralization system and clarify the power and obligations of the central government and local governments, respectively.**

The overall debt of the society is a substantial topic that calls for coordination and cooperation between all parties. Government plays an important role in economic development and social transformation, so the central government and local governments at all levels should be clear about their responsibility and take the initiative to coordinate and guide the society in terms of debt control and supervision.

The central government should play an exemplary role in confirming the debt size and assuming risk. It should be bold enough to utilize debt instruments to boost economic development at the right time and assess the driving force of the overall debt on the economy instead of being too timid to promote economic development. And it cannot focus only on the positive impact of debt on economic development; rather, macroeconomic risk should be considered as well. If the overall debt level is too high, enormous pressure will fall on the society and the economy. The pile-up of government debt will impact fiscal balance as well. Therefore, the central government should have the right understanding of debt instruments and a clear picture of the macroeconomy – not only to set a good example for local governments, but to help other debt entities with appropriate debt level assessments and risk controls.

Local governments should think carefully as to whether to relax their grip on the right to issue bonds. In a power division, both the need and the repayment capacity of localities should be taken into consideration. Fiscal difficulty caused by the abuse of power by local governments can be prevented by properly dividing fiscal power and improving the transfer payment system and economic development can be driven by proper debt levels.

4. **Actively adjust the relationship between the real economy and the virtual economy, and encourage the development of the real economy.**

At present, the scale of the virtual economy has far exceeded the development needs of the real economy in China, and this has exerted a negative impact on the latter. To better regulate and control debt – part of the virtual economy – we suggest that access to financial institutions and the capital market should be tightened. We should (1) ensure that the pace of development of the virtual economy is coordinated with that of the real economy, (2) prevent liquidity from getting detained in the virtual economy and (3) direct funds into the real economy in a targeted and efficient way.

As for the virtual economy, the conditions for the establishment of financial institutions and access to the capital market first should be tightened to put the development of the financial market in order. A stricter policy requirement is needed for the access standard in such aspects as product design, risk control, capital restriction, industry experience and technological applications. When necessary, licensing supervision should be adopted to impose stricter access requirements. Second, the very core of financial innovation should be profoundly understood. We need to implement the so-called channel-type and copy-type financial innovations including P2P and crowdfunding. This should improve the efficiency of serving the real economy and reduce financial and systemic risk. Third, for institutions in the banking sector and other sectors that have rather ordered risk management systems, the focus of supervision should be shifted from business to capital to further strengthen capital supervision. Constraint of capital can force and encourage commercial banks to optimize their asset structures, raise the efficiency of capital allocation and support the banking institutions in transforming to a low capital consumption mode.

As for the real economy, structural reform, supply-side reform and a transformation of industry development should be realized. Contribution of technological progress, organizational innovation, specialization and production innovation for the real economy shall be promoted as well. In addition, the virtual economy should be an important support of the real economy. Multi-pronged measures should be put in place to ensure that funds flow to the real economy, effectively addressing the difficulties in – and the high costs of – financing. Trends in social capital flow to the virtual economy – rather than to the real economy – should be firmly checked to prevent "innovation" that may circumvent supervision and deviate from the needs of economic development.

In sum, this was an exploratory research study on the relationship between debt and GDP in China. Though some preliminary conclusions were made, the limitations of this study are evident because of the lack of sufficient data. The accessibility of data from local governments was relatively low, so the continuity of subsequent research cannot be guaranteed. Also, there were no clear data specification standards for contingent liabilities, so this part of debt could not be sorted and analyzed; this weakens the reliability of our conclusions and excluded the possibility for us to employ more complicated statistical methods.

Future work should focus on further collecting and sorting debt data – especially that of each province – to study the relationship between debt and GDP in China with an emphasis on regional differences, to improve the validity of research results. And an analysis of the impact of contingent debt on economic growth should be added. If conditions permit, normalized research on the impact of the contingent liabilities of government and different industries on economic growth could be conducted.

Chapter 3
A Study of China's Government Debt

Globally, government debt is a factor intimately related to macroeconomic activities in the development of all economies. International experience over the past several decades has demonstrated that excessive expansion of government debt is detrimental to the macroeconomy. Hence, aside from recognizing the positive influences of government debt, it is important to identify the enormous risks of letting debt expansion go unchecked. There have been many studies regarding government debt around the world, but there have been relatively few that have targeted China – especially those related to quantitative metering and measurement of government debt. Given these restrictions, the studies of government debt and macroeconomy have not been theoretically solid – hence the significance of our study.

China's government debt over time – particularly local government debt – has accounted for a relatively large proportion of the total GDP. In 2014, the central government debt amounted to 15.0% of the GDP and the local government debt amounted to 24.2% of GDP. Together they accounted for nearly 40% of the GDP. Among government debts, the proportion of central government debt was decreasing, while local government debt was increasing; and the increase of local government debt was higher than that of central government debt.

As for the influence of government debts on economic growth, it can be concluded that **central government debt is still positively related to economic growth, while local government debt has been harming economic growth since debt exceeded the turning point years ago.** In other words, a further increase in local government debt would pose a more significant negative impact on the GDP performance. Therefore, at the current stage and for the foreseeable future, it is essential that China prioritize the assimilation of local government debt in policymaking and improve financial transparency, to promote economic restructuring and industrial adjustment as well as propel the healthy and sound development of domestic economic activities.

X. Zhu et al., *A Study of the Turning Point of China's Debt*,
https://doi.org/10.1007/978-981-13-1325-7_3

3.1 Definition and Characteristics of Government Debt

3.1.1 Definition of Government Debt

Government debt, or a public loan, is a function in which a creditworthy government raises funds as a debtor; the money is used to close fiscal deficits and conduct macro regulation. The government then repays its creditors. Specifically, government debt refers to government bonds issued by the government in both domestic and foreign markets and government loans from foreign governments and banks.

The government debt of China falls into two main categories: central government debt and local government debt. The former refers to the debt of the central government borrowed as fiscal funds. China's current financial revenues and expenditures show that treasury bonds are an important source of funds for the central government. China's central government debt is comprised primarily of treasury bonds which create a debtor-creditor relationship created by raising fiscal funds from the public. The central government must repay investors, with promises of interest – in addition to principal – in due time. Local government debt refers to the debt directly borrowed by construction companies for public infrastructure projects. The liability of local public institutions and the debt are guaranteed by local governments.

By issuing treasury bonds, the central government can pool superfluous savings on the credit market and reinvest them in infrastructure, the social security system and people's livelihoods, thus meeting the demands of economic growth.

Compared with other fiscal instruments, treasury bonds have several advantages – especially in times of economic recession. During a recession, the actual national income is lower than the potential national income, so the government's budget deficit will be very high. If the government chooses to increase state revenue and reduce deficits with higher tax rates, people would have less money in their pockets and bank accounts, resulting in less social capital for investment. This would ultimately aggravate the economic recession. However, if the government chooses to turn public savings into an investment by issuing treasury bonds, it would be able to close the gap on the fiscal deficit while avoiding tax increases (which would curb growth).

Despite their merits, treasury bonds should be kept within a reasonable range. Excessive treasury bonds negatively influence long-term interest rates and social investment. They also worsen the fiscal imbalance and can trigger a bank or currency crisis. Increasing debt and issuing currency to repay government debt is equally detrimental to the economy.

Local government debt is good for economic growth in two ways. First, it is an important tool of macro-control for local governments to pool the capital necessary for local economic regulation. This is especially true in places where local government is financially inadequate and local financial institutions are not mature. Second, issuing debt enables local governments to provide better public products and services, as money raised through debt issuance is usually spent on local infrastructure and public-profit product production, thus boosting local development and improving people's living conditions.

Like central government debt, local government debt also can have a negative impact. The amount of debt that regional fiscal revenue can afford is limited. If a local government issued more debt than it could repay, it would struggle indefinitely. Once the government fails to make a payment on the due date, its expenditures would soon be compromised, stopping the government from operating its ongoing projects and even from performing necessary functions. Moreover, a debt crisis eventually would be transferred to the central government, which adds to the fiscal pressures.

In this book, central government debt refers to treasury bonds, and the balance of central government debt refers to the balance of treasury bonds. Data for our research were derived from statistical yearbooks published by the Ministry of Finance and figures released by the National Bureau of Statistics. Bond issuances with a maturity of 1 year were counted by the par value, and short-term discount bonds with maturity of less than 1 year were counted by the actual amount raised. The local government debt included local government debt at various levels.

3.1.2 A Trend Analysis of the Size of China's Government Debt

There is a great difference between central and local government debt, so this study separately elaborates on the two types of debt. Government debt has four characteristics reflected in the data:

1. **Central and local government debt is increasingly large.**

An analysis of the sizes of central and local government debt with available data showed that the absolute sizes of the debt have been increasingly large. Central government debt soared from around RMB 54.182 billion in 1986 to more than RMB 9.565545 trillion in 2014. Therefore, the absolute size of government debt is rather large and keeps expanding (see Fig. 3.1). From 2012 to 2014, the size of local government debt was bigger than that of the central government debt. In 2014, central government debt amounted to 15.0% of the GDP. In other words, government debt has provided a very large share of China's economic growth. Furthermore, the proportion of government debt in China's overall debt was considerable. Using the first method to calculate total debt, it seems that central government debt made up just 7.4% of China's total debt.

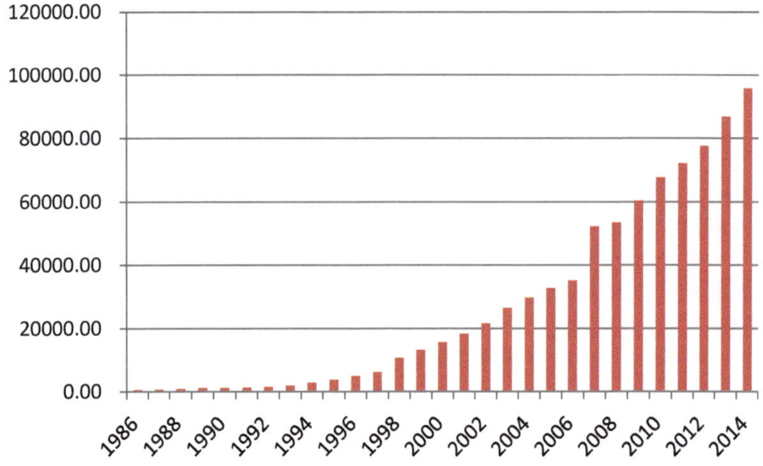

Fig. 3.1 Central government debt in China

2. **The proportion of central government debt is decreasing, while that of local government debt is increasing.**

The proportion of central government debt decreased from 68% in 2007 to 38% in 2014, while the proportion of local government debt increased. From 2007 to 2011, though on a decline, the proportion of central government debt was kept at a level of more than 50% – higher than that of local government debt. Then from 2012 to 2014, the situation reversed.

3. **Local government debt has grown faster than central government debt.**

Among various debt entities, local governments were taking on debt at a relatively fast pace, while central government debt was increasing relatively slowly. For example, in 2003, central government debt totaled RMB 264 million, and in 2014, the figure was 6.92 trillion – registering the slowest annual increase of 14.7%. The proportion of debt in GDP was notable as well. In 2007, the central government debt accounted for 19.4% of the GDP, while in 2014, the proportion decreased by around four percentage points to 15.04%. This suggests that, in recent years, China's central and local governments adopted different strategies and methods for handling debt. In comparison, the local governments were more active in issuing bonds to raise funds.

4. **Growth rates of central and local government debt have fluctuated, but local government debt has been more volatile.**

We first calculated the annual growth rates of China's GDP, total debt, central government debt and local government debt. We then calculated the standard deviation of the growth rate of each entity. The standard deviation serves as a key index in assessing discrete characteristics of the data: a larger standard deviation indicates higher variability. As shown in Fig. 3.2, the standard deviations for both central and local government debt growth rates were high – especially for local

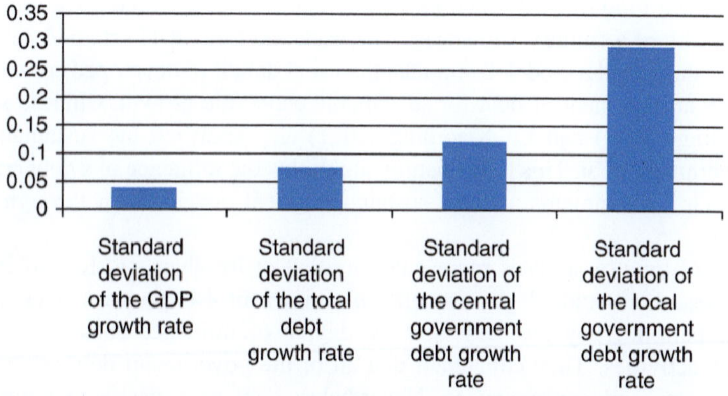

Fig. 3.2 A comparison of the volatility of China's government debt growth rates

government debt. While the growth rates of both central and local government debt fluctuated considerably, the latter fluctuating even more so.

3.2 Literature Review

Ever since its emergence in China, debt has attracted much attention. Thus extensive studies have focused on payment risks associated with high level of debt, the appropriate ways to manage debt and methods to avoid debt risks. As noted by Tian Huimin and Tian Tian (2016), in the aftermath of the 2008 global financial crisis, nearly all countries in the world witnessed a continuously increasing leverage ratio. The severity of the debt issue attracted even more attention from the academic community. This section presents a review of the literature on central and local government debt.

3.2.1 Central Government Debt

Available studies of central government debt fall into three categories. The first is the study of the government debt crisis. For instance, when the European debt crisis began, many scholars tried to explain the reasons from the perspective of welfare (Gao Haihong and Yu Yongding 2010) or internal wealth imbalance (Greenspan 2011) and probed solutions to existing debt problems by adopting improved policies. Some believed that, ultimately, government debt was to blame for the economic crisis. Burnside (2004) viewed the economic crisis in Southeast Asia as a result of worsening government debt. Furceri and Zdzienicka (2010) also studied the banking crisis and found evidence of the impact of government debt on macroeconomic risks.

The second kind of study focuses on the relationship between government debt and the health of a country's finances. Auerbach and Lee (2011) studied debt in the U.S. and established a model to simulate the fiscal deficit of developed countries and the proper arrangement of debt for sustainable economic growth. Chinese scholars Zhang Ming (2009) and Lu Xiaoming (2011) also analyzed the sustainability of U.S. government debt. This type of study highlights the influence of a debt crisis and tries to help governments achieve sustainable fiscal development through proper modeling.

The third type of study is represented by that of Reinhart and Rogoff in 2010. These researchers studied government debt crises in 44 countries over a recent 200-year period. They also assessed the degree of influence each crisis had on economic activities. They concluded that all of the government debt crises shared similar causes and consequences. Nevertheless, out of a desire to maintain its credibility, the government experiencing the debt crisis tends to mislead the public into thinking that there were other causes. This approach provides a more objective assessment of the causes and hazards of government debt crisis. Research by Abbas in 2011 also was a seminal work in the study of government debt since 1880. Data from 178 countries were collected, and a landmark literature review on government debt was compiled.

Though the researchers have taken different approaches, all of them have acknowledged that – regardless of the sizes and maturity periods – government debt has exerted an important influence on the macroeconomy. Most notably, excessive government debt has resulted in macroeconomic instability. Larger government debts distort the issue of taxation. In cases where the government is unable to solve debt problems, it's inclined to resolve a fiscal crisis by raising taxes (Barro 1979). As Sargent and Wallace (1981) and Feng Wencheng and Liu Ying (1993) noted, large-scale issuance of government debt implies imminent inflation. Baldacci and Kumar (2010) further stated that instead of boosting economic growth, this might dampen the economic growth rate in the long run. Empirical studies by Saint-Paul (1992) and Aizenman and Lee (2007) and many other scholars have found evidence of the negative relationship between medium- and long-term debt and the per capita growth rate of GDP.

Since government debt adversely affects the economy, many scholars have proposed ways to lower the size of government debt and thus improve fiscal conditions. Research has shown that scaling down social security expenditures, streamlining government (Alesina and Perotti 1995), reducing infrastructure budgets, practicing fiscal restraint (Mcdermott and Wescott 1996) and making structural adjustments with policy instruments with a smaller multiplier all can effectively help downsize government debt.

We can infer from previous studies that econometric models may overemphasize the way to consolidate fiscal revenue to ensure sustainable fiscal development. And the data-based conclusions offered limited guidance for realistic practice.

3.2.2 Local Government Debt

Why do local governments issue debt? Current studies tend to summarize the reasons as the demand for economic development (Hildreth and Miller 2002), a decline in fiscal revenue (Mikesell and Mullins 2011), the imperfection of management systems (Levine 2011) and political requirements (Geys 2006). The expansion of local government debt has pressured debt management and has diverted scholars' attention to local debt management.

In Western countries, local governments have a longer history of debt issuance and hence have more experience in this regard. First, in local government debt management, administrative means alone are not enough; it's also necessary to use market forces for regulation. By proactively rating the government, the market maintains its credibility and debt performance (Folkerts-Landau et al. 1993). Second, a constraint of the government's right to debt issuance centralizes the rights of the central government, thus preventing irrational debt issuance. It also facilitates local government debt management. Lastly, Plekhanov and Singh (2006) contended that employing reasonable risk-warning indicators can effectively prevent local governments from running into debt risks. In cases where a local government's fiscal deficit or the degree of debt reliance goes too high, the government would be restrained from issuing further debt as a means of better controlling relevant risks.

The local debt problem in China – as well as its academic study – dates to the taxation reform of 1994. There have been three stages of domestic research. The first stage occurred prior to the mid-1990s. However, due to China's national conditions back then, not much data is available. Most of the studies at this stage focused on theoretical exposition and analysis and served political purposes. For instance, Zhang Qiang and Chen Jiyu (1995) pointed out the significance of local government debt. They proposed that improving the fiscal investment and financing system of local governments would be the key to settling local government debt risks in China.

The second stage, marked by the outbreak of the Southeast Asian financial crisis in 1997, extended from the mid-1990s through 2008. To avoid an economic recession, China promulgated expansionary fiscal policies, which, to some extent, increased local government debt. According to Lin Guoqing (2002), at that time, many scholars started to look at local government debts in light of relevant phenomena and employed regional data for analysis. Guo Lin and Chen Chunguang (2002) asserted that the formation of local government debts could be attributed to deficiencies in the fiscal system. They thought that local governments should work to avoid fiscal risks by increasing financial revenue, regulating public expenditures (Rui Guijie 2003) and establishing methods for debt repayment (Lin Sheng 2005).

The third stage refers to the period after 2008. Following the global financial crisis and the continuous introduction of proactive financial policies, China has seen remarkable growth of local government debt. What's more, the study of debt in China has increasingly influenced foreign countries. The perspectives of debt study have diversified, but the approaches have become more standardized. Hu Wenjun (2010) and Yin Shouxiang (2009) and other scholars have discussed the feasibility of authorizing local governments to issue debts based on domestic conditions and international experience. They have contended that by issuing debt independently, the local governments could ease fiscal tensions as well as promote economic development. Nevertheless, some have questioned this view. Miao Lianying and Cheng Xueyang (2009), for example, noted that China's institutions were insufficient to support local governments in doing so; their arguments were extremely heated at this stage. Some researchers have introduced international studies on local government debt, hoping to learn from others and thus establish a management arrangement appropriate for China.

In fact, for countries like China which are undergoing economic restructuring, apart from domestic scholars, foreign experts also have a great interest in conducting research. Mello (2009) believed that as countries in transformation develop rather rapidly, their governments would be confronted with a cash crunch for infrastructure projects; hence these governments might raise funds by issuing debt. However, Hogye (2002) opined that since these governments are rather powerful during economic restructuring, they had better not to take a market-based view in considering local government debt. Their debt issuance has the characteristics of a planned economy, and the financial revenue and expenditures also are highly planned. Therefore, it's unlikely that government debt will go higher.

In summary, studies of local government debt have made substantial progress. But most of these studies have been theoretical rather than empirical. This may be because of a "data desert." Therefore, this book focuses on empirical studies of government issued debt in an effort to better understand – and solve – the problems associated with it.

3.3 A Comparison of Chinese and Foreign Government Debts

The development of China's central government debt and local government debt can be better understood in the context of government debts of the U.S., Japan and European countries. China can learn from these countries how to handle current and future government debt.

3.3.1 A History of China's Government Debt

1. **Central government debt**

Since the founding of the People's Republic of China, the country's central government debt – i.e. treasury bonds – has transformed dramatically from their birth, followed by a depression, a recovery, an expansion and a more recent ballooning.

China's government debt was first issued between 1950 and 1958. As a newly founded nation, the PRC was faced with huge difficulties and severe challenges. To provide sufficient supplies for the revolutionary war and change the underdeveloped economy which was characterized by faltering production, inflation and trade contraction, in 1950, the Chinese government issued the People's Victory bonds with a total value of RMB 30.2 billion. This was the first type of treasury bonds issued in the PRC. After 3 years of economic recovery, China entered a planned economy. During this period, to address the funding gap and further accelerate economic development, China drew on past experience and issued government bonds. They were issued in five lots from 1954 to 1958 and amounted to RMB 836 million, RMB 619 million, RMB 607 million, RMB 684 million, and RMB 798 million, respectively (RMB 3.544 billion in total). Since these government bonds were primarily used to facilitate the country's economic growth, they were known as economic construction bonds.

From 1959 through 1980, China experienced a depression of central government debt. For historical reasons, the Chinese government declined any form of foreign capital or other assistance for economic growth and did not consider domestic debt for economic construction. As a result, China did not issue any domestic treasury bonds for 22 years. Meanwhile, the Chinese government, with astonishing speed, repaid all its domestic and foreign debts in 1964 and 1968, respectively. During this period, China assumed neither domestic debt nor foreign debt.

From 1981 to 1993, the Chinese central government debt started to accelerate. In the 1980s, due to the economic reform and opening-up, the distribution pattern between government and businesses was adjusted. Although enterprises benefited from tax cuts, these cuts hurt the central government. National income fell, while enterprises and local governments had much more money at their disposal. With the changes in national income distribution, the fiscal income of the central government was insufficient for expenditures. Hence the country was saddled with alarming budget deficits in 1979 and 1980. In 1981, to handle the fiscal problems, China decided to issue treasury bonds again. From 1981 to 1987, the Chinese government issued treasury bonds worth RMB 5.95 billion on average per year – which was a relatively small amount. Meanwhile, the treasury bonds were not sufficiently diversified: most were medium- and long-term bonds which would mature in 5–9 years, with few three-year Projects Construction Bonds. Since 1986, the central government planned to regulate the overheated economy. The *Provisional Regulations of the People's Republic of China on the Control of Banks* clearly stated that finance departments might not overdraw on the People's Bank of China. Hence for a long time, the fiscal deficits were primarily addressed by issuing currency. In this way, a small part of the PBC's borrowing was covered by treasury bonds. As the Chinese government was working to administer the economic climate and regulate the economic order, its fiscal burdens became heavier in 1988. As a result, the central government had to issue ad hoc capital construction bonds to bridge fiscal deficits. Overall, however, the fiscal deficits were covered by central government bonds and PBC overdrafts or borrowing. Thus the size of China's government debt remained small.

The central government debt in China expanded from 1994 to 2007. To untangle the relationship between banks and financing and to sever the direct link between inflation and fiscal deficit, the Chinese government – with documents issued in 1993 – stated that the Ministry of Finance was forbidden from borrowing from the PBC. Further, the fiscal deficit was to be covered by treasury bonds. Thus after 1993, treasury bonds became the only way for the central government to reduce fiscal deficits and pay interest and principal on its debt. As a result, the issuance size of treasury bonds increased significantly, and government debts ramped up substantially as well. In 1994, the issuance of treasury bonds exceeded RMB 100 billion for the first time. Since the Asian financial crisis began in 1997, the Chinese government adopted a proactive fiscal policy to lessen its impact. Thus the government expanded treasury bond investments from 1998 to 2004. However, this led to the dramatic increase of government debts and fiscal deficits. From 2004 to 2007, the Chinese government replaced its proactive fiscal policy with a prudent one, yet deficits remained. In 2007, as bubbles built up in the stock market and as taxes – such as the stamp duty of stock deals – increased, China ran a budget surplus for the first time in 25 years amid its economic surge.

China's central government debt began to balloon in 2008. The outbreak of the global financial crisis in 2008 sent the country back to fiscal deficits. To deal with the impact of the financial crisis on the economy, the Chinese government resumed its proactive fiscal policy and launched a RMB four trillion stimulus package. This led to another round of booming investments and resulted in the largest government debt ever seen in China.

2. **Local government debt**

After the founding of the People's Republic of China, local government debt underwent similar phases to that of central government debt: initial development, initial expansion, sharp expansion, constant growth and ballooning.

The initial development of local government debt occurred from 1979 to 1992. In 1958, the Chinese government issued the *Decision on Issuing Local Government Debts*, making clear that local governments could issue construction bonds when necessary. The local government debt in China first appeared in 1979, when eight counties and districts assumed local government debts. After 1979, local governments at all levels began issuing debt. From 1981 to 1985, a total of 28 provincial governments (including municipalities with independent planning status) began facilitating government borrowing. By constantly issuing debt, local governments could invest heavily in infrastructure. However, aimless investment practices resulted in a series of problems, such as overcapacity and inflation. To address the situation, the State Council issued the *Notice on Suspending the Issuance of Local Government Bonds*, forbidding local governments from issuing debt.

From 1992 to 1997, local government debt expanded. Note that in 1992, China became a socialist market economy. Local economies grew rapidly, and local government debt issues surfaced. After the reform of the tax system in 1994, the financial powers were shifted upward – and administrative power distribution shifted downward. The imbalance further aggravated the expansion of local government debt. To facilitate local economic growth, local governments at all levels expanded their debts to a different extent – regardless of their own finances. To curb the unregulated borrowing of local governments, the *Budget Law* dating from 1995 banned local governments from debt issuance. However, after the 1997 Asian financial crisis, risks associated with local financial institutions came to the fore. To maintain a stable financial system and social order, the local governments had to address the payment shortfall.

Local government debt expanded sharply from 1998 to 2004. In the second half of 1998, the Chinese government introduced proactive fiscal policies featuring treasury bond investments, aiming to address issues such as the Asian financial crisis. After the central government and local governments entered into on-lending agreements, local governments were allowed to use most treasury bonds. In the meantime, local governments had to arrange matching funds. Therefore, during the implementation of proactive fiscal policies, local governments and other functional departments had to issue debts or raise funds with methods such as establishing investment companies. That, in a way, resulted in the sharp expansion of local government debt. According to rough estimates by the Development Research Center of the State Council in 2003, the local government debt at that time amounted to at least RMB one trillion. Additionally, from 1998 to 2005, more than RMB 300 billion of local government debts arose from the on-lending programs of treasury bonds.

The period between 2004 and 2007 witnessed continued growth of local government debt. The Chinese government fell back on prudent fiscal policies and large deficits remained. Though local governments at all levels had taken aggressive steps to control and address local government debt, it kept growing.

Local government debt has ballooned since 2008, the year when the global financial crisis broke out. The following year, China was confronted with great challenges in economic development. To handle the impact of the financial crisis on the economy, the Chinese government resumed proactive fiscal policies. These policies were characterized by issuing additional treasury bonds and running larger deficits. To facilitate local governments to invest massively in construction and ease their financial stress in unfolding the RMB four trillion stimulus package, the Ministry of Finance – for the first time – issued local bonds totaling RMB 200 billion on behalf of local governments. Meanwhile, the expansion of local government investment increased local government debt to a certain extent. In 2009, local debt jumped to RMB nine trillion from RMB 5.56 trillion at the end of 2018, reporting a year-over-year increase of 61.7%. By the end of 2014, the local government debt in China totaled RMB 15.4 trillion, which represented 24.2% of GDP.

3.3.2 A History of U.S. Government Debt

U.S. government debt dates to the founding of the country. The U.S. has been involved in many large-scale wars. To satisfy the funding requirements of prewar preparedness, wartime army supplies and reconstruction of strategic regions, the government has had to constantly expand its debts. Thus government debt was played an increasingly important role in macroeconomic growth. The history of U.S. government debt includes four stages: its birth, development, expansion and recent ballooning.

When the U.S. was founded, the Continental Congress was held. One of its charges was to issue war bonds – the earliest form of U.S. government debt. After the U.S. federal government was established in 1789, the principal and unpaid interest of the nation's domestic and foreign debt – at their face values – were translated into the federal government's long-term treasury bonds totaling approximately $750 billion. They were not paid off until 1835.

The first boom of U.S. treasury bonds took place during the Civil War. In 1860, the U.S. treasury bonds amounted to only $65 million. However, after the war began, the figure rocketed to $2.7 billion. There was then a year-over-year drop. Later, the breakout of World War I prompted the surge of U.S. treasury bonds, which sharply increased to $27.4 billion in 1919 (from $5.7 billion prior to the war).

After the 1930s, President Franklin Roosevelt adhered to Keynesian macroeconomic theories to overcome the international economic crisis. Thus the U.S. government worked to stimulate economy by assuming huge debts – a policy known as "the New Deal." A large amount of government debts were issued to cover the fiscal deficit, leading to the sustained and rapid increase of U.S. treasury bonds. The growth trend continued until World War II. By 1946, the U.S. government debt had reached $269.4 billion. After the war ended, few years witnessed shrinkage of government debt; overall, the U.S. government debt continued to expand at an increasingly fast speed – reaching $256.7 billion in 1950, $290 billion in 1960 and $382.6 billion in 1970.

Since the 1980s, the U.S. government debt kept increasing rapidly. In 1985, the U.S. went from being the world's largest creditor to the largest debtor, which ended its creditor status (which began in 1914). After that, the U.S. macroeconomy gradually became a debt-dependent one.

Since 2000, U.S. government debt has continued on an upward trend. After the U.S. Internet economy bubble burst, health care benefits and the "war on terrorism" called for larger portions of the fiscal budget. Fiscal deficits remained at a high level, and the financial situation became worse with the U.S. subprime mortgage crisis beginning in 2007. This global financial event had significant negative consequences on the U.S. macroeconomy and made U.S. fiscal expenditures rise even faster than before. To address the adverse effects, the U.S. government announced a third round of "quantitative easing," or QE3, to significantly reduce the federal funds target rate. The proactive fiscal policy and monetary easing policy saved the U.S. financial system to some extent, but also further drove up U.S. government debt. For example, in 2013, the U.S. government debt was as high as $16.719 trillion or 100.6% of GDP; if the states' debt ($1.191 trillion) and local government debt ($1.792 trillion) were included, the total debt reached $20.531 trillion or 118.5% of GDP.

3.3.3 A History of Government Debt in Japan

Japan's government debt has a short history. In the beginning, it remained at a relatively low level. It was not until the 1970s that Japan's government debt increased rapidly – more rapidly than any other country in the world. The history of Japan's government debt includes three stages.

The first stage occurred from 1965 to 1990. After WWII, an economic crisis hit Japan. Japanese industrial production plummeted and so did the government's tax revenue. To ease the pressure of government operation and stimulate the economy, the Japanese government – for the first time – issued a small amount of debt. This involved major adjustments to Japanese fiscal policies, which shifted from the balanced budget policy to the Keynesian deficit spending policy. The first treasury bonds were primarily used to invest in public works. The global oil crisis in 1974 also dealt a blow to Japan's macroeconomy. As a result, private investment and consumption contracted sharply. The overall economy was shattered as production costs soared and private capital spending experienced a slippery slope. To boost economic growth, the Japanese government had to issue a huge amount of deficit-financing bonds. This trend remained strong until the 1980s.

The second stage ranged from 1991 to 2007. After Japan's economic bubble burst in the early 1990s, the country's economy declined sharply. Total investment and consumption plunged. Meanwhile, the Japanese government issued a large number of treasury bonds from 1993 to 1995. Nevertheless, as the economy picked up after 1996, the Asian financial crisis broke out in 1998. To combat the crisis and stimulate the economy, the issuance of Japanese treasury bonds hit a record high, amounting to nearly JPY 40 trillion.

In 2008, government debt in Japan has entered its third stage, which involved even more growth. An international financial crisis began in 2008 and sent ripples throughout global markets. To address the international financial tsunami, the Japanese government had to – again – increase the issuance of treasury bonds. In 2009, the issuance of Japanese treasury bonds was at an all-time high, totaling JPY 53 trillion. After that, the Japanese government debt continued to expand, and the amount of treasury bonds reached JPY 1009 trillion in 2014.

3.3.4 A History of European Government Debt

After the financial crisis broke out in 2008, member states of the European Union (EU) – most notably Greece – became mired in a debt crisis, which attracted worldwide attention. According to the EU *Stability and Growth Pact*, each country had to keep its annual budget deficit below 3% of GDP and keep total public debt below 60% of GDP. In December 2009, Greece's deficit/GDP ratio reached 12.7%, and its debt/GDP ratio reached 113%. Both figures were far above the thresholds specified in the pact. Within just 1 month, the Big Three credit rating agencies –

Standard & Poor's (S&P), Moody's and Fitch Group – downgraded Greece's sovereign ratings, which instantly fueled the spread of market fears. Investors in the debt market dumped Greece's treasury bonds. In fact, the Greek debt crisis had shown huge negative impacts before breaking out: the stock markets of the U.S. and European countries reported declines of more than 1% shortly after the opening bell. Meanwhile, other EU members like Spain, Portugal, Ireland and Italy also faced similar grim fiscal outlooks: the fiscal debts were too large and accounted for a high share of GDP, and their ratings were downgraded to different extents.

In early 2010, the crisis hit Spain. On Feb. 4, 2010, the Spanish Treasury published a report and submitted it to the European Commission, targeting a general government deficit at 9.8% of its GDP for 2010. The statement triggered strong reactions in the market. On Feb. 5, 2010, the Spanish stock market plunged 6%, marking the largest decline in 15 months. Since Spain had been a relatively strong economy among EU countries, its debt crisis led to wild economic swings, and the euro was dragged down sharply. Starting with Greece and Spain, the debt crisis then spread to the entire euro zone. Many countries which had had robust economics – such as Belgium – even experienced a crisis.

With the contagion of Europe's sovereign debt crisis, the debt ratings of Greece, Spain, Italy and other countries were downgraded. Even the better-off Germany experienced a rapid increase in its debt, and its debt/GDP ratio exceeded the EU standard. On Jan. 13, 2012, S&P cut the triple-A rating of France and Austria to AA +; meanwhile, the agency lowered its ratings for Portugal, Italy and Spain by two notches. And the S&P downgraded the long-term credit ratings of nine euro zone governments. These moves meant that Europe's sovereign debt crisis had spread from peripheral countries to core countries, from smaller economies to bigger economies – and it quickly escalated.

3.4 A Metrological Analysis of Government Debt

Since there is big difference between the debt of the central government and that of local governments, this study illustrates the impact of both types of debt on economic growth. However, the conclusions might not be as accurate due to limited data. For example, in the analysis of the impact of local government debt, only data from 2007 to 2013 are available, which limits our conclusions.

3.4.1 Central Government Debt

We examined the total volume of central government debt and GDP as the major variables of an econometric model for overall debt:

Table 3.1 The regression results for central government debt

Model		Unstandardized coefficient				
		B	Standard error	Standardized coefficient	T	Sig.
1	(Constant)	17,138.047	9380.507		1.827	0.082
	Central government debt	2.897	0.980	0.458	2.957	0.008
	Square of debt	0.0001749	0.000	0.541	4.027	0.001
	One-year loan IR	−109.861	859.827	−0.006	−0.128	0.900

$F = 611.009^{**}$
Adjusted $R^2 = 0.987$
**Significantly correlated at 0.01 level (tow-tailed)

$$\begin{aligned} GDP_{t+1} &= C + b_1\text{central government debt}_t + b_2\text{central government debt}_t^2 \\ &\quad + b_3\text{one-year loan interest rate}_t + e \end{aligned}$$

Results of the least squares regression are shown in Table 3.1.

The table shows that both central government debt and its square were significantly positively correlated with economic growth. This means that an increase in central government debt exerted a strong, positive influence on economic growth. Thus there was a noticeable difference between central government debt and China's overall debt in terms of their respective influence on the macroeconomy since there was no downward turning point in central government debt. Therefore, the positive influence of central government debt on the economy will most likely continue to rise. The continued increase in central government debt will still positively affect GDP.

The scatter plot of central government debt and GDP is shown in Fig. 3.3, in which a relatively evident upward quadratic relationship is evident.

3.4.2 Local Government Debt

We also examined local government debt and GDP, which were the major variables in this econometric model:

$$\begin{aligned} GDP_{t+1} &= C + b_1\text{local government debt}_t + b_2\text{local government debt}_t^2 \\ &\quad + b_3\text{one-year loan interest rate}_t + e \end{aligned}$$

Results of the least squares regression are shown in Table 3.2.

The table indicates that local government debt was positively correlated with economic growth, while its square was negatively correlated with the latter. However, the coefficient was not statistically significant – probably because of limited data. It can be roughly inferred that local government debt had a relatively weaker positive influence on economic growth. Nonetheless, this influence also had a turning point. The deduced turning point of local government debt was reached

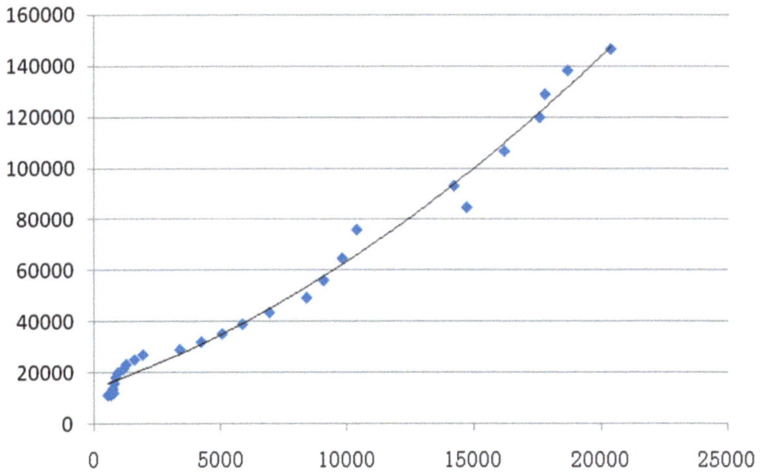

Fig. 3.3 The relationship between central government debt and GDP

Table 3.2 The regression results for local government debt

Model		Unstandardized coefficient		Standardized coefficient	T	Sig.
		B	Standard error			
1	(Constant)	74,133.014	12,4219.111		0.597	0.593
	Local government debt	6.089	2.344	2.024	2.598	0.081
	Square of debt	−0.00002874	0.000	−1.068	−1.390	0.259
	One-year loan IR	11,629.475	14,689.249	0.122	0.792	0.486

F = 15.797*
Adjusted $R^2 = 0.940$
*Significantly correlated at 0.05 level (tow-tailed)

when the volume of debt was RMB 10.69 trillion (the 2003 price) or RMB 14.96 trillion (the 2015 price).

Moreover, the data show that local government debt may have reached its turning point before 2014. This means that China's local government debt has become negatively correlated with GDP, and its marginal effect on GDP has become negative. The continued rise of local government debt will exert a stronger negative influence on GDP.

3.5 Summary and Suggestions

The relationship between government debt and economic growth illustrated in this study was based on current debt data. Our analyses revealed that the expansion of central government debt in China still has had a positive influence on macroeconomic growth to some extent. This means that it is still feasible to stimulate economic growth by expanding central government debt. This positive influence likely will last for a while, which is considerably different from the situation in the foreign countries we analyzed. Countries stricken by the European sovereign debt crisis exhibited problems in regard to debt issued by the central government. Therefore, we conclude that the influence of central government debt and the overall debt in an economy is evidently different given that there was no downward turning point for central government debt.

But for local – as opposed to central – government debt, the situation was completely the opposite. And the problems with local government debt seem to be specific to China's unique conditions. In foreign countries, the size of local government debt has not been a significant issue. But in China, the problem of local government debt is far more complicated than that of central government debt, due to the characteristics of tax allocation between local governments and the central government and the intrinsic motivation of local governments in stimulating economic growth. According to the data, local government debt generally has had a weak positive influence on economic growth, and, after a certain turning point, it has had a negative influence. In fact, China's local government debt already has exceeded the turning point. At this stage, the expansion of local government debt will exert a strong negative influence on economic growth. Thus maintaining a high level of local government debt is akin to provoking a debt crisis.

Considering the unique characteristics of China's government debt and drawing on some successful government debt management experience from the U.S., Japan and Europe, we offer the following suggestions for China:

1. **The function and role of government in economic growth should be properly defined to achieve the maximum market efficiency on the premise of appropriate and moderate intervention.**

The recurrent worldwide financial crises and debt crises facing many countries have led people to rethink the role and function of government. As noted by economic theories, the market alone is not perfect. Further, there are defects of various degrees in market resource allocation – sometimes even to the disadvantage of economic growth. Even so, the function and role of government in economic growth should not be overamplified. Neither should we think that government can address every aspect of an economic or financial crisis. From studying the reactions of different countries in financial crises, we found that government undoubtedly plays an important role in regulating markets and stimulating economic growth. However, this does not mean that the market can be replaced by government. We still should look squarely at the relationship between government and markets as well as the role and position of government in economic growth.

China also faces a grim external development environment. Its domestic consumption market, private investment and labor market are all under huge pressure. Thus it is more important to have the right view of the function of government. If the function of government is overly stressed and amplified, the self-regulation capacity of the market will be compromised. And if this is the case, it is not difficult to anticipate the government issuing debt for macro regulation.

China's government debt indicates that local government debt has already become negatively correlated with economic growth. Though this is not the case with central government debt, we cannot afford to neglect its absolute volume. To effectively put government debt – especially local government debt – under control, it is critical to properly recognize the role of government and the negative influence of debt. In the face of intricate macroeconomic issues, a clear line should be drawn between the government and the markets. Government should give full play to the advantages of its command of information and formulation of rules, avoid its shortcomings, and clarify the border of free competition to maximize market efficiency with appropriate and moderate intervention.

2. **China should accurately gauge the intensity and timing of a fiscal stimulus plan and moderately control the total volume of central government debt.**

Although the data showed that China's central government debt is still positively correlated with economic growth, we should maintain sharp vigilance against the expansion of debt. Countries in the West have long been issuing debt to "pay deficit down with deficit" and "repay debt with debt," which has caused a daunting debt crisis. This is an important alarm for China.

While recognizing the positive effect of the increase in central government debt, it is of significance to think carefully about a possible crisis that could be brought about by excessive debt. As mentioned above, an understanding of the role and position of government is essential. But it is not necessary for the government to take care of everything that can be addressed by the self-regulation of the market. Nor is the government capable of going beyond its power in this regard. Rational analysis and assessment of the realistic macroeconomic problems are needed to manage the timing and intensity of effective fiscal policy. In particular, we need to take precautions prior to the breakout of macroeconomic problems, to achieve sound regulation at a low cost. Otherwise, sound implementation cannot be guaranteed – no matter what measures are taken. On the contrary, economic fluctuations might arise which shift the economy from overheating to overcooling.

We believe that whatever fiscal measures are taken, moderate control of the total volume of central government debt should be the goal. Although the data suggest room for expansion, we should remain vigilant. Since our data and econometric model were exploratory, the variables could not fully reflect the law of macroeconomic operations. Hence the influence of central government debt on economic growth may change when more macroeconomic elements are incorporated into the model. As a result, our conclusions are suggestive rather than absolute. Moreover, macroeconomic activities have much uncertainty, making prediction difficult. When the external environment changes significantly, the boundaries adopted in this study may change, leading to changes in the relationship between central government debt and economic growth. Therefore, moderate control of central government debt still will be needed – especially given the complicated economic situation in China and its high level of central government debt.

3. **China's fiscal transparency needs to be improved gradually, and its government funds should be used more efficiently.**

Sound fiscal transparency is necessary for managing government debt, building modern government and improving government administration. In light of China's integration into global social, economic and cultural affairs, fiscal transparency will play an important role in helping China increase its economic exchange and raise its international image and presence. Also, it is important for the government to proactively manage its debt and improve its efficiency, while preventing waste and debt expansion. According the definition proposed by the International Monetary Fund, fiscal transparency means that government reports to the public regularly on its organizational structure and the function of its departments, orientation of the fiscal policy and the fiscal position and plan of the public sector. Raising fiscal transparency means that the government regularly should disclose all relevant financial data including details regarding the budget, taxation, assets and debts.

Compared with other countries – especially developed countries in Europe and North America – China's fiscal transparency is relatively low. In China, only general budget reports have been provided to the public. Moreover, extra-budgetary fiscal revenues and expenditures have accounted for quite a large share of the country's debt, making fiscal budget management almost pointless. Since information on China's government debt is incomplete, it is very difficult to conduct meaningful research on the subject. In effect, compared with that of the central government, the fiscal transparency of local governments is even more ambiguous. Much information disclosed by local governments is only fragmentary fiscal data, which doesn't consider budgets, assets and debt. In addition, data disclosed by governments have regional differences as there are no unified standards. Thus it's hard to make horizontal comparisons. In fact, this was the major challenge in our study in trying to determine the relationship between debt and economic growth. The lack of statistics at the regional (provincial) level has compromised the validity of our results at the local level.

Fiscal transparency is the basis for the state and government to create macro policy. And it is needed to provide the basic conditions for the analysis of government assets, debts and debt management. We believe that we should learn about fiscal transparency from foreign governments, so we can gradually narrow the gap between China's fiscal transparency and the international standard. Improvements in fiscal transparency can force the government to formulate fiscal policies in a more reasonable way to avoid excessive debt.

4. **Local government debt management needs to be improved by enhancing debt capital at different stages.**

The root cause of the government debt problem lies in the lack of a complete and systemic debt management system in government at all levels. Consequently, the first step in effectively dealing with the local government debt problem is to strengthen the legal supervision system for government bonds. This will stipulate such aspects of local government debt issuance as debt issuer qualifications, use of funds, targeted areas, debt repayment, information disclosure, crisis response and disciplinary actions. Local government debt management and risk control also will rely on this legal system.

A debt issuance review system should be established regarding the debt issued by local governments. Scientific assessment of the debt-financed projects launched by local governments – in particular, meticulous argumentation of the size of debt, source of funds and benefit of projects – should avoid unreasonable government debt issuance. Budget management of debt financing should be emphasized in the debt issuance review to clarify the scope of use and supervision system of the funds.

As for the debt already issued by local governments, management of the debt should be tightened to avoid deviation from its original purpose. We should establish – and clarify – a scientific and reasonable procedure for debt financing, and designate a responsible person to oversee the use and impact of the funds. Meanwhile, we should establish a tracking mechanism for debt repayment. Local governments and agencies should be required to strictly comply with their debt agreements, eliminate bad debts on a regular basis and effectively hedge various debt-related risks.

It may be possible to classify the debt generated on a local government financing platform based on its liquidity. Then financial innovation can transform low-liquidity assets or asset portfolios that can generate a stable cash flow into tradable securities products. These products can bring some cash flow in the future, so they could help local governments make their debt more refundable. They also could resolve the short-term default risk of local government debt.

Governments at all levels can refer to the practices of Westernized countries when formulating annual budgets; this will involve setting aside a certain proportion of the funds as debt reserves to reduce insolvency risks.

5. **Local government financing and private capital can be expanded to finance regional construction.**

To solve the problem of excessive local government debt, we should expand local governments' financing options. Local governments issue debt with the aim of financing local economic development. But there are difficulties inherent in alternative financing channels for financing debt. If other financial sources are available, then the current debt financing mode of local governments can be replaced.

In local economic development, a public-private partnership should be vigorously promoted to fully introduce private capital into the local economic construction. This should ease the pressure of local governments caused by economic construction and fiscal expenditures. When drawing private capital into economic construction – and infrastructure in particular – we should observe the principles and laws of market operation, to develop a mutually beneficial, sustainable outcome. This will make private capital benefit from local economic construction, and bring strong sustainability to this mode.

6. **Measures of local government performance should emphasize culture, ecology and living conditions (rather than political achievements).**

The main problem with China's local government debt – in terms of the sustainable development of the economy – is closely related to the current economic growth model. The extensive economic growth model refers to the model of increasing output or value of output based on the increase in the input of production factors including capital, labor and material resources. In this model, local governments have adequate motivation to issue debt for funds and increase the value of output through debt financing. The transformation of the economic development mode would require concerted efforts between the central and local governments. The central government can encourage industrial transformation, support emerging industries and guide the transformation of the economy through means of policy-based funds, guarantees, interest subsidies and tax incentives. And local governments should consciously transform the mindset of economic growth, carry out corresponding incentive policies at the regional level, and facilitate the adjustment and transformation of the industrial structure.

Excessive local government debt is interlinked with the current assessment system of political achievements of China's government agencies. Currently, in our opinion, the measurement of local government performance has an undue emphasis on economic indicators such as GDP growth rate, fixed investments, the amount of attracted investments, the number of businesses, and the development level and aesthetic measure of municipal construction. In contrast, few indicators are related to social and cultural conditions, the ecological environment or people's livelihoods. The current system places a greater emphasis on political achievements which has given rise to the desire of local governments to blindly pursue debt to invest in infrastructure. In the short term, this debt-driven development model can increase GDP to some extent, but in the long term, it will exert a strong negative influence on economic activities and increase the debt risk for local governments. Therefore, revising the current system based on local political achievements and replacing it with a system based on societal accomplishments in regard to culture, ecology and living conditions as core indicators is necessary to reduce the size and risk of local government debt.

Chapter 4
A Study of China's Bank Debt

At present, China's traditional financial service model with banks at its core is confronted with external challenges. Firstly, as the marketization presses ahead, the industrial competition among banks intensifies. Secondly, as the social financing structure profoundly changes, the phenomenon of financial disintermediation is becoming more and more prominent. Thirdly, pro-cyclical businesses of banks are exposed to risks. Fourthly, as technical disintermediation accelerates, Internet and other technologies are marginalizing banks' payment and financing function. Fifthly, the debt capacity and structure of banks is approaching the turning point. Sixthly, the liquidity risk management is the most critical issue in the leverage ratio management of commercial banks. Meanwhile, there are some internal problems in the transformation of China's banking industry. Firstly, banks with single-large shareholders have some inherent defects in their corporate management, and the de-administration of banks remains a huge task. Secondly, the functions of commercial banks are converging. Thirdly, the customer-oriented operation logic has not been formed yet. Fourth, the information technology capability of banks is not strong enough to fully release productivity.

This chapter mainly focuses on the size of bank debt and its relationship with economic growth. Statistics show that the debt of China's banking industry was more than twice the GDP in 2014, and accounted for an ever-increasing proportion of the economy. Quantitative analysis confirms that, an increase in the bank debt by one unit could increase the GDP by 0.479 unit. Moreover, the regressive relationship between the square of the debt indicators and GDP is highly negative. **This proves the existence of the turning point of bank debt. If we consider the debt of RMB 197.54 trillion (in 2015s prices) as the turning point, the influence of bank debt on GDP has already turned or is about to turn negative.**

In view of the law of international banking development, there is always an end to the scale expansion of commercial banks, and value management is the development trend of China's commercial banks. During this process, the central government needs to introduce regulatory policies to lead commercial banks towards the path of "value banks". The suggestions are as follows: firstly, guide commercial banks back

X. Zhu et al., *A Study of the Turning Point of China's Debt*,
https://doi.org/10.1007/978-981-13-1325-7_4

to the rational operation philosophy of ensuring "security, liquidity and profitability" in a proper way; secondly, construct an assessment mechanism oriented on capital return rather than rules and regulations, and promote commercial banks to be transformed from "scale banks" into "value banks"; thirdly, be cautious about the absolute size of debt of financial industry, and take appropriate measures to reduce debts.

4.1 Definition and Characteristics of Bank Debt

4.1.1 Definition of Bank Debt

In a broad sense, the financial industry includes the banking sector, the securities industry, futures, trust, insurance companies, and other financial institutions. The previous chapters have looked into the virtual markets such as the securities market and bond market that mainly engaged in direct financing. And all the cash deposit and insurance funds charged by securities companies, futures companies, trust companies and insurance companies need to be entrusted to banking institutions and thus become the debt of these institutions. Therefore, the debt held by China's banking sector can be roughly equated with the debt of the financial industry by reckoning up and sorting out the assets and debt mutually held by financial institutions.

Based on simplified estimation of the debt sizes of different business forms in the financial industry, the debt of the banking sector accounts for the majority among such industries as the banking, securities, insurance, fund and futures sectors. At the end of 2014, the debt size of the banking institutions in China was RMB 155.85 trillion while that of the insurance sector, securities sector, fund sector and futures sector were RMB 8.83 trillion, RMB 3.17 trillion, RMB 14 billion and RMB 11 billion respectively. In terms of their proportions, the banking sector accounted for as high as 92.83%, far higher than other industries. In regards to the importance, bank debt can on the whole represent the changing trend of the debt size of the entire financial industry (Table 4.1).

Table 4.1 Debt sizes and proportions of China's major financial industries in 2014

	Debt size (RMB 100 million)	Proportion
Banking sector	1,558,479.00	92.83%
Securities industry	31,694.81	1.89%
Insurance industry	88,336.21	5.26%
Fund industry	140.61	0.01%
Futures industry	107.75	0.01%

Sources: China Banking Regulatory Commission, China Securities Regulatory Commission and China Insurance Regulatory Commission. Total debt sizes of industries are the difference between total asset and owner's equity (net asset)

Table 4.2 Asset correlations between China's major financial industries

	Banking financial institutions	Securities companies	Insurance companies
Banking financial institutions	1	.795*	.994**
Securities companies	.795*	1	.851**
Insurance companies	.994**	.851**	1

*Significantly correlated at 0.05 level (tow-tailed)
**Significantly correlated at .01 level (tow-tailed)

According to the asset correlations between the banking, securities and insurance industries from 2007 to the end of 2015, the correlation between the banking and insurance industries is 99.4% and that between the banking and securities industries is 79.5%, so the changing conditions of the asset and debt in the banking sector can basically reflect that in the securities and insurance sectors (Table 4.2).

Given the above analysis, all of the cash deposit and insurance funds charged by financial institutions in such industries as securities and insurance industries except for the banking sector needs to be entrusted to banking institutions and thus become the debt of commercial banking institutions. Notably, simple accumulation might enlarge the debt size of the financial industry or lead to wrong analysis. Moreover, the absolute amount of bank debt accounts for over 90% of the total of the financial industry, which is significantly correlated with the debt sizes of other forms and can represent the overall trend and characteristics of the financial industry. Thus, the debt of the financial industry studied in this book mainly refers to the debt of the banking sector.

Statistics, deposit statistics for example, are all collected from those published by National Bureau of Statistics. Debt represents all of the economic responsibilities assumed by the bank for its debtors. Looking from the perspective of the banking business, deposits and derivative deposits consist of the majority of bank debt. The amounts due to banks, loans or inter-bank borrowing or issued bonds are also part of the bank debt.

4.1.2 *Characteristics of Bank Debt*

1. **The size of bank deposits keeps increasing**

Various types of deposits taken by the banking sector constitute one of the major forms of bank debt. Since China opens its economy to the world, the size of bank debt has been on the rise, only at a slower rate nowadays. There are mainly four stages of the expansion of bank debt.

The period from 1978 to 1994, the 1st days when China implemented the reform and opening-up policies, marked the stage of stable expansion of bank debt. With a wide range of reform being carried out after 1978, and as social economy and people's livelihood were considerably improved, the size of bank debt also increased. In 1978, the balance of deposit items in China's financial institutions was only RMB 115.501 billion. Yet, it grew at a rate of around 20% each year, reaching RMB 200 billion in 1981, and exceeding RMB one trillion in 1989 and two trillion RMB in 1992. As soon as in 1994, the volume hit RMB four trillion, up by 36.60%. As for the overall economic development conditions, China's economic growth rates rose year after year after 1978, standing at 14.2% in 1992. It could be concluded that the expansion of deposit size is closely related to the overall macroeconomic growth. In 1988, as the so-called "making a breakthrough of commodity prices" started, a rush for goods emerged, and then the soaring inflation. In order to tackle the problem, the People's Bank of China (PBC) raised the interest rate for multiple times. In 1993, the rate went as high as 10.98%. At the same time, the government began to reflect on problems resulted from the practice of "making a breakthrough of commodity prices" and addressed them by resorting to such measures as raising the purchasing prices of agricultural products and prices of textiles and other light industrial goods, pushing forward with the price reform in an orderly fashion, and implementing a "double-track price system" containing both planned and non-planned prices for heavy industry products and some strategically important products while retaining directive prices for products and services concerning national interest and people's livelihood.

The period from 1995 to 2000 marked the stage of slow expansion of deposit size. In 1994, China established three policy banks for major policy-related lending as specialized state banks while such specialized state banks as Industrial and Commercial Bank of China (ICBC), the Agricultural Bank of China (ABC), Bank of China (BOC) and China Construction Bank (CCB) were transformed into four state-owned commercial banks afterwards. Furthermore, the government put in place a series of measures, which facilitated the "soft landing" of economic development. Although the economic growth rate reduced from 13% in 1993 to 7.8% in 1998, the price index went back gradually to around 1%. As for bank deposits, it took only 6 years for the balance of deposits to rocket to RMB ten trillion in 1999, a tenfold increase in a decade.

The period from 2000 to 2010 marked the stage of stable rise of the deposit size. In about 2000, as many reform measures including the SOE reform, higher education reform and personal housing reform were implemented, foreign trade gained momentum after China accession to the WTO and China's overall economic strength improved, volumes of various types of deposits in the banking sector started to grow rapidly and the growth rate of deposit volume reduced from the high level of 28% to around 16% and remained stable for a period. As for the size of deposits, it stood at RMB 14.3 trillion in 2001, exceeded RMB 20 trillion in 2003 and RMB 30 trillion in 2006, and reached RMB 59 trillion with a decade-record-high growth rate of 28.21% in 2009. This period was also the "golden time" of China's banking sector as the major commercial banks including the ICBC, ABC and CCB completed shareholding system reform in an orderly fashion and got listed in Hong Kong and Shanghai consecutively with those transformations. As a result, they achieved diversified property ownership, set the operation goal as market-based operation and the maximization of shareholders' interest, and basically established the corporate governance framework for modern financial companies. Since then, the commercial banks became responsible for their business operations, profits and losses, and bear their own investment and operational risks. The development and improvement of various types of financial institutions in the banking sector served as an important foundation and guarantee of the "golden ten years" of China's economic development. According to statistics released by China Banking Regulatory Commission (CBRC), by the end of 2008, there were 5 large-scale commercial banks, 3 policy banks, 12 joint-stock commercial banks, 136 municipal commercial banks, 4965 rural credit cooperatives, 22 rural commercial banks and 163 rural cooperative banks in China's banking sector.

The period from 2011 to the present marks the stage of the slowing down of deposit growth. The global financial crisis in 2008 hit regional economies including the US and Europe hard, which led to the shrinkage of overseas consumption demand. Against this backdrop, China's foreign trade was affected significantly. From the end of 2008 to the first half of 2009, to cope with the shock of the global financial crisis, China carried out a "four trillion yuan stimulus package", with a series economic stimulus plans being implemented by both central and local governments. The hedging force of the open market was reduced by the monetary policy; the issuance of central bank bills decreased; and in order to ensure liquidity, the benchmark interest rate and required reserve ratio were cut for five and four times respectively. In terms of the fiscal policy, measure included the 4 trillion yuan stimulus package, adjustments of the export rebate rate, and revitalization plans for multiple industries. In this process, China's commercial banks provided considerable credit support. The size of credit in 2009 grew at excessive rate, securing fund supply for many development projects and playing an important part in helping the national economy recover at a fast pace. Yet, the stimulus package also has certain negative impacts, especially contradictions faced by industries with overcapacity. After the year 2011, influenced by de-capacity efforts and economic restructuring, the economic growth rate decreased to below 8% and even 6.9% in 2015. In this macro-economic context, the overall size of deposits in the financial institutions in the banking sector is still expanding, but at evidently slower pace, down from over 15% in the past to merely 9.10% in 2014, lower than 10% (Fig. 4.1).

As of 2015, the total debt volume of China's banking institutions reached RMB 179 trillion (according to statistics released by the CBRC), up by 14.84% and an acceleration of 1.79 percentage point compared with the previous year. According to statistics published by listed banks, the average growth rate of the balance of debt of state-holding commercial banks was 8.22%, up by 1.29 from the level of the previous year; and that of the national small- and medium-sized joint-stock commercial banks was 16.41%, up by 0.68% year on year. The debt volume of the listed state-holding commercial banks was RMB 75.97 trillion, accounting for 42.44% of the total debt of banking financial institutions; and that of the national small- and medium-sized joint-stock commercial banks took up 17.22%, which shows that listed state-holding commercial banks are at an absolute dominant position in the debt market of banking financial institutions.

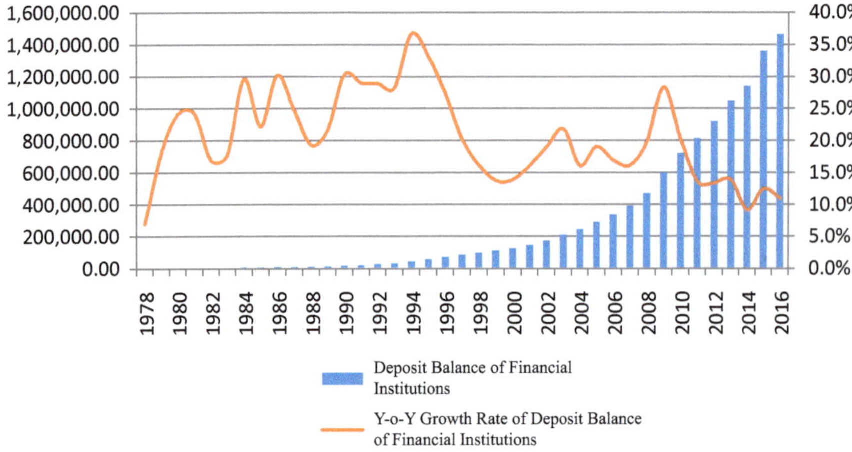

Fig. 4.1 Sizes and growth rates of deposits in China's financial institutions (1978–2015)

(1) Types of bank deposits generally settle out

From the perspective of proportions of different types of deposits, there are three stages:

The first stage was before 1990 when corporate deposits accounted for the largest proportion in the total. Before 1990, the Chinese economy was mainly a state-owned one featuring cheaper labor costs, so the proportion of corporate deposits was the largest, even reaching 64.18%. Yet, the proportion gradually decreased, down to around 35% by 1990. As resident income grew, the share of deposits began to rise. Its share, only 21.8% in 1978, grew to exceed the share of corporate deposits, became the largest in 1987, and then reached 61.32% in 1990. Throughout this period, the share of fiscal deposits was on the decline, down from 26.36% in 1978 to 3.68%.

The second stage was from 1991 to 2000 when the proportion structure of various deposits remained basically stable. The share of saving deposits roughly stayed above 60% while that of corporate deposits and fiscal deposits around 35% and 5% respectively. The rather large share of saving deposits was both an inevitable result of increase in resident income and related, to some extent, to the not-fully-opened consumption market and pent-up consumption demand in the 1990s.

The third stage starts from 2001 when the share of saving deposits was on a steady decline, that of corporate deposits remained basically stable, and that of fiscal deposits edged up. The proportion of saving deposits fell gradually from 57.47% in 2001 to around 50%, that of corporate deposits stood stably at around 40%, and that of fiscal deposits rose from 2.31% to over 4%, with 5.36% as the largest. The rise of the share of fiscal deposits and decline of saving deposits were particularly noticeable in 2009 and 2010. The major reasons were: on the one hand, in order to cope with global financial crisis and reverse the downward trend of economic growth, China carried out proactive fiscal policies and loose monetary policies in 2009 and

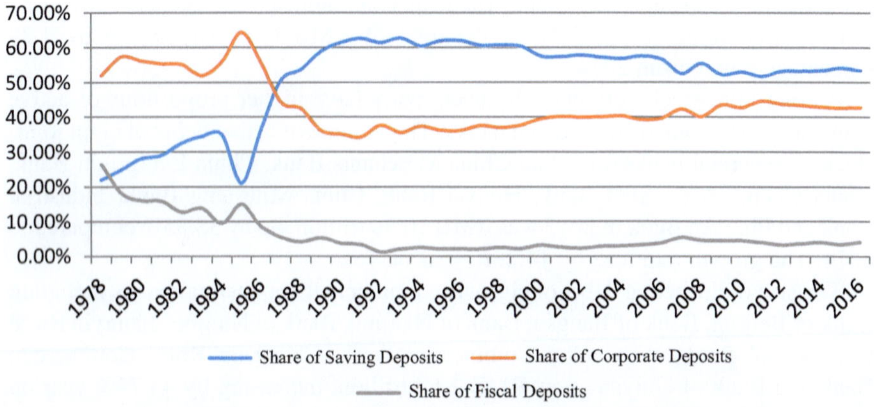

Fig. 4.2 Changes of deposit shares of China's major listed commercial banks

2010. Expenditures of both central and local governments grew tremendously. Correspondingly, financing platform companies sprang up. Various companies, institutions and other operation entities were in easy circumstances of cash flow, and their fixed asset investment volume and growth rate were high, generating large amount of fiscal deposits. On the other, as for saving deposits, after 2009, China issued a series of policies stimulating consumption and encouraging individual housing loan, which directed a large amount of personal finances flowing to such areas as the housing market and automobile market, thus driving down the share of saving deposit. Since 2010, the share of saving deposits has jumped a bit as both fiscal and monetary policies came back to normal, but the overall trend has remained downward (Fig. 4.2).

(2) Active bank debt grows faster and the share increases

According to the definition of *Report on the Development of China's Commercial Bank*, active debts include: deposits from other banks and financial institutions, borrowings from the central bank, loans, trading financial liabilities, derivative financial liabilities, financial assets sold for repurchase and bonds payable. Seen from the proportions of active debts in total debts of China's major listed commercial banks from 2006 to 2015, it can be concluded that the sizes of active debts of these banks were all on gradual rise.

Among state-owned commercial banks, in 2015, the volume of active debts of the ICBC was RMB 3.29 trillion, accounting for 16.12% in its total debt of RMB 20.41 trillion, up by 1.37 percentage points from the level of 2014; that of the ABC stood at RMB 2.51 trillion, taking up 15.15% in its total debt of RMB 16.58 trillion, an increase of 1.95 percentage points from 2014; that of the BOC reached RMB 2.99 trillion, accounting for 19.33% in the total of RMB 15.46 trillion, up by 0.24 percentage point from 2014; that of the CCB was RMB 2.82 trillion, taking up 16.67% in the total of RMB 16.90 trillion, rising by 2.34 percentage points compared to 2014; and that of the Bank of Communications reached RMB 1.87 trillion, accounting for 28.32% in the total of RMB 6.62 trillion, up by 1.28 percentage points from 2014.

Among joint-stock commercial banks, many have higher proportions of active debts than state-owned commercial banks. The volume of active debts of eight joint-stock commercial banks including China Merchants Bank, China Everbright Bank, China CITIC Bank, SPD Bank, Huaxia Bank, China Minsheng Bank, Industrial Bank and Ping An Bank in 2015 was RMB 10.30 trillion, up by 38.35% compared to 2014. The growth rate rose by 14.28% year on year.

The size of the active debts of eight listed municipal commercial banks including Bank of Beijing, Bank of Jiangsu, Bank of Nanjing, Bank of Ningbo, Jiangyin Rural Commercial Bank, Wuxi City Commercial Bank, Changshu Rural Commercial Bank and Bank of Guiyang was RMB 1.67 trillion, increasing by 44.74% year on year and registering an acceleration of 8.88 percentage points.

The proportions of active debts in the total debts of joint-stock commercial banks and municipal commercial banks are higher than that of state-owned commercial banks. The shares of active debts of state-owned commercial banks are mostly in the range of 15–20%, with 28.32% of the Bank of Communications being the largest; and those of joint-stock commercial banks are mainly over 25%, with 48.39% of Industrial Bank being the largest. The proportions of active debts of municipal commercial banks vary greatly, with 42.39% of Bank of Ningbo being the largest while 14.76% of Jiangyin Rural Commercial Bank being the smallest.

In terms of the active debts of major commercial banks, in 2015, the average growth rate of active debts of 14 major listed commercial banks was 28.19%, 16.02 percentage points higher than that of the total debts (12.17 percentage points) in the same period. Among them, the growth rate of active debts of municipal commercial banks is the highest, standing at 44.47%, 18.56 percentage points higher than that of the total debts (25.91 percentage points) of these banks; the active debt growth rate of joint-stock banks was 38.35%, 21.26 percentage points higher than that of the total debts (17.09 percentage points); and the growth rate of active debts of five state-owned banks was 19.77%, 10.26 percentage points higher than that of the total debts (9.51 percentage points) (Fig. 4.3).

The major reasons for accelerated growth rates of active debts are: first, with the implementation of new commercial bank capital management policies, the capital adequacy ratios of some banks fall short of the requirement of the CBRC, which forced commercial banks to accelerate active debt businesses in order to improve the stability of long-term debt sources and financial liquidity. Second, the implementation of loose monetary policies and proactive fiscal policies since 2008 have made commercial banks increase their lending considerably, hence the rise of loan-to-deposit ratio. And as a result, commercial banks have to conduct active debt management strategies to increase their asset liquidity and profitability. Third, conventional credit business of commercial banks was under huge pressure. Out of considerations of profit, risk, liquidity and others, and to deal with the negative impacts of decline of profit in conventional credit business and deficient demand, banks have to carry out proactive asset and liability policies.

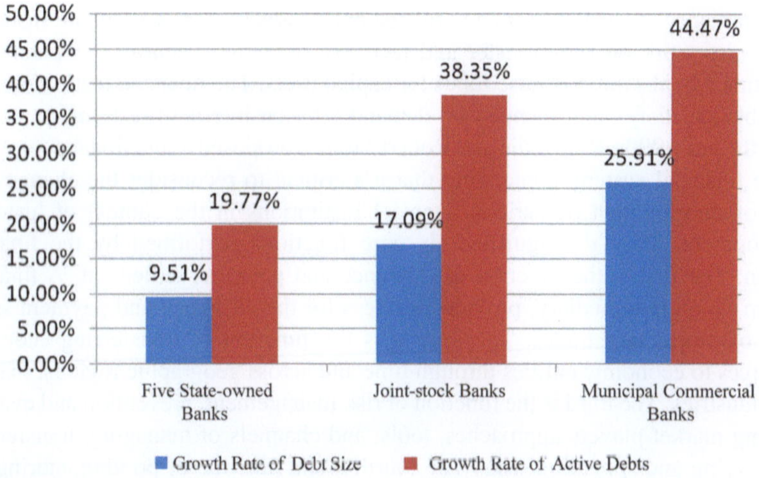

Fig. 4.3 Changes of active debt growth rates and total debts growth rates of different types of Chinese commercial banks in 2015. (Sources: Banks' annuals)

4.2 Bank Debt and Economic Growth

4.2.1 Bank Debt's Role in Economic Growth

After the 2008 global financial crisis, more and more scholars and financial practitioners came to realize that, the development of the financial industry must be geared to real economy; in other words, the reform and innovation of the financial industry must be premised on better serving the growth of real economy. The development history of the financial industry overseas and in China both demonstrates that, it's not until the real economy has entered a certain development stage, where the demand for capital flow management expands, that the financial industry starts to rise. As early as in the sixth century B.C., the Greek temples had already conducted money custody and interest-charging, money-lending businesses. Then in the fifth to third century B.C., as trade sprung up and economy grew, businessmen dealing with money and commercial institutions similar to banks appeared in Athens and Rome. In 1694, Bank of England – the first commercial bank of the modern financial industry was established in the UK. Since then, the financial industry in almost all capitalist states developed rapidly, which greatly facilitated capital aggregation and production concentration. In the late nineteenth and early twentieth century, major capitalist states entered the development stage of monopoly capitalism. Bank monopoly centering on credit activities was interpenetrated with industrial monopoly capital, hence creating the financial capital.

Currently, the forms of financial business in China are mostly commercial banks, insurance companies, securities companies and investment banks. Functionally, commercial banks are mainly engaged in basic businesses such as saving, lending and remittance, as well as currency-related businesses such as settlement; insurance companies work on risk transfer and recovery of losses; security companies and investment banks directly raise funds for capital users. The financial institutions take on debts to satisfy other companies' demand for their internal functions.

In the late 1990s, Zvi Bodie and Robert Merton proposed a functional perspective of the financial system, contending that it's critical to reconsider the changes and laws of development of various financial institutions in the context of historical development. They distinguished six core functions performed by the financial system. The first is the function of clearance and payment settlement. A financial system, as an intermediary, provides services for the clearance and payment settlement of proprietary trades. The second is the function of transferring economic resources to economic entities through time and across geographic regions, markets and industries. The third is the function of risk management, prevention and evasion, offering market players approaches, tools, and channels of managing, transferring, diversifying and spreading risks. The fourth is the function of pooling, storing and splitting capital and shareholdings. Through financial intermediaries of all kinds, the financial system can, on the one hand, pool funds together for investment, and on the other, enable diversified and detailed fund usage, thus spreading risks and facilitating capital flows. The fifth is the function of providing information. The financial system can bring together and make full use of all information across geographic regions, markets and industries, and get it reflected in prices of financial assets, so as to help the market players make targeted decisions. The sixth is the function of dealing with the incentive problem. That is, the financial system can provide dealers with an incentive and restraint mechanism through the money market, capital market and relevant financial derivatives, thus relieving the problem of information asymmetry, reducing moral hazard, and handling the problem of adverse selection. So to speak, financial institutions, products and markets are all carriers for the realization of the six core functions.

4.2.2 Correlations Between Bank Debt and Economic Growth

According to the statistics concerning China's aggregate economic volumes, bank debt size and non-bank size as of 2015, in 2003, the total debt of China's banking sector amounted to RMB 26.60 trillion, while the GDP was only RMB 13.65 trillion. The size of bank debt was 1.95 times of that of GDP. In addition, as mentioned earlier, the non-bank debt size totaled RMB 20.40 trillion; so the size of bank debt had well exceeded GDP and the debt levels of other entities.

Firstly, the ratio of bank debt to economic growth keeps escalating. In 2009, financial institutions, represented by banks, had a total debt worth of RMB 75 trillion, 2.17 times of the GDP, an increase of 0.30 percentage point than the previous year. Since then, the ratio of bank debt to GDP kept rising, standing at 2.34, 2.40 and 2.45

in 2012, 2013 and 2014 respectively, with bank debt outweighing relatively a great deal than that of corporate debt and the total non-financial debt. At end-2015, the debt of China's banking institutions added up to RMB 179.05 trillion, 2.61 times of the GDP, which implies that the role of financial industry debt in supporting GDP growth was on a decline.

Secondly, the ratio of bank debt to debt of non-bank enterprises levels off. In 2005, the non-bank enterprises' debt amounted to RMB 15.52 trillion, and the ratio of bank debt to non-bank debt stood at 1.90. Then, the ratio started to fall, 1.89 in 2006, 1.87 in 2007, and the lowest 1.77 in 2008. Nevertheless, it picked up again, and rose to 1.95 in 2012.

Thirdly, the ratio of bank debt to central government debt gradually increases. From 2003 to 2015, despite a rather low figure 9.62 in 2007, the ratio of bank debt to central government debt was generally on a rise. The ratio of bank debt to central government debt reached 10.07 in 2003, and then 11.91 in 2006. After a temporary decline in 2007, the figure rose rapidly after 2008. This reveals the ever enlarging of the gap between bank debt and central government debt. In 2009, the ratio soared to 12.46, and in 2012, 16.11. At end-2015, the figure stood at 16.80, registering a 0.5 percentage point increase than the previous year.

Fourthly, the ratio of bank debt to local government debt gradually decreases. Since 2007, while the size of central government debt kept expanding steadily, that of local government debt increased by leaps and bounds. Therefore, from 2007 to 2015, the ratio of bank debt to local government debt gradually declined, a stark contrary to the ratio of bank debt to central government debt. In 2007, due to the relatively small size of local government debt, the ratio stood at 20.44; then in 2008, the ratio edged down to 19.23; the next year, influenced by the policies China issued to mitigate the global financial crisis, this figure plunged to 13.38. After marginal rises in 2010 and 2011, it resumed a downward trend, decreasing to 12.98 in 2012, and 11.63 in 2013, thus presenting a scissors gap compared with the ratio of that to central government debt. At end-2015, according to the statistics released by the National People's Congress, China's local government debt amounted to RMB 17.18 trillion, and the ratio of bank debt to local government debt stood at 10.42 (Fig. 4.4).

Fifthly, the growth rate of bank debt is generally consistent with that of China's total debt. Through a comparison of the annual growth rates of GDP, China's total debt, bank debt, and central government debt (See Fig. 4.5), it can be referred that, before 2008, the gap between the growth rate of bank debt with that of GDP and China's total debt was relatively small, basically ranging between 10% and 20%. Nevertheless, after 2008, the growth rate of bank debt started to differ from that of GDP, but maintained closeness to that of China's total debt and both reached the peak in 2009. However, the two rates then plunged. So to speak, the growth of bank debt was also closely correlated with the 2008 global financial crisis and the ensuing adjustments to macroeconomic policies. The similarity and correlation between bank

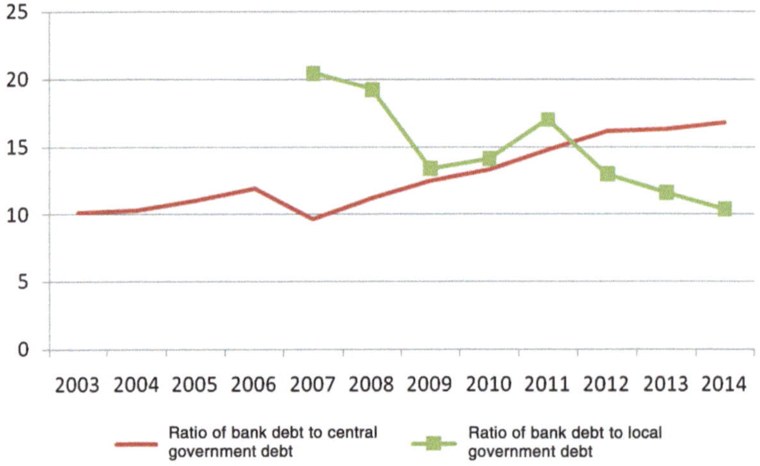

Fig. 4.4 Ratios of bank debt to government debt

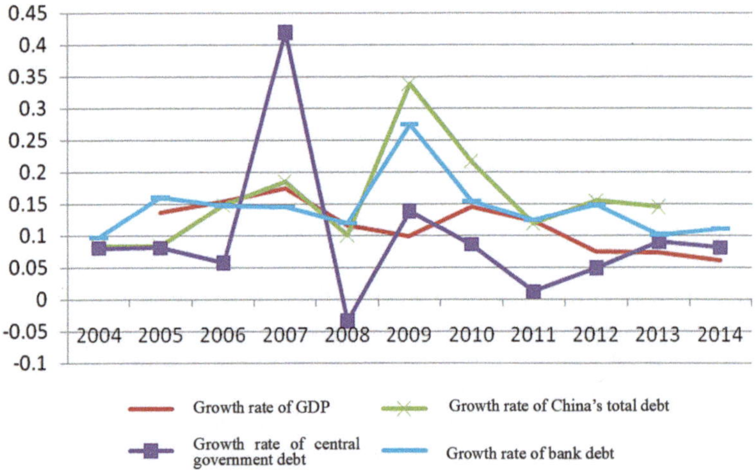

Fig. 4.5 Debt growth ratios since 2004

debt and China's total debt in their growth is likely to be a result of the fact that the debt of the banking sector itself accounts for a large proportion in China's total debt.

With the analysis above, it can be concluded that, though one of the important functions of banks is to fund real economy and promote economic development, both the ratio of bank debt to GDP and that of bank debt to debt of non-bank enterprises show that, to some extent, the development of the banking sector has deviated away from that of real economy, especially in terms of bank debt expansion and GDP growth.

Table 4.3 Regression results of bank debt

Model		Unstandardized coefficient		Standardized coefficient	t	Sig.
		B	Standard error			
1	(Constant)	−36743.702	19859.649		−1.850	0.107
	Bank debt	0.732	0.046	1.872	16.067	0.000
	Square of bank debt	−0.000000273	0.000	−0.900	−7.765	0.000
	One-year loan IR	4140.901	3034.045	0.025	1.365	0.215

$F = 1018.589^*$
Adjusted $R^2 = 0.997$
* Significantly correlated at 0.05 level (tow-tailed)

4.3 A Metrological Analysis of Bank Debt

4.3.1 Metrological Model and Analysis Results

The banking sector plays an important role in national or regional economic activities, so we also study the relationship between bank debt and economic growth separately. Similarly, the aggregate of bank debt and GDP are taken as two major variables of the econometric model and the interest rate of one-year loan as the controlling variable. This econometric model is shown below:

$$\begin{aligned} GDP_{t+1} = & C + b_1\text{Bank Debt}_t + b_2\text{Bank Debt}_t^2 \\ & + b_3\text{One-year Loan Interest Rate}_t + e \end{aligned}$$

Results of the least square regression conducted with this formula are shown in Table 4.3.

Statistics show that bank debt has positive influence on economic growth. One unit of increase in bank debt can lead to 0.732 unit of increase in GDP. Meanwhile, the square of bank debt is highly negatively correlated with GDP, which proves the existence of the turning point.

It should be noted that limited data have made unit root test and co-integration test pointless. Therefore, considering model normality, this model falls into the category of an exploratory one aiming to discover and study the possible quantitative relation between bank debt size and GDP. Further data collection and variable definition are needed for a more standard and rigorous study.

4.3.2 Identification of Bank Debt Turning Point

The turning point of bank debt is in fact the critical value of bank debt size. Before reaching the critical value, every unit of increase in bank debt can pull the GDP

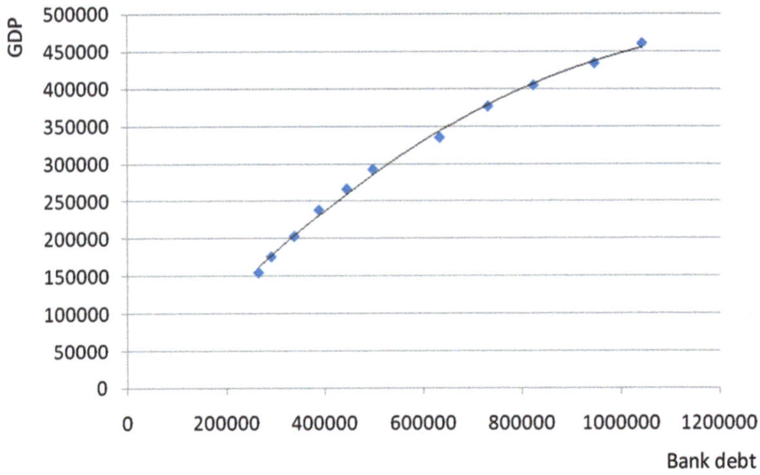

Fig. 4.6 Relationship between bank debt and GDP

higher. That means bank debt has positive impacts on economic growth. Nevertheless, with diminishing marginal utility, the contribution of every unit of increase in bank debt declines progressively. When reaching a certain size, the marginal contribution of bank debt to economic growth will turn to zero. This very point can be defined as the turning point of bank debt. At this point, the size of bank debt is also the critical value of reasonable size of debt in the banking sector.

The regression coefficients of the model show that the square of bank debt is highly negatively correlated with GDP; and statistical result also implies that bank debt may reach the turning point when its volume stands at RMB 134.07 trillion (the 2003 price) or RMB 188.09 trillion (the 2015 price). Taken the latter figure as an example, assuming that external factors, business structures of all banking institutions, and product innovation conditions remain unchanged, before the volume of bank debt reaches RMB 188.09 trillion, the increase or decrease in the debt volume of the whole industry has positive effects on real economy development; nevertheless, once the volume exceeds RMB 188.09 trillion, the effects will turn negative. In other words, once bank debt accumulates to a certain size that it passes the turning point, it will only have negative influence instead. Every unit of increase in bank debt, rather than propelling economic growth, will dampen the process (Fig. 4.6).

4.3.3 Current Effects and Development Trend of Bank Debt

Data reveal that, currently, the size of China's bank debt is standing around the turning point. The influence of the size of China's bank debt on GDP has reached or is reaching the "critical point" of the descent stage. Available data show that, the total volume of bank debt amounted to RMB 124.95 trillion in 2012, RMB 141.18

Table 4.4 Prediction of the turning point of bank debt

Year	Bank debt
2012	124.95
2013	141.18
2014	160.02
2015	181.38
2016	205.58
Turning point calculated with the price of 2003	142.06
Turning point calculated with the price of 2015	188.09
Passed or not	Passed

trillion in 2013, and RMB 160.12 trillion in 2014 (price of the same year). If based on our calculated turning point of RMB 188.09 trillion (the 2015 price), the current China's bank debt is already standing around the turning point which might be reached roughly between 2015 and 2016. Therefore, currently, bank debt is exerting negative effects on economic growth. Provided that external factors remain relatively stable, the increase of bank debt will dampen the growth of GDP (Table 4.4).

4.4 Pressure and Challenges Facing the Banking Sector

Nowadays, the banking sector is faced with tremendous operation pressure. On one hand, analysis of data shows that, the volume of bank debt is now around the turning point, and debt expansion is about to impact negatively economic growth. On the other hand, as Chinese economy and society transform, the banking sector itself is faced with many challenges, especially in terms of external pressure and internal management, which has made the transformation of the industry both imperative and urgent.

4.4.1 External Pressure

(1) Industrial competition intensifies as market-based development is pressed ahead.

The inherent advantages of China's traditional banks are a result of market under-competition. Now, the industry is increasingly opening to private capital. As of the end of 2011, among the total capital stocks of joint-stock commercial banks and municipal commercial banks, private capital (including domestic corporate shares, natural person shares and other public shares) accounts for 42% and 54% respectively. In the total capital stock of small-and medium-sized rural financial institutions, private capital makes up 92%. The basic legal framework for such issues as the legalization of capital market, bond market and private financing channels has been put in place. All these market-oriented processes not only propel social development, but exert profound influence on the operation model of banks.

(2) Financial disintermediation worsens as social financing structure profoundly changes.

In recent years, the social financing structure is rapidly changing from "relying mainly on indirect inter-bank financing" to "focusing on both direct and indirect financing." According to statistics of the People's Bank of China, in 2012, the RMB loans accounted for only 52.1% of the total social financing; however, 3 years later in 2015, the figure soared to as high as 95%, conveying a critical signal that financial disintermediation has reached its a new peak. Financial disintermediation advances from the two perspectives of assets and liability simultaneously, affecting negatively traditional business of banks, which in one aspect, results in lowered demand for loans from banks, and in the other, diverts the capital of high-quality customers. Besides, financial disintermediation requires commercial banks to go beyond their traditional services of deposits, loans and remittance to carry out "functional reform". Otherwise they can hardly satisfy the diversified needs of clients.

(3) Banks' pro-cyclical businesses exposed to risks as economic growth decelerates.

Amidst changes of business cycles, the operation of banks is highly pro-cyclical. During economic expansion, as enterprises have higher capital demand and sound credibility, banks tend to expand their business; whereas during economic depression, as corporate revenue declines and credibility goes down, banks tend to stint loans. This pro-cyclical feature results from market competition, and, just as risks, cannot be eliminated. Nevertheless, excessive synchronization might drive the banks to "collectively absorb" all kinds of losses, and end up ruining themselves and being a victim of the financial crisis. Just as after the 2008 global financial crisis broke out, banks in Europe, the US and many other countries collapsed one by one. As for China's banking sector, generally it is also closely related to the economic cycle. Corporate business is the focus of most banks, and the main products of personal financial business, such as financial products based on real estate credit assets are also highly linked to the business cycle. Once the economic development slows down, there will be great fluctuations of the banks' margin interest for sure.

(4) Internet and other technologies marginalize banks' payment and financing functions as technical disintermediation accelerates.

Recent years have witnessed rapid development of Internet finance, an emerging financial mode capable of financing, payment and infomediary by feat of Internet technologies and mobile telecommunication technologies. Hence it has great substitute effect on traditional commercial banks. Currently, the business scope of third-party payment companies has extended from payment and settlement to online loans, and even providing business solutions to the entire industrial chain. Internet enables traditional banks to compete beyond the scope of the industry. Notably, it's a historical phenomenon that Internet operators engage in payment business. As the banks concentrate more on financing than payment in their services, the market space for Internet operators takes its shape. It's unlikely that such a space expands further in the future. However, it's risky for Internet operators to get involved in credit financing. The ambition of Internet operators to provide direct financing is in fact a business illusion in the absence of proper regulation. Despite that, it should be noticed that, technical disintermediation is posing threats to the operation mode of traditional banks.

(5) Space for debt expansion is limited as banks are under great capital replenishment pressure.

As banks are now under great capital replenishment pressure, it is difficult to sustain the increase of leverage ratio and thus the expansion of bank debt. To replenish capital, banks resort to either internal accumulation or external financing. At the current stage, with macro-economic growth slowing down, and interest rate liberalization basically completed, commercial banks are stressed out in business operation. Since 2014, the growth rate of the net profit of Chinese commercial banks had kept decreasing. As of end June 2015, the industry-wide profit only edged up by 1.54% compared with the previous year, inflicting seriously upon the banks' internal accumulation of capital. In terms of external financing, as their market value is on the brink of falling below the net asset value, traditional commercial banks are confronted with a much lower financing amount and the difficulty to issue more debts. Thus, under both internal and external limitations of capital replenishment, commercial banks find it hard to develop through business expansion just as they did before.

(6) Net spread sharply narrows down to the level of advanced international banks.

The major source of profits of Chinese commercial banks is still net interest income. However, currently, influenced by development strategies of commercial banks, interest rates of the local financial market, social deposit and loan structure, as well as expectations of the market rates, the net spread sharply narrows down, declining to that of global advanced banks before the global economic crisis broke out in 2008, even lower than that of Citibank, Bank of America and some other traditional commercial banks.

On December 30, 2003, the State Council reviewed and passed the *General Plan for Shareholding System Reform of Bank of China and China Construction Bank*, in which it was decided that the two state-owned banks start the shareholding system reform as pilots. The state foreign exchange reserves were used as their capital fund, to enhance asset quality and expand capital scale. In 2004, as the first among the four major commercial banks to complete the shareholding system reform, the Bank of China was officially renamed as Bank of China Limited. Since then, the reform took place among major commercial banks nationwide. Through the reform, in accordance with the requirements of modern commercial banks, standardized corporate governance structures and strict and impartial power and responsibility systems were established; and effective financial discipline and internal risk prevention mechanisms were enforced. Besides, the banks conducted financial restructuring, to rapidly dispose non-performing assets and replenish the capital; and put in place a sound financial foundation and strict financial standards. Then, all major commercial banks rose to be modern financial companies featuring adequate capital, rigorous internal control, sound operation and good performance in service and benefits. The operation capacity was also substantively enhanced, stabilizing the net spread at a certain level.

The People's Bank of China lowered the benchmark interest rate for a total of 14 times from 2007 to 2015, and only raised it four times around 2011. The deposit and loan rates gradually decline. For instance, the one-year loan rate shrank from the highest 7.47% to 4.35% at the end of 2015 (See Fig. 4.1). Furthermore, since 2014, the deposit rate of commercial banks has been allowed to float freely within a certain range, which further narrowed down the general deposit-loan spread of commercial banks to almost the same level as or even lower than the level before the global financial crisis. The net spread of the five major state-owned commercial banks declined to from the highest 2.83% in 2008 to 2.30% at the end of 2015; and that of joint-stock banks decreased from the highest 2.87% to 2.30%. Similarly, the net spread of Citibank, Bank of America, JP Morgan and other major global banks stood at 2.89%, 3.08% and 2.78% respectively after the 2008 global financial crisis broke out. Therefore, the entrenched thought that Chinese commercial banks had too high a "net spread" should be changed.

In terms of long-term development, as China has basically completed the market-based determining reform of interest rate, the net spread of Chinese commercial banks is sure to maintain relatively narrow. To offset the negative influence of a narrowing spread on the traditional interest income, the commercial banks will have to adjust and optimize loan structure, improve assets and liability management, enhance business value and proactively increase income from intermediate businesses.

4.4.2 Problems of Internal Management

(1) Banks with single-large shareholder have inherent defects in corporate management, and de-administration process remains an arduous task.

At present, not only the "Big Five" commercial banks, namely the Industrial and Commercial Bank of China, Agricultural Bank of China, Bank of China, China Construction Bank, and Bank of Communications, are under absolute control of China's Ministry of Finance and Central Huijin Investments, but many joint-stock banks and urban commercial banks are wholly owned by local governments or government-related entities. Under the context where state-owned shares dominate, it's hard to bring corporate governance into full play, or to avoid excessive influence of political intention on banks' operation. In other words, banks can hardly get rid of the "quasi-administration" features. "Quasi-administration", nevertheless, has such advantages as being effective in transmitting policies, which is especially true when China fought against the global financial crisis. (With regard to Europe and the US, though governments and central banks released the strong signal of bailing out the market, and pumped in much liquidity into the banking sector, the major banks were still reluctant to issue loans). However, "quasi-administration" governance also has evident defects. Aside from with the rights and interests protection problem of minority shareholders, depositors and employees, a unified administrative intention tends to synchronize major banks' decisions. Once some decision-making bias surfaces in some period, after transmission of major banks and amplification of financial leverage, it may cause systematic risks.

(2) Banks' functions are converging, and the "customer-oriented" philosophy is yet to form.

Currently, almost all Chinese banks share similar operating strategies and management models, and even so in terms of products, technologies and talents. Behind this, there's a lack of market segmentation. Some problems are becoming more and more prominent: Firstly, banks, no matter big or small, compete in similar fields, while putting less effort in the issues related to "small businesses", "agriculture, rural areas, and rural residents" and others. An imbalance of resource allocation not only affects financial fairness, but leads to impairment of financial efficiency; Secondly, the high homogeneity of functions and products will result in homogeneity of risks. Apparently, the risks are spread among all banks; however, once there is any adverse change, the risks will be amplified. Just as in the 2008 financial crisis, the banks swarmed to buy in products or keep some trading positions at first, but as soon as problems arose, they scrambled to undersell, which resulted in a single market. The prices avalanched as a result, and the market suffered irrational fluctuations.

Generally, Chinese commercial banks still follow the conventional way to mark off target markets based on such dimensions as deposits/loans, RMB/foreign currency, or fixed loan/current loans. Though the management of each target market seems to be gradually refined, the banks are still "departmental banks" – they assign tasks in different target markets to different functional departments. By making such arrangements, banks only consider "internal convenience", and impose their logistics of internal management to customers with different labels. It is a very backward management mode. There are many problems; the cost of management and coordination is high; and the customer experience unsatisfactory. In fact, a real-sense market-oriented enterprise must be one that differentiates markets according to customer elements (target customer groups), allocates operation and management resources in a customer-oriented manner, and design system and processes accordingly. However, Chinese commercial banks lag far behind in these regards.

(3) IT capability is not strong enough to fully release productivity.

Since the 1980s, global banking sector has been developing by leaps and bounds, mainly driven by modern information technologies. According to statistics, over 90% financial innovation is backed by information technologies. As knowledge-incentive enterprises, banks must avail themselves of these technologies to improve productivity. In recent years, China's banking sector has made rapid progress and substantive achievements in the application of information technologies. But in general, as many works still rely on human labor, technology intensity is yet to be improved. Besides, the public complain about having to queue up for a long time at local branches, which is owing to not only service problems, but insufficient technical capability. For one thing, many local branches do not have enough ATMs and e-channels for customer diversion; for another, with a low degree of IT application and intensity, business of front and back offices mingles, and loads of works pile up in front offices. Hence low efficiency, low customer satisfaction, and operation risks resulting from "management fatigue" persist. By optimizing working procedures with modern information technologies, banks can free lots of employees from cumbersome labor, and focus them on customer services. There is much room for improvement.

(4) HR mechanism remains imperfect, and the market for professional managers is yet to be fostered.

At present, managers at all levels of large-scale banks in China, explicitly or implicitly, have their "administrative ranks." In many customer marketing and business cooperation events, "rank equivalence" is often stressed. So, Chinese bankers are actually a combination of "quasi-bankers" and "quasi-officials". This is a situation existing not only in large-scale banks, but newly founded joint-stock commercial banks and municipal commercial banks. Since the "objective functions" of politics and business are inconsistent, the blurred line between politics and business would easily result in distorted operating behaviors of banks. Bankers in a mature market environment, by virtue of their expertise, achievement and personal integrity, can gain a higher value acting as professional managers. However, as a professional managers' market is yet to take shape in China, bankers cannot demonstrate their "values". Under this background, "administrative ranks" seem to have become an alternative incentive to outstanding bankers. Therefore, it's understandable that some good bankers naturally become officials. From the perspective of the market-based and professional development of the banking sector, the absence of professional bankers will be an ever more prominent problem.

4.5 Summary and Suggestions

To sum up, in view of the current external environment of the banking sector, though maintaining fairly rapid growth, China's economy shows a clear downward trend. As the economic growth slows down, the financing needs in society decrease, which then weakens the external driving force for the continued expansion of banks. Meanwhile, the capital replenishment channels in the banking sector are strictly constrained. Banks seek to replenish capital primarily through two approaches, i.e. internal accumulation and external financing. In terms of internal accumulation, although the average return on equity (ROE) of listed banks is as high as approximately 20% at present, their core capital posts an annual growth of around 14%, after the cash dividends which account for nearly 30% of the total on average are deducted. Moreover, with the increasing influence of interest rate liberalization and other factors, the growth rate may go further lower in the future, hence the incapability to support banks' current 17–18% growth. Regarding the external financing, instruments like stock, subordinated debt, and hybrid debt are all severely restricted. Given all that, this study holds that **value management is the future of commercial banks**.

Price is the monetary expression of value. In the long run, price remains the monetary tag of value. In the case of the banking sector, the value of banks is reflected only in the price of assets. Those short-term, extreme factors aside, the trading price of stock can reflect the value of banks at a certain point. The market has a well-established assessment system for banks, which involves indictors such as profitability, risk profile, and management level. But the most important indicator is ROE, which comprehensively represents the overall operation and management of banks and how much shareholders can reap from their investment. In this sense, the price of assets is the value of banks; the value of banks is determined by whether they can earn sufficient returns on assets.

We shall not simply define value management as the maximization of market value or profit. "An enterprise which seeks to maximize profit will collapse." That is because the practice of considering profit as the measure of value is inherently questionable. First, profits can only represent the history, not the future. Secondly, profit as a financial indicator is, in itself, easy to manipulate, as evidenced by the Enron scandal and Arthur Andersen's demise in the US. Thirdly, if banks seek profit maximization blindly, they will inevitably squeeze costs excessively. As a result, banks may lose control of long-term interests, remain fixated on short-term targets, and finally head downhill. Therefore, while profit is important, it is solely a means of survival, not the end. As long as banks can hold onto the long-term targets of survival and development, they will make profits.

"Value bank" is not a vacuous concept, but a construction built upon the concrete features of banks. Five things are especially important for Chinese banks.

1. **To implement the strategy of developing "capital-light" businesses.**

As capital regulations become tighter, it is increasingly difficult and costly to raise exogenous capital. As a result, capital will be the most prominent constraint on banks' development in the future. Banks need to focus on tapping internal potentials, and establish a strategy of developing "capital-light" businesses by actively adjusting the business structure. Firstly, banks should make capital weigh less in the business structure. They need to shift the focus of their business development onto capital-light industries with fewer risks, and optimize their profit structure. For example, in terms of public products, banks should prioritize the development of short-term credit, investment banks, international settlements, cash management, financial market, interbank business, and custody business; commercial banks should focus on developing small business loans, consumer loans, credit card overdraft, mobile payment, agent business, etc. Secondly, banks shall strive to facilitate intermediary businesses. In fact, part of intermediary revenues in China's banking sector relies on banks' assumption of risks or is directly transferred from their interest income. Hence, to avoid the rapid development of subsequent businesses, prevent banks from being more exposed to risks, and curb the increasing capital pressure, the banks need to firstly shift intermediary businesses from financing to green businesses such as payment and settlement. Payment and settlement are basic functions of banks. Therefore, banks can better serve customers by making payment a product. Meanwhile, to avoid the situation in which competition among market players is so fierce that they become indistinguishable, banks should consider about their business advantages and strategic positioning and build peripheral businesses with broad prospects into the main offering, thus creating distinctive features of the sector, and acquiring differentiated competitive advantages. Thirdly, banks should arrange businesses in a countercyclical manner. They should steer clear of the destructive power of the swings of the economic cycle, keep to the bottom line at any stage of the economic cycle, and ensure sound operation. Banks needs to make arrangements in risk control, asset and liability management, industry structure, term structure, industrial policies, business strategies, and financial resource scheduling, actively distance resources and credit investments from the economic cycle, and ward off the sharp swings in the cycle.

2. **To strengthen intensive approaches of capital replenishment, and maintain the limited expansion.**

Excessively frequent equity financing not only damages investors' interests, but also constantly adds to the difficulty and costs of bank financing, which runs contrary to the over-riding goals of a "value bank". Meanwhile, as currently the internal capital accumulation is not strong enough to support their development, banks have to address problems of capital replenishment with equity financing. Then how to break this dilemma? Banks need to take measures from two aspects, i.e. earning more and saving more. Firstly, banks need to continue improving profitability, enhance the internal capital accumulation, and achieve intensive development; meanwhile, they must proactively study and explore the application of innovative capital instruments, seek to replace high-level capital with low-level capital, and gradually reduce their reliance on equity financing. Secondly, banks need to attach great importance to capital management, and with a focus on the risk-adjusted return on capital (RAROC), constantly optimize the structure of risky assets, reduce improper capital consumption, prioritize the development of capital-light businesses like consumer loans, strive to facilitate intermediary businesses, maintain limited expansion, and decrease the demands for capital replenishment. By earning more and saving more, banks can extend the financing cycle and shrink financing scale, so as to minimize the sharing of refinancing among existing shareholders, proceed towards the path of capital discipline and stable dividend, and achieve sustainable growth of banks' value.

3. **To establish stable expectations of return on investment (ROI).**

It is obligatory on listed companies to reward investors. A sound ROI mechanism enables higher earnings estimates, boosts investor confidence, enhances investors' desire to invest, and thus promotes sustainable and healthy development of enterprises. For historical reasons, listed companies in China have not established strong mechanisms of ROI and capital discipline; the policies regarding cash dividends in most banks remain ambiguous, and there have been considerable fluctuations in the revenue sharing over the years – such uncertainties, in a way, make investors less willing to invest. Throughout the world, the dividend level of listed companies is an important criterion for investors to make decisions. Hence, in order to promote the steady increase in banks' value, we need to establish and improve a stable ROI mechanism. Banks should work to develop clear, sustainable dividend policies, achieve sufficient information disclosure, increase investors' earnings estimates in real terms, and protect consumers' interests. Meanwhile, banks must keep equity refinancing to a minimum, and avoid diluting the existing shareholders' equity.

4. **To optimize the shareholding structure and facilitate capital flows.**

The shareholding structure determines the governance structure which, in turn, determines the management structure. To meet the inherent requirement of increasing banks' value, we need to build a moderately dispersed shareholding structure. For one thing, a reasonable shareholding structure can help to establish a sound governance structure: it shall not only prevent excessive interventions of the majority shareholder in banks' operations, but also handle the insider control problem when shareholdings are too dispersed. After reorganization and listing financing, state-owned banks and shareholding banks have diversified their shareholdings to some extent and improved their cooperate governance. Yet overall, most banks are still controlled by one single de facto controlling shareholder, and the excessive concentration of shareholdings has not been ultimately addressed. Although major commercial banks in China may at present, and for a long time to come, remain firmly state-controlled, we can work to further optimize the way of state ownership. For example, we can increase the shares held by state-owned enterprises, state-owned asset managers, and insurance companies, and introduce an appropriate amount of private capital. Through the moderately dispersed shareholding structure, banks can reduce the influence of big shareholders, strengthen the role of the market, and constantly improve corporate governance. For another, dispersed shareholdings can facilitate capital flows, and reflect capital values in a more reasonable manner. The values of commodities are achieved through exchanges, and prices shall attain a unity with values in the long-term, sufficient exchanges. When one single shareholder owns the majority stake, its capital has a prohibitively high price and no sales are reported; as a result, it's difficult to realize its capital value in a real sense. Meanwhile, excessive concentration of shareholdings may constrain market activeness, and dampen the increase in banks' valuations to a certain extent; in this way, the value of bank capital held by other investors cannot be reflected reasonably either.

5. **To replace scale-oriented drivers with technology-oriented ones.**

Business environment are changing profoundly. There used to be lots of "one-trick ponies" in the past. But now, technological advances have rapidly shattered the barriers in information, channels, and policies, and the cycles in which enterprises gain or lose edges contract sharply. In the future, to achieve greater development, the banks need to replace scale-oriented drivers with technology-oriented ones, adapt to industry trends and new, diversified customer demands by innovating various financial products and non-financial services. And sustainable growth relies on innovation instead of capital inputs. For instance, an evident substitution effect is taking place as the fast-growing Internet finance has been challenging traditional channels of commercial banks in recent years, which also enables new revenue sources in the banking sector. The innovation approaches of banks have always focused on businesses, with information technologies and systems playing the auxiliary and supporting role. Banks are typically passive followers of new technologies, rather than active initiators. As the market competition inside and outside the industry becomes increasingly fierce, banks, in order to maintain competitive edges, must transform the "business-driven" approaches into those driven by both businesses and technologies or even dominantly by technologies, facilitate innovation of business models with technological innovation, translate customers' "potential demand" into "effective demand" by leveraging new technologies, and provide steady driving forces for business development. If banks can "think bigger" in terms of data application and technological innovation, they can create "data banks" in the big-data era with no limit to their growth.

In addition to the reform inside the banking sector, government agencies shall also proactively implement regulatory policies to steer commercial banks towards "value banks".

First, government agencies shall appropriately bring commercial banks back to the rational operation principles of "safety, liquidity and profitability". In 2003, the revised *Law of the People's Republic of China on Commercial Banks* put safety on the top agenda and continued doing so since then, making it the primary principle in banks' operations. In view of the rise and fall of the world's banking sector over the past 300 years, banks' survival is based on their conservatism and prudence. Banks are firstly service providers for national economy, and then promoters. This requires banks to stick to prudent operations, risk-averse modes, and conservative stance. In terms of innovation practices, banks need to prudently fuel innovation within reach of their risk management capability and risk tolerance, rather than implement radical reforms.

Secondly, government agencies shall establish a review mechanism oriented towards return on capital instead of built upon rules and regulations and enable the shift from "scale banks" to "value banks". At present, China's economy has been transitioning from a phase of high growth to a stage of moderate to slow growth – this is not short-term volatility. As the economic growth is moderating, the financing needs in the society may decrease, which will then weaken the external driving force for the continued expansion of banks. Meanwhile, the capital replenishment channels in the banking sector are strictly constrained, and the drive for the scale expansion is receding. That calls for government agencies to act based on their review systems, guide commercial banks in shaking off the scale-oriented conventional thinking, and head towards value-added operations and value management by improving profitability, risk conditions, and management capabilities and steadily enhancing returns on capital (primarily ROE).

Thirdly, government agencies need to be wary of the absolute size of debt in the financial industry and take appropriate measures to reduce its debt levels. Statistics show that debt in the financial industry accounts for the biggest share of China's total debt. Moreover, there exists a huge gap between financial industry debt and corporate debt, which fully demonstrates a deviation of the financial industry from the real economy. Essentially, the financial industry is to serve the real economy; however, its overextension, especially debt expansion, will weaken its role in promoting real economy growth. A crushing burden of debt will expose the financial industry to huge operations risks, and even impact the economic order of the whole nation. Therefore, China shall focus on debt in the financial industry in its future debt management.

Chapter 5
A Study of China's Corporate Debt

Propelled by an RMB 4 trillion stimulus package in 2008, Chinese enterprises took on debts for business expansion. Over the years, they have accumulated a large amount of debt – hence the heavy burden now. The seriousness of China's corporate debt is relatively obvious. But how can we determine if an individual enterprise has a serious debt problem? In the various economic sectors, which are overburdened? Based on the studies of the turning point of China's debt in the previous chapters, we will now interpret the turning point of Chinese enterprises from the perspective of "debt turning points of industries."

In this chapter, the history of the debt scale of China's real economy is discussed. The status quo of debt leverages of pillar industries is analyzed according to the industry classification system of China's National Bureau of Statistics. We found that after 2009, there has been an explosive growth of debt in the real economy, with the stock of debt surging. However, the debt leverages of different industries has varied, as the leverage of some industries keeps rising while that of others decreases. Thus we utilized an analysis model for marginal profits from investments and found that the differences in industrial profits can account for the leverage differentiation among various industries. Given that the changes in debt leverage among industries have been different, a single holistic approach cannot meet all the requirements of this research. So we selected some relatively important industries in China's economy, conducted an elastic analysis and an industry analysis of debt effects, and made a preliminary judgment of the industries' turning points.

The chemical fiber manufacturing industry and the petrochemical industry are two typical industries with overcapacity. A study of these industries showed that **the debt of the chemical fiber manufacturing industry might have reached its turning point around 2014 when purified terephthalic acid (PTA) capacity peaked, while the debt in the petrochemical industry have might crossed its turning point around 2011.**

X. Zhu et al., *A Study of the Turning Point of China's Debt*,
https://doi.org/10.1007/978-981-13-1325-7_5

5.1 Status Quo and Development History of Corporate Debt

5.1.1 Status Quo of China's Corporate Debt

The current situation of China's corporate debt is closely correlated with the bank-dominated financial system, government debt and economic development model – none of which can be analyzed as a separate element. Surging corporate debt is the combined result of domestic and foreign economies situation, national policies and corporate behaviors. By some estimates, the debt ratio of China's real economy reached 156% by the end of 2015; 65% of the debt was attributed to state-owned enterprises (mostly through indirect financing). China's financial system is dominated by banks, and it is usually state-owned enterprises and large joint-stock banks that have played an important role in financing the real economy. Therefore, the corporate debt problem in China involves several closely-related actors, including enterprises, banks, the financial system and even the nation's finances. That is what makes the problem so complicated and troublesome (Fig. 5.1).

The figure above shows that the total social financing (TSF) increased significantly after 2008, reaching RMB 13.9 trillion in 2009 and reporting a year over year increase of nearly 100%. It is safe to say that the nationwide stimulus package, through the efforts of governments and banks, worked at the corporate level: driven by policies, the demands for enterprises' products increased, and the enterprises were willing and able to secure financing, increase their debt leverages and expand production. Though the TSF kept fluctuating in the following years, its absolute level remained high. It seemed that China's real economy had developed a "path dependence" on debt to some extent. Enterprises in the real economy, especially the state-owned ones, had been used to facilitating businesses and expanding production with the "cheap money" borrowed from banks. Why not increase debt leverages

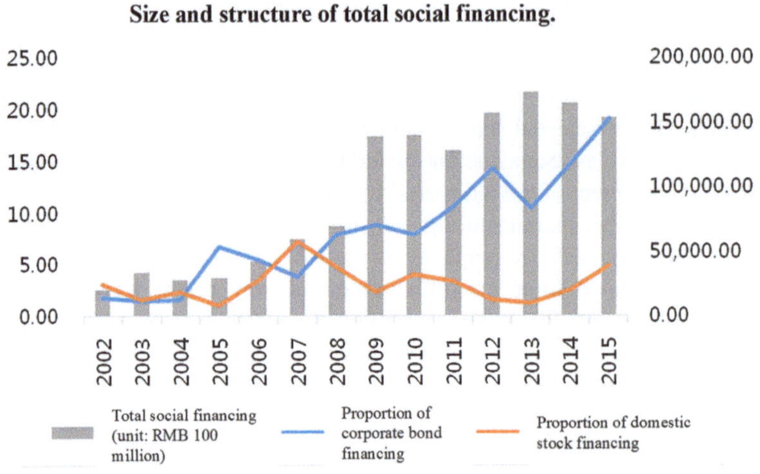

Fig. 5.1 Size and structure of total social financing in China, 2002–2015

when bank loans were easily available? Meanwhile, the problem of poor productivity in state-owned enterprises had not been resolved. Due to slower economic growth and corporate mismanagement, Chinese real enterprises – especially those with overcapacity problems – have not generated satisfactory profits. Even worse, they had to spend a considerable proportion of profits on debt interest payments, hence gloomy financial numbers. Enterprises with weak profits were certainly unable to handle the high stock of debt accumulated for historical reasons. As a result, refinancing their debt seemed to be the most acceptable approach, so that old debts could be rolled over with new borrowing, and they could stave off the imminent liquidity risk.

In reviewing the internal structure of social financing, we found that indirect financing from banks remained the major funding source of enterprises. The proportion of bond financing in the TSF increased significantly, reporting an average annual growth of 20% from 2002 to 2015. This indicates that China had attained initial achievements in the improvement of its direct financing system and the construction of a multilevel capital market. However, bond financing still accounted for less than 20% of the TSF. The proportion of domestic stock financing was even smaller at 4.9% in 2015 and peaking at 7.3% in 2007. The figure stayed below 10% because of a correlation with the bullish stock market.

Can the TSF comprehensively reflect the status quo of the total debt of enterprises in China's real economy? The existing TSF recordkeeping system considers only basic underlying assets like entrusted loans and undiscounted bankers' acceptances, but not shadow loans. Hence to some extent, the TSF figures may underestimate the total corporate debt and debt growth. The sum of the TSF and banks' claims on non-bank financial institutions is not the perfect answer either. The calculation has two major defects. First, an enterprise's shadow loans also involve other financing channels such as the banks' off-balance-sheet financial products, so we cannot get the total figure by solely adding banks' claims on non-bank financial institutions. Second, since the basic underlying assets of some shadow loans have already been included in the TSF, there may be double counting that leads to an overestimated result. Thus it can be difficult to get the real numbers of corporate debt with available data. We believe that, so far, the TSF and the annual figures of corporate debt released by the National Bureau of Statistics are relatively reliable, valid and publicly available compared with others, which thus can best reflect the situation of corporate debt. From the description of the TSF in this section, we can, at least, clearly understand the current situation of the total size, internal structure and recent development trends of corporate debt. In the following sections, the researchers will analyze the corporate debt figures released by the National Bureau of Statistics.

5.1.2 A Development History of China' Corporate Debt

Since 2009, the corporate debt in China has exploded with an average annual growth rate of 24.84%. By the end of 2014, the corporate debt of non-financial enterprises in

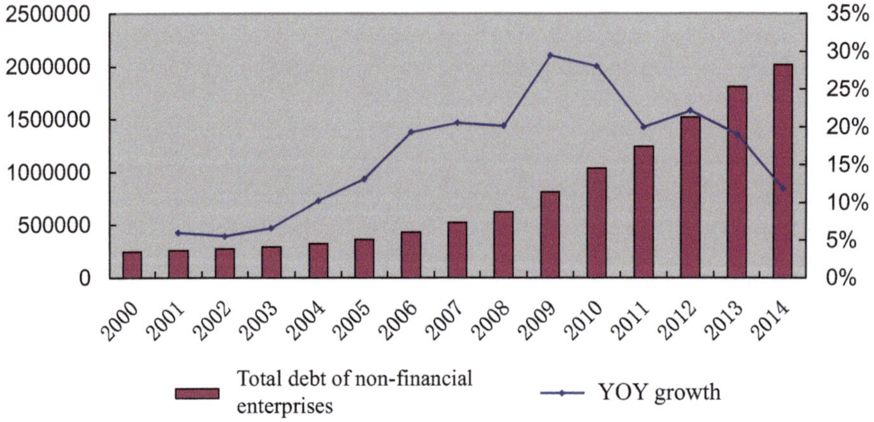

Fig 5.2 Total debt of non-financial enterprises in China, 2000–2014

China amounted to RMB 201.87 trillion, a year over year increase of 11.81% and 2.5 times that of the corporate debt at the end of 2009. Though the debt growth began to slow in 2012, due to a large stock offering, the annual increment amounted to approximately RMB 25 trillion (Fig. 5.2).

Although corporate debt increased rapidly after 2008, the asset-liability ratio, hereinafter referred to as the asset-liability ratio of enterprises, remained stable. At the end of 2014, the asset-liability ratio of non-financial enterprises in China was 60.0%, an increase of 1% compared with that at the end of 2013.

We can first analyze the relationship between enterprises' asset-liability ratios and GDP growth. Since 2000, the relationship between the asset-liability ratio of non-financial enterprises and GDP growth passed through three stages. In the first stage (2000–2007), the asset-liability ratio continually decreased, and the economic growth kept accelerating. In the second stage (2007–2011), the enterprises' asset-liability ratio and GDP growth remained basically the same. Due to the financial crisis in 2008, China's economic growth slowed, and enterprises' asset-liability ratio decreased as well. In 2009, the debt leverage of enterprises expanded, reversing the downward turn of economic growth and effectively facilitating economic recovery; after that, enterprises' asset-liability ratios and GDP growth moved in the same direction. In the third stage (2011–present), the debt leverage presented a significant scissors gap compared with the economic growth: the overall asset-liability ratio of enterprises increased from 56% in 2010 to 60% in 2014; the GDP growth decreased from 9.5% to 7.3%; and the growth of industrial added value decreased from 13.9% to 8.3%. Therefore, overall, debt expansion in the non-financial industry in China has exceeded its turning point. Thus debt has started to take a toll on economic growth since 2011(Fig. 5.3).

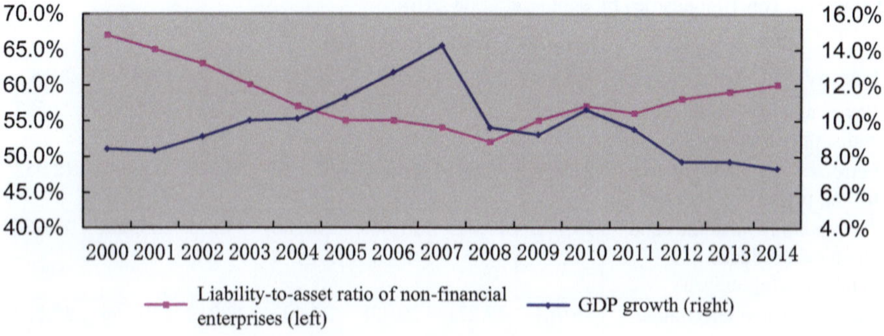

Fig.5.3 Liability-to-asset ratio of non-financial enterprises (left). (Source: National Balance Sheet, National Bureau of Statistics)

5.2 A Comparison of Debt Leverages of Various Industries

5.2.1 Debt Size of Various Industries

In view of the total debt volumes of major industries, the top five industries were the power and heat production and supply industry, the ferrous metal smelting and rolling processing industry, the chemical raw materials and chemical products manufacturing industry, the electronics and telecommunications equipment manufacturing industry, and the coal mining and processing industry, which all assumed a huge amount of debt. For example, the debt of the power and heat production and supply industry was RMB 7.26 trillion in 2014, which was RMB 3.27 trillion more than that in 2008. The debt of the coal mining and processing industry reached RMB 3.46 trillion, an increase of RMB 2.32 trillion compared to 2008 and almost three times that in 2008. In contrast, the ferrous metal mining and processing industry, the furniture manufacturing industry, the tobacco manufacturing industry, the non-ferrous metal mining and processing industry, and the other minerals mining and processing industry had smaller debt sizes (Table 5.1).

In view of the debt growth of major industries from 2008 to 2014, industries including the ferrous metal mining and processing industry, the coal mining and processing industry, the gas production and supply industry, the food processing industry, and the non-metallic mining and processing industry reported considerable growth. In particular, the ferrous metal mining and processing industry and the coal mining and processing industry saw their debt double during this period (Table 5.2).

In regard to the proportions of the various industries' debt as part of the total debt, most industries in the national economy and typical industries with overcapacity accounted for considerable shares. According to the data at the end of 2014, for example, industries accounting for more than 5% of the total debt were the power and heat production and supply industry, the ferrous metal smelting and rolling processing industry, the chemical raw materials and chemical products manufacturing industry, the electronics and telecommunications equipment manufacturing

Table 5.1 Top 10 industries by debt size, 2008–2014

	Year (unit: RMB 100 million)						
Industry	2008	2009	2010	2011	2012	2013	2014
Power and heat production and supply industry	39,817	44,675	50,505	55,801	61,410	67,772	72,557
Ferrous metal smelting and rolling processing industry	22,306	26,087	30,192	35,120	39,123	43,675	42,952
Chemical raw materials and chemical products manufacturing industry	15,172	17,725	21,588	25,166	30,351	35,601	39,667
Electronics and telecommunications equipment manufacturing industry	15,761	17,271	20,438	24,402	27,012	30,566	35,172
Coal mining and processing industry	11,483	14,051	17,419	22,558	27,205	31,775	34,632
Electric machinery and equipment manufacturing industry	11,994	14,044	18,290	21,901	24,540	27,371	30,139
Non-metallic mineral products industry	10,056	11,396	13,901	16,154	19,406	22,712	24,935
Non-ferrous metal smelting and rolling processing industry	8166	9813	12,363	14,755	17,691	20,748	23,061
General equipment manufacturing industry	11,627	12,907	15,492	16,626	17,401	19,671	21,366
Special-purpose equipment manufacturing industry	8087	9086	11,030	12,839	14,680	16,994	18,023

industry, the coal mining and processing industry, the electric machinery and equipment manufacturing industry, and the non-metallic mineral products industry. These were all major industries or typical industries with overcapacity in the national economy. Among the top five industries, the proportions of the power and heat production and supply industry and the ferrous metal smelting and rolling processing industry in the total debt slightly decreased compared to those in 2008. Meanwhile, the proportion of the coal mining and processing industry in the total debt rose gradually from 5.23% in 2008 to 7.20% in 2014 (Table 5.3).

In reviewing the trends of various industries' proportions in the total debt from 2000 to 2014, we found that in industries with high absolute volumes of debt, the debt probably accounted for increasingly smaller proportions, while the proportions of those with relatively low absolute volumes of debt could rise. This indicates that we should stay alert to debt burdens within all industries – even those with a limited amount of debt – due to the potential risks associated with rapid debt expansion. Among the industries witnessing an increase in debt proportions from 2008 to 2014, those with excess capacity – like the coal mining and processing industry, the

Table 5.2 Top 10 industries by debt growth, 2008–2014

Industry	Debt growth from 2008 to 2014 (unit: RMB 100 million)	Cumulative growth rate in 6 years (%)
Ferrous metal mining and processing industry	4298	281.47
Coal mining and processing industry	23,149	201.59
Gas production and supply industry	2348	191.21
Ferrous metal smelting and rolling processing industry	14,895	182.40
Food processing industry	10,216	170.21
Non-metallic mining and processing industry	1074	164.72
Chemical raw materials and chemical products manufacturing industry	24,495	161.45
Non-ferrous metal mining and processing industry	1650	157.29
Electric machinery and equipment manufacturing industry	18,145	151.28
Other minerals mining and processing industry	3	150.00

Table 5.3 Top 10 industries by debt proportions of in total debt, 2008–2014

Industry (unit: RMB 100 million)	2008 (%)	2009 (%)	2010 (%)	2011 (%)	2012 (%)	2013 (%)	2014 (%)
Power and heat production and supply industry	18.13	17.78	16.94	16.12	15.67	15.25	15.09
Ferrous metal smelting and rolling processing industry	10.16	10.38	10.13	10.15	9.98	9.83	8.93
Chemical raw materials and chemical products manufacturing industry	6.91	7.05	7.24	7.27	7.74	8.01	8.25
Electronics and telecommunications equipment manufacturing industry	7.18	6.87	6.86	7.05	6.89	6.88	7.32
Coal mining and processing industry	5.23	5.59	5.84	6.52	6.94	7.15	7.20
Electric machinery and equipment manufacturing industry	5.46	5.59	6.14	6.33	6.26	6.16	6.27
Non-metallic mineral products industry	4.58	4.54	4.66	4.67	4.95	5.11	5.19
Non-ferrous metal smelting and rolling processing industry	3.72	3.91	4.15	4.26	4.51	4.67	4.80
General equipment manufacturing industry	5.29	5.14	5.20	4.80	4.44	4.43	4.44
Special-purpose equipment manufacturing industry	3.68	3.62	3.70	3.71	3.75	3.82	3.75

non-ferrous metal smelting and rolling processing industry, and the chemical raw materials and chemical products manufacturing industry – all had relatively large debt loads. Hence, they deserve special attention.

5.2.2 Debt Leverages of Various Industries

(1) A comparison of debt leverages of various industries in the industrial sector

In terms of corporate operations, debt includes both interest-bearing loans from banks and other financial institutions and non-interest debt between enterprises. In order to reflect the debt leverages of industries in a more objective and comprehensive manner, we considered the asset-liability ratio as a measure of debt leverage and reviewed the movements of debt leverages of 30 major industries in the industrial sector from 2000 to 2014. The industries and data were selected based on the industry classification standards proposed by the National Bureau of Statistics and covered most sectors in the national economy. Since the data for the culture and education industry and the transportation industry were incomplete, these industries were not included on the final list (Table 5.4).

To fully demonstrate the characteristics of the post-financial crisis era, we calculated the average asset-liability ratios of various industries in the industrial sector from 2008 to 2014 and then presented them in a descending order (see Table 5.5). The results show that the ferrous metal smelting and the rolling processing industry, the power and heat production and supply industry, the petroleum processing and coking industry, the non-ferrous metal smelting and rolling processing industry, the chemical fiber manufacturing industry, and the coal mining and processing industry had relatively high debt leverages (all above 57.8%, the average debt leverage of industries above a designated size).

(2) A comparison of debt leverages of different industries

In comparing the asset-liability ratios of the retail industry, the wholesale industry, the real estate industry, the power and heat production and supply industry, the gas production and supply industry, and the water production and supply industry, we can draw several conclusions.

The asset-liability ratio of the retail industry remained at a relatively high level with minor fluctuations, but it had a slightly downward trend, mainly due to the overall increasing profitability of the retail industry and a larger growth rate of assets than debts. The total retail volume of consumer goods can be considered a measure of the retail market. In fact, the total retail volume of consumer goods kept rising from 2000 to 2014, with its growth rate edging up amid general stability. This was a testament to the stable asset-liability ratio in the retail industry.

The asset-liability ratio of the wholesale industry had a downward trend. After the 2008 global financial crisis, the industry suffered weak foreign demand and

Table 5.4 Top 10 industries by debt-to-asset ratio, 2008–2014

	2008	2009	2010	2011	2012	2013	2014
Industries above a designated size	57.7	57.9	57.4	58.1	58.0	58.1	57.2
Petroleum processing and coking industry above a designated size	61.9	62.4	60.9	63.0	65.0	66.0	66.3
Coal mining and processing industry above a designated size	59.0	59.1	58.2	59.5	60.7	64.8	66.2
Ferrous metal smelting and rolling processing industry above a designated size	63.4	63.6	65.7	67.5	67.2	67.5	65.8
Power and heat production and supply industry above a designated size	64.0	64.7	65.8	66.6	66.7	66.1	64.8
Non-ferrous metal smelting and rolling processing industry above a designated size	57.8	59.6	60.9	62.2	62.9	64.2	63.7
Chemical fiber manufacturing industry above a designated size	59.7	60.8	60.1	61.9	62.8	63.5	62.1
Electronics and telecommunications equipment manufacturing industry above a designated size	58.3	58.1	54.2	58.8	58.2	58.5	58.6
Chemical raw materials and chemical products manufacturing industry above a designated size	55.0	55.7	55.7	56.0	56.9	58.1	57.9
Electric machinery and equipment manufacturing industry above a designated size	57.8	58.0	57.7	58.3	58.0	57.6	57.6
Water production and supply industry above a designated size	51.9	53.3	54.1	53.8	55.8	56.3	57.6

Source: National Bureau of Statistics

experienced decreased profits from its core businesses. Meanwhile, the government's RMB 4 trillion stimulus package affected the demand for steel, so some enterprises – represented by steel dealers – significantly expanded their debt, which in turn drove up the asset-liability ratio.

The debt leverage of the real estate industry fluctuated around 75%. Before the 2008 financial crisis, the ratio remained basically stable at around 74%; yet after the crisis, it rose slightly from 72.30% to 77.00% in 2014. (This problem will be further discussed in later chapters.)

The asset-liability ratios of the sub-industries of power and heat gas production and supply, and water production and supply increased modestly. Among them, the debt leverage of the power and heat production and supply industry fluctuated around 65%; the debt leverage of the gas production and supply industry was stable at around 55%; that of the water production and supply industry rose significantly, increasing from 51.9% in 2008 to 57.6% in 2014.

Enterprises in the power and heat, gas, and water production and supply industries are mostly public institutions and government financing platforms. Due to the

Table 5.5 Average asset-liability ratios of industries in the industrial sector, 2008–2014

Industry	Asset-liability ratio (%)
Ferrous metal smelting and rolling processing industry	65.8
Power and heat production and supply industry	65.5
Petroleum processing and coking industry	63.7
Non-ferrous metal smelting and rolling processing industry	61.6
Chemical fiber manufacturing industry	61.6
Coal mining and processing industry	61.1
Electric machinery and equipment manufacturing industry	57.8
Electronics and telecommunications equipment manufacturing industry	57.8
Gas production and supply industry	57.5
Papermaking and paper product industry	57.4
Special-purpose equipment manufacturing industry	56.5
Chemical raw materials and chemical products manufacturing industry	56.5
Textile industry	56.2
General equipment manufacturing industry	56.1
Metal products industry	54.7
Water production and supply industry	54.7
Non-metallic mineral products industry	54.6
Food processing industry	53.9
Rubber and plastic products industry	53.0
Ferrous metal mining and processing industry	52.7
Furniture manufacturing industry	52.6
Food manufacturing industry	49.7
Instruments, meters, cultural and office machinery manufacturing industry	49.6
Drink manufacturing industry	49.0
Non-ferrous metal mining and processing industry	48.0
Non-metallic mining and processing industry	47.1
Petroleum and natural gas extraction industry	45.4
Pharmaceutical manufacturing industry	44.6
Other minerals mining and processing industry	38.1
Tobacco processing industry	23.9

properties of government financing platforms and their special relationship with local governments, the figures on their financial statements cannot objectively, effectively or comprehensively reflect whether the enterprises operate well in the market. Local governments can, to some degree, intervene in the balance sheets of government financing platforms by leveraging capital injection and asset evaluation. Meanwhile, the debt of government financing platforms is closely related to the government debt issue, and they can affect one another. Therefore, we did not further explore the debt in this industry in our study of industrial debt (Table 5.6).

Table 5.6 Asset-liability ratios of various industries, 2000–2014

	Power and heat production and supply industry	Water production and supply industry	Gas production and supply industry	Retail industry	Wholesale industry	Real estate industry
2000	60.5	39.2	45.7	73.0	81.5	75.6
2001	60.6	41.1	44.7	72.1	77.5	75.0
2002	61.5	42.0	47.5	72.3	76.9	74.9
2003	63.3	43.6	48.6	73.3	75.5	75.8
2004	55.2	45.3	46.9	71.9	72.5	74.1
2005	56.7	47.8	51.5	72.9	71.9	72.8
2006	57.2	50.5	54.7	73.0	70.6	74.1
2007	58.2	51.5	56.3	73.4	70.9	74.4
2008	64.0	51.9	55.8	69.9	69.5	72.3
2009	64.7	53.3	64.8	70.3	70.4	73.5
2010	65.8	54.1	55.6	71.8	71.9	74.5
2011	66.6	53.8	55.7	71.2	73.3	75.4
2012	66.7	55.8	57.0	71.9	73.6	75.2
2013	66.1	56.3	57.6	72.1	73.9	76.0
2014	64.8	57.6	55.8	71.6	73.9	77.0

Note: The National Bureau of Statistics did not release data concerning the real estate industry in 2013

In sum, the debt sizes of all industries were rising by the end of 2014, and nearly all of the asset-liability ratios of various industries in the industrial sector remained below the warning line of 70%. Industries once had an asset-liability ratio of more than 70% and will embrace a reduction to nearly 70%. Although the asset-liability ratios of some industries with significant overcapacity problems kept rising in recent years, the warning line is unlikely to be passed.

Among the 30 major industrial categories, the asset-liability ratios of the ferrous metal mining and processing industry above a designated size, the petroleum and natural gas extraction industry above a designated size, the coal mining and processing industry above a designated size, the non-ferrous metal smelting and rolling processing industry above a designated size, the water production and supply industry above a designated size, and seven other industries were on the rise. Those showing a significant upward trend were mostly industries with severe overcapacity problems: for example, the asset-liability ratio of the coal mining and processing industry in 2014 increased by 7.2% compared to that in 2008. The asset-liability ratios of the other 18 industries were declining overall.

The trends of various industries' debt leverages clearly diverged. Although the absolute debt volumes of major industries in the industrial sector were increasing, their asset-liability ratios were moving in different directions. Meanwhile, the asset-liability ratios of the retail industry, the wholesale industry and the real estate industry all exceeded 70%; the wholesale industry, in particular, saw a significant increase in its asset-liability ratio.

5.3 Debt Leverages and Profit Margins in Different Industries

5.3.1 Model and Hypotheses

It is important to analyze the causes of debt leverages in various industries from the perspective of their profit margins. Thus we propose a simple model for marginal profits of investment. We used this model to analyze the differentiation between trends of the debt leverage of industries based on basic mathematical logic. The logic of the model is as follows: The asset-liability ratio is the quotient of total debt divided by total assets. In accounting, total assets is the sum of total debt and shareholder equity. Total debt can be further categorized as debt with – or without – interest. Most debt without interest is related to sales on credit and operations activities of upstream and downstream businesses and inside the industry. Specifically, it includes accounts receivable, account payable and other items, and it is a necessary operational instrument with different turnover rates in industries with different characteristics. The volume of total debt cannot directly reflect the debt burden of a company. The major issues we studied were the debt stock, debt burden and debt risk of industries, so we were concerned with debt with interest (rather than without).

$$\text{Asset-liability ratio} = \frac{\text{Total debt}}{\text{Total debt} + \text{Shareholder equity}} = \frac{\text{Debt w/interest} + \text{Debt w/o interest}}{\text{Total debt} + \text{Shareholder equity}}$$

$$= \frac{1}{1 + \dfrac{\text{Shareholder equity}}{\text{Debt w/interest} + \text{Debt w/o interest}}}$$

In daily operations, debt without interest is usually related to the established business model of an enterprise, which may maintain a relatively stable rate of change in a short, fixed observation period. Therefore, we can assume that changes in debt were driven by debt with interest. We analyzed the rate of change of debt with interest when considering changes in total debt. After much consideration, we concluded that an increase in debt with interest was primarily a result of the increase in the investment growth of an industry. Moreover, the motives for enterprises to take on debt can be divided into the following three categories: long-term debt raised for long-term strategic development, short-term loans assumed to solve the problem of fund shortages in the short run and accounts payable generated in daily operations.

The cause for money-borrowing in the third category has been explained earlier, and it can be excluded from the scope of debt with interest. As for the other two categories, considerable changes often take place within them. The second category of demand for debt was the result of a bigger share of funds occupied by long-term projects, leading to a shortage of capital in short-term operations. The first category, in fact, represented enterprises' investment expansion. Thus we can further assume that debt with interest is driven by the growth of industry investment, which is particularly true with traditional resource-intensive industries.

As for shareholder equity, we think that the shock of additional offerings to shareholder equity was not the focus of discussion. Meanwhile, dividends of domestic listed companies were generally low, so it can be assumed that changes in shareholder equity were driven mainly by net profit.

In summary, based on these assumptions, in the simple model of the marginal profit of investment, changes in the total debt were driven by debt with interest, and the changes in debt with interest reflected the investment expansion of an industry. Changes in shareholder equity were linked to changes in net profit. That is to say, "growth of profit" and "growth of debt with interest" jointly determined changes in the asset-liability ratio of an industry. The investment marginal profit model was a proper fraction with very simple mathematical logic, i.e. changes in both numerator and denominator determined the value of the fraction. If the numerator increased and the denominator decreased, the value increased; but if the numerator decreased and the denominator increased, the value decreased.

Referring to the interpretations of concepts including the marginal effect of investment in classical theories, we improved the economic definition of the model. The marginal profit of investment referred to the net increment of profit brought by every unit of increase in investment. If one unit of new investment can bring less than a one unit of increase in profit, it means that additional investment cannot bring profit to the enterprise. Since the fund for further investment is raised from debt with interest, it may add to the financial burdens of the enterprise. In contrast, if a one unit of extra investment can bring more than a one unit increase in profit, the expansion of investment is favorable since it can benefit the enterprise. According to our research assumptions, the model can be further simplified as follows:

$$\begin{aligned}\text{Asset-liability ratio} &= \frac{\text{Total debt}}{\text{Total debt} + \text{Shareholder equity}} = \frac{\text{Debt w/interest} + \text{Debt w/o interest}}{\text{Total debt} + \text{Shareholder equity}} \\ &= \frac{1}{1 + \frac{\text{Shareholder equity}}{\text{Debt w/interest} + \text{Debt w/o interest}}} \\ &= \frac{1}{1 + \frac{\text{Netprofit}}{\text{Debt w/interest} + \text{K}}}\end{aligned}$$

In this model, K is a consonant or a value with a fixed growth rate. It can be ignored in the study of changes in the asset-liability ratio where only the correlation between changes in profit and investment needs to be considered.

When studying the static value of the asset-liability ratio, the focus should be on the relative value of net profit and debt with interest. And when studying the dynamic trend of the ratio, the focus should be on the relative value of net profit and the rate of change of debt with interest.

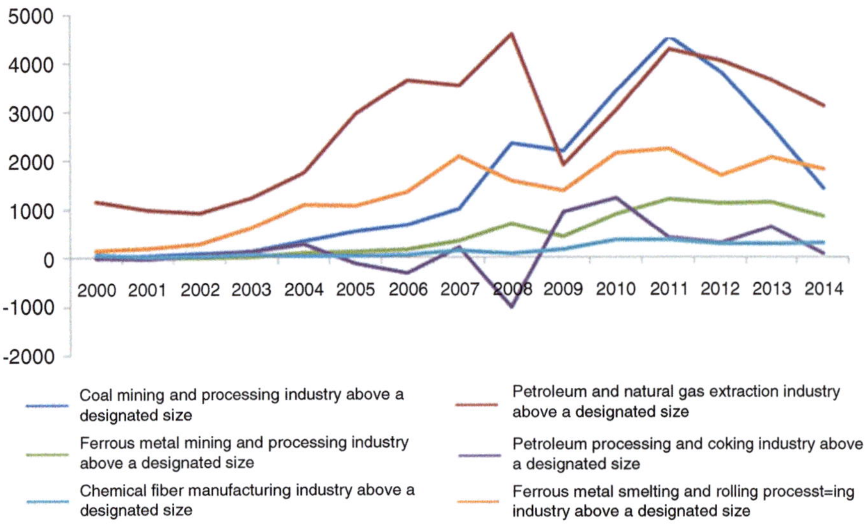

Fig. 5.4 Profitability of industries with positive growth of debt leverage, 2000–2014

5.3.2 Model Application

After elaborating on the model, we tested the application of the model with actual data. The empirical study uncovered a noticeable downward trend after 2012 in the profit of enterprises in industries above a designated size. These industries included coal mining and processing, petroleum and natural gas extraction, ferrous metal mining and processing, petroleum processing and coking, chemical fiber manufacturing, and ferrous metal smelting and rolling processing (Fig. 5.4).

Comparatively, during the observation period, the overall profitability grew considerably in beverage making (debt leverage grew by −1.98%), tobacco processing (−5.32%) and pharmaceutical manufacturing (−1.92%) (Fig. 5.5).

The profit curve of the real estate industry showed an upward trend, but the average annual growth remained positive. This would seem to contradict the statement that profit facilitates the differentiation of debt leverage – but it doesn't. The average annual growth rate of the total debt in the real estate industry was as high as 28.45% – far higher than its average annual growth rate of profit (1.89%), thus driving up the debt leverage of the industry. The root cause was still the mismatch of the growth of profit and that of debt leverage, i.e. excessively low profit growth and excessively high debt growth. This resulted in an increase in the debt leverage of the real estate industry.

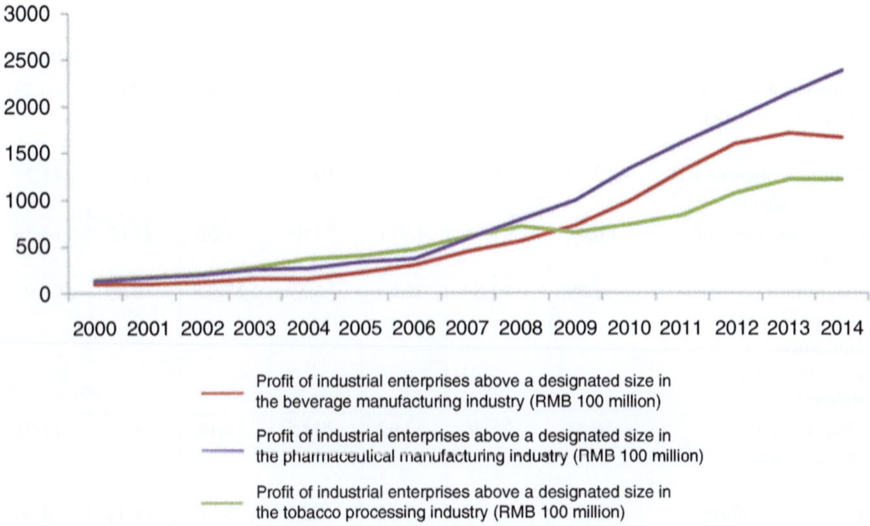

Fig. 5.5 Profitability of industries with negative growth of debt leverage, 2000–2014

5.3.3 Changes in the Profitability of Various Industries

The above model has shown that industry profitability was the major cause for the differentiation between trends of industry debt leverages. Primary data shows that the absolute sizes of debt in all industries were rising against the context of debt expansion in the society, but only six industrial enterprises above a designated size – coal mining and processing, petroleum and natural gas extraction, ferrous metal mining and processing, petroleum processing and coking, chemical fiber manufacturing and ferrous metal smelting and rolling processing – realized a positive average annual growth in their asset-liability ratios. Combining profitability data of various industries, we concluded that industry profitability was the main cause for the differentiation between trends of debt leverages in different industries.

We also analyzed industries with an increase (or a decrease) in profit from 2008 to 2014. During this period, 28 industries saw their profits rise (see Table 5.7).

Given that the 2008 financial crisis was a watershed, we sorted the average profitability of different industries from 2008 to 2014 as a reference to assess the overall profitability of industries after the crisis. The median profit of these industries from 2008 to 2014 was RMB 150.281 billion. Industries with profit higher than the median included: metal products; non-ferrous metal smelting and rolling processing; pharmaceutical manufacturing; textile, ferrous metal smelting and rolling processing; special-purpose equipment manufacturing; power and heat production and supply; food processing; general equipment manufacturing; electronics and telecommunications equipment manufacturing; coal mining and processing; non-metallic mineral products; electric machinery and equipment manufacturing;

Table 5.7 Profitability growth in major industries, 2008–2014

	2008	2009	2010	2011	2012	2013	2014
Average of industries above a designated size	12.55	13.02	53.58	15.73	0.84	10.45	−0.33
Water production and supply industry	−12.37	−6.35	137.67	19.55	0.72	43.53	45.22
Gas production and supply industry	66.01	41.56	43.11	23.83	1.58	17.62	14.39
Electronics and telecommunications equipment manufacturing industry	6.69	13.84	63.59	−1.59	12.97	19.79	11.92
Pharmaceutical manufacturing industry	36.41	25.36	33.92	20.65	16.18	14.3	11.71
Electric machinery and equipment manufacturing industry	46.70	19.89	43.66	6.22	3.31	11.79	8.90
Instruments, meters, cultural and office machinery manufacturing industry	17.02	15.45	42.91	13.91	−6.08	15.26	8.65
Furniture manufacturing industry	28.38	31.63	52.93	21.12	13.49	11.61	8.12
Power and heat production and supply industry	−74.34	153.8	52.47	−2.38	42.89	43.63	7.40
Chemical fiber manufacturing industry	−49.18	108.79	110.31	2.44	−26.33	1.14	6.68
Food manufacturing industry	24.19	46.4	41.67	21.35	15.49	15.73	5.93
Other minerals mining and processing industry	35.71	3.51	235.59	−28.79	79.43	−43.08	3.47
Metal products industry	40.78	14.55	58.90	13.26	19.28	13.70	3.07
General equipment manufacturing industry	35.45	12.40	51.88	12.70	−10.46	12.27	2.55
Non-metallic mineral products industry	42.75	25.40	53.97	25.49	−4.15	17.51	2.24
Textile industry	21.09	17.66	55.60	15.25	−3.20	13.80	0.57
Tobacco processing industry	17.20	−8.78	12.85	14.51	27.48	14.10	−0.12

(continued)

Table 5.7 (continued)

	2008	2009	2010	2011	2012	2013	2014
Rubber and plastic products manufacturing industry	59.93	43.13	9.34	0.21	8.01	21.15	−0.60
Chemical raw materials and chemical products industry	4.62	13.87	66.5	21.82	−7.01	9.72	−1.60
Beverage manufacturing industry	25.46	30.41	36.03	32.69	21.82	7.15	−2.69
Non-metallic mining and processing industry	55.02	9.90	48.76	29.69	7.43	10.66	−2.90
Special-purpose equipment manufacturing industry	30.44	17.27	56.56	16.14	−0.46	8.84	−3.10
Food processing industry	35.84	23.67	56.12	19.27	14.58	8.46	−6.04
Paper-making and paper product industry	14.05	16.08	44.06	4.58	1.81	0.22	−6.31
Non-ferrous metal smelting and rolling processing industry	−27.93	9.01	75.28	27.57	−14.87	1.71	−7.45
Ferrous metal smelting and rolling processing industry	−24.63	−12.54	56.19	4.21	−24.16	21.32	−11.05
Non-ferrous metal mining and processing industry	−4.86	−16.74	68.68	42.48	−3.41	−15.36	−12.58
Petroleum and natural gas extraction industry	30.15	−58.63	59.01	42.05	−5.83	−9.99	−14.54
Ferrous metal mining and processing industry	100.66	−37.28	103.29	35.5	−6.39	0.34	−25.12
Coal mining and processing industry	129.75	−5.97	56.07	32.33	−16.5	−29.62	−46.86
Petroleum processing and coking industry	−563.88	−192.83	31.13	−65.35	−29.06	111.95	−87.73
Educational and sports goods manufacturing industry	1.11	42.15	48.38	41.05	212.09	25.81	27.84

petroleum and natural gas extraction; and chemical raw materials and chemical products. Those with profit lower than the median included: other minerals mining and processing; water production and supply; chemical fiber manufacturing; gas production and supply; non-metallic mineral mining and processing; furniture manufacturing; petroleum processing and coking; educational and sports goods manufacturing; instruments, meters, cultural and office machinery manufacturing; non-ferrous metal mining and processing; paper-making and paper products; ferrous mining and processing; tobacco processing; food manufacturing; and beverage manufacturing (Table 5.8).

Table 5.8 Average profit in various industries, 2008–2014 (Unit: RMB 100 million)

Industries	Average profit
Other minerals mining and processing industry	1.43
Water production and supply industry	73.23
Chemical fiber manufacturing industry	259.72
Gas production and supply industry	285.19
Non-metallic mineral mining and processing industry	316.12
Furniture manufacturing industry	318.95
Petroleum processing and coking industry	369.53
Educational and sports manufacturing industry	388.31
Instruments, meters, cultural and office machinery manufacturing industry	544.72
Non-ferrous metal mining and processing industry	595.65
Paper-making and paper product industry	672.02
Ferrous metal mining and processing industry	909.04
Tobacco processing industry	921.87
Food manufacturing industry	1181.26
Beverage manufacturing industry	1226.33
Rubber and plastic products industry	1502.81
Metal products industry	1517.16
Non-ferrous metal smelting and rolling processing industry	1523.89
Pharmaceutical industry	1586.43
Textile industry	1698.75
Ferrous metal smelting and rolling processing industry	1847.10
Special-purpose equipment manufacturing industry	1849.24
Power and heat production and supply industry	2373.61
Food processing industry	2541.95
General equipment manufacturing industry	2584.86
Electronics and telecommunications equipment manufacturing industry	2900.35
Coal mining and processing	2925.25
Non-metallic mineral products industry	3055.98
Electric machinery and equipment manufacturing industry	3115.77
Petroleum and natural gas extraction industry	3519.79
Chemical raw materials and chemical products industry	3609.89
Industrial enterprises above a designated size	53,999.21

5.4 An Analysis of the Elasticity of Debt Effect in Various Industries

5.4.1 *Definition of the Elasticity of Debt Effect*

An assessment of the debt effect in different industries can be done with a debt-profit elasticity coefficient and a debt-income elasticity coefficient, according to the financial leverage effect and the diminishing marginal utility of debt. The former coefficient defined the reaction of a profit increase to a debt increase, i.e. the ratio of the profit growth rate to the debt increase rate. If the elasticity were larger than 1, it meant that a one unit of increase in debt would bring more than a one unit increase in profit; but if it were smaller than 1, it implied that every one unit of increase in debt brought less than a one unit increase in profit. The latter coefficient defined the reaction of income increases to debt increases, i.e. the ratio of the income growth rate to the debt increase rate. If the elasticity were larger than 1, a one unit increase in debt resulted in more than a one unit of increase in income. But if were smaller than 1, it meant that a one unit of increase in debt brought less than a one unit increase in income. Both center on the profitability of a specific industry. The debt-profit elasticity involves cost changes based on debt-income elasticity. These two indicators provide a reference for studying favorable debt levels from the perspective of relative quantity.

If the debt-profit/income elasticity kept declining – or even turned negative – it meant that the driving force of debt on the profitability of an industry was gradually weakening and could have a negative influence on profit/income. If the elasticity follows an upward trend, it implies that the current debt level of the industry were healthy and favorable since debt can facilitate improvements in profit/income growth and capacity. In China, both the debt-profit elasticity and the debt-income elasticity were on a downward trend. In particular, the debt-profit elasticity had a precipitous drop and reached −0.04 in 2014 (Fig. 5.6).

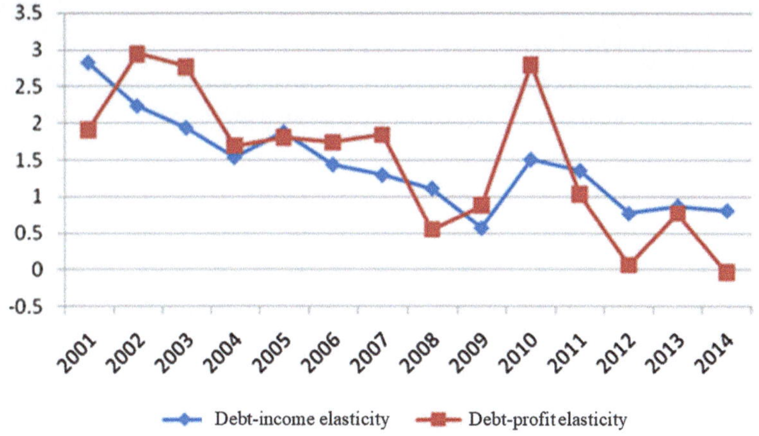

Fig. 5.6 Overall debt-income and debt-profit elasticity of industries in China

5.4.2 An Analysis on Debt Elasticity Coefficient of the Industrial Sector

Using statistics from the National Bureau of Statistics, we analyzed the debt elasticity of major industries in the national economy from two aspects: the debt-profit and debt-income.

Among the 30 industries studied, the number of industries with debt-profit or debt-income elasticity smaller than 1 was evidently on the rise since 2012. Regarding the debt-profit elasticity, before 2011, the highest share of industries with an elasticity smaller than 1 was 43.33%, which only appeared once; while in the 3 years after 2012, the figure exceeded 60%, even reaching as high as 93.33% in 2014 when only two industries had an elasticity larger than 1. The trend of debt-income elasticity was basically the same as that of debt-profit elasticity. Prior to 2011, there were no more than 10 industries with an elasticity smaller than 1 except in 2009. Yet in each of the 3 years after 2012, there were more than 20 industries with an elasticity smaller than 1, but the range of change was not as big as that of the former (Table 5.9).

5.4.3 An Analysis on the Debt Elasticity Coefficient of Other Industries

The above is the analysis on the sub-sectors in the industrial sector. Apart from that, such industries as retail, wholesale and construction also were considered important. Table 5.10 lists the debt-profit elasticity and debt-income elasticity of these industries. The results show that in the construction industry, the debt-income elasticity and debt-profit elasticity have presented a prominent polarization trend.

Table 5.9 Debt elasticity of 30 industries

	Debt-profit elasticity smaller than 1		Debt-income elasticity smaller than 1	
	No. of industries	Share (%)	No. of industries	Share (%)
2004	9	30.00	5	16.67
2005	10	33.33	5	16.67
2006	5	16.67	3	10.00
2007	4	13.33	5	16.67
2008	11	36.67	6	20.00
2009	13	43.33	19	63.33
2010	2	6.67	4	13.33
2011	11	36.67	5	16.67
2012	25	83.33	26	86.67
2013	19	63.33	20	66.67
2014	28	93.33	20	66.67

Table 5.10 Debt elasticity in different industries

	Debt-profit elasticity of the construction industry	Debt-income elasticity of the construction industry	Debt-profit elasticity of the retail industry	Debt-income elasticity of the retail industry	Debt-profit elasticity of the wholesale industry	Debt-income elasticity of the wholesale industry	Industrial added value elasticity of the real estate industry	Fixed asset investment elasticity of the real estate industry
1996	−0.39	1.18						
1997	6.81	0.71						
1998	−1.93	0.93						
1999	−1.28	1.21						
2000	−1.89	1.66	1.64	2.03	1.17	0.96		
2001	−0.58	2.97	2.56	6.83	0.50	0.73		
2002	−0.71	1.50	0.97	1.87	0.86	1.00	0.44	0.74
2003			0.39	1.26	0.72	1.19	0.24	0.51
2004	−1.18	1.61	0.39	1.26	0.72	1.19	0.24	0.51
2005	−0.33	1.43	5.58	1.65	−0.57	−0.67	0.11	0.26
2006	−0.80	1.43	2.77	1.47	1.36	1.17	−0.17	−0.37
2007	−0.81	1.13	1.56	1.24	1.13	0.98	0.19	0.35
2008	−0.42	1.11	1.23	1.20	1.63	1.40	2.29	3.82
2009	−0.36	1.22	2.52	1.39	−358.87	−140.31	5.68	14.84
2010	−0.20	1.04	0.34	0.83	1.91	1.44	−0.32	−1.08
2011	−0.48	0.76	0.99	1.14	2.88	2.28	0.17	0.32
2012	−1.61	0.87	1.09	0.95	3.89	1.83	−0.65	−1.43
2013			0.59	0.65	0.98	−0.73	−0.46	−1.19
2014			1.51	1.03	3.92	4.68		

In the retail and wholesale industries, different from the sub-sectors in the industrial sector, there was no noticeable decline in either the debt-income elasticity or the debt-profit elasticity. In general – except for the abnormal value enabled by the financial crisis in 2008 – the elasticity coefficients improved in 2013 compared with those in 2000. The retail sales volume in the whole society kept growing. A sound sales environment laid a foundation for the profitability in the retail and wholesale industries. These two industries cannot be regarded as typical cyclical ones. Although their profitability can be hit hard by major events like a financial crisis, the impact of an ordinary industrial cycle and product cycle on them is much smaller compared with other industries in the industrial sector. A sluggish macroeconomy has put some pressure on household consumption, but with the emergence in recent years of financing via the Internet, the rapid development of e-commerce has accelerated the flow of off-line traffic to an online shopping mode, driving its profitability.

As for the real estate industry, its development was evidently in sync with the economic cycle due to its unique operations, and it has contributed significantly to the development of the macroeconomy. Therefore, the debt elasticity of this industry was analyzed from the following two aspects: the industrial added value elasticity and the fixed asset investment elasticity which have experienced three stages since 2002. The first stage was the period before 2005 which witnessed declining elasticity. The fixed asset investment elasticity dropped from 0.74 in 2002 to −0.37 in 2005. The second stage was from 2006 to 2008, which saw an upward trend. In fact, in 2008, the fixed asset investment elasticity was as high as 14.84. The third stage was the period from 2009 to the present when the fixed asset investment elasticity has been on a downward trend. For example, in 2011 and 2012, the elasticity coefficients were lower than 0, so it could be concluded that the debt effect crossed its turning point.

In sum, comprehensive analyses debt leverage and elasticity have shown that at present, the asset-liability ratio in most industries is on a downward track. We believe that this is what we should attend to. The debt-profit/income elasticity in most industries is on the decline, which indicates that every additional unit of debt is bringing increasingly lower profit. The industries faced with this problem are mainly those with overcapacity – coal, steel, building materials and non-ferrous metal. For one thing, their profits have fallen considerably because of the shock of the macroeconomy. For another, constant input and expansion of new capacity during the period of decreasing demand has resulted in a huge amount of debt, which makes the situation worse. Therefore, in the industries of non-financial enterprises, deleveraging becomes the focus in industries with overcapacity including the coal, steel, building materials and non-ferrous metal industries, as well as the real estate industry. Thus our follow-up analyses will be centered on these industries.

5.5 Analysis of the Turning Point of the Debt of Important Industries

Our study probed into the debt effect elasticity and profit margin of the chemical fiber manufacturing industry and petrochemical industry – two typical industries with overcapacity. We then made initial judgments on the possible turning point of their debts.

5.5.1 Chemical Fiber Manufacturing Industry

1. **Industry status quo**

The chemical fiber manufacturing industry, with Dacron and Spandex as its major products, is at the upstream of the fiber industry. In recent years, the chemical fiber manufacturing industry has been confronted with extreme overcapacity, a result of both internal problems and external impacts. Internally, since the technology related to China's fiber industry has been limited regarding fiber materials and fabrics as well as product development and design, homogeneous competition among products prevails, and the gross margin is low. A majority of enterprises have expanded their production capacity and utilize the scale effects to earn profits. The *Report on the Industry Competitive Landscape and Investment Strategy Consultancy on China's Chemical Fiber Manufacturing Industry (2015–2022)* shows that since 2009, the production of chemical fibers was on the rise for six consecutive years. According to data released on chyxx.com (a website providing industry information in China), as of the first half of 2015, there were 1905 chemical fiber manufacturers above a designated size. Among them, 445 ran at a loss, and the loss amounted to RMB 2.358 billion. The chemical fiber industry, capital-incentive as it is, had to expand production capacities by increasing loans and debt financing. Therefore, as the capacity rapidly expanded, the debt burden has grown considerably (Table 5.11).

Purified terephthalic acid (PTA) is one of the major raw materials used in the chemical fiber manufacturing industry. Therefore, the capacity of PTA correlates with the supply-demand pattern and product prices of the chemical fiber industry and the downstream fiber industry. In fact, 90% of PTA is used for producing polyester fiber, while 80% of polyester is used for the production of Dacron, a synthetic fiber with the largest production volume.

Since 2012, the problem of overcapacity in China's PTA production has become increasingly prominent. After 5 years of heavy investment, the production capacity of PTA expanded from fewer than 15 million tons per year in 2010 to more than 46 million tons in 2015, registering a growth rate of more than 200%. The surge in the production capacity of PTA led to a decline in product prices and weakened the

Table 5.11 Assets and debts of the chemical fiber industry

	Asset (RMB 100 million)	Debt (RMB 100 million)	Asset-asset-liability ratio(%)
2000	1808.44	1034.70	57.22
2001	1531.20	917.77	59.94
2002	1563.10	930.52	59.53
2003	1595.13	933.56	58.53
2004	2122.46	1269.08	59.79
2005	2461.41	1454.84	59.11
2006	2736.40	1633.10	59.68
2007	3462.37	2106.29	60.83
2008	3366.01	2008.85	59.68
2009	3389.56	2059.93	60.77
2010	4204.80	2526.73	60.09
2011	5236.96	3242.19	61.91
2012	5737.44	3605.60	62.84
2013	6205.37	3942.19	63.53
2014	6455.37	4008.63	62.10

Table 5.12 PTA supply and demand in China

Year	Output	Import	Export	Apparent consumption	Growth rate of consumption	Self-support ratio
2007	981.0	599.3	0.0	1580.2		62.10%
2008	935.0	497.0	0.9	1431.8	−9.40%	65.30%
2009	1196.0	508.0	0.1	1703.9	19.00%	70.20%
2010	1413.5	540.2	0.4	1953.3	14.60%	72.40%
2011	1648.0	537.7	2.7	2183.0	11.80%	75.50%
2012	2050.0	419.5	0.9	2468.6	13.10%	83.00%
2013	2700.0	213.7	12.6	2901.0	17.50%	93.10%
2014	2655.0	98.1	46.3	2706.8	−6.70%	98.10%
2015		68.7	62.3			

Sources: General Administration of Customs, National Bureau of Statistics

profitability of chemical fiber enterprises. In 2012 and 2014, there were two rounds of massive PTA production without much limitation, with growth rates of 64% and 29.4%, respectively. In 2014, the amount of newly produced PTA reached 43.1 million tons. Meanwhile, the growth rate of consumption plummeted below zero for the first time after the 2008 financial crisis (Table 5.12).

The chemical fiber industry does not have an evident cycle or seasonal changes. Therefore, with the macroeconomy heading down due to sluggish demand from the real economy, the industry's overcapacity problem can be alleviated through an overall production restriction, technological upgrade and industry chain extension. Compared with cyclical industries, the chemical fiber industry has stronger self-control. The policy of "protecting prices by restricting production" proves effective

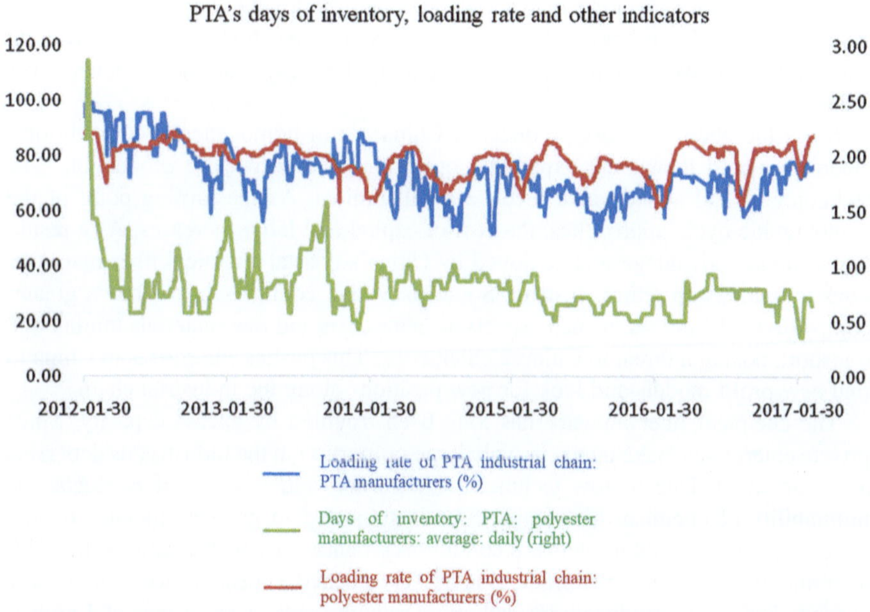

Fig. 5.7 PTA's days of inventory, loading rate and other indicators

in destocking, with PTA's days of inventory gradually decreasing and the loading rate of PTA and polyester factories picking up. This not only provides a basis for storage pressure relief and price margin increases, but it helps chemical fiber manufacturers and increases their profitability (Fig. 5.7).

2. **Industry development trends and identification of the debt's turning point**

The problem of PTA overcapacity is expected to be greatly alleviated – benefiting from supply-side reform – and the supply and demand of PTA will be tightly balanced. Because of controls on capacity expansion, there will only be 3 million tons of new capacity in the coming 2 years. With a stable demand for polyester and Dacron, the overall condition of the industry is expected to improve.

The chemical fiber industry features a high concentration of production capacity. The top five large-capacity enterprises – Xianglu Petrochemicals, Yisheng Dahua Petrochemical, Zhejiang Yisheng Petrochemical, Hengli Petrochemical and Far East Petrochemical – accounted for 14%, 13%, 12%, 10% and 7% of the total production capacity, respectively, and 56% combined. A high concentration of capacity is conducive to increasing their bargaining power with upstream and downstream enterprises, as well as improving corporate profits.

However, as a typical industry with excess capacity, the chemical fiber industry is still faced with the arduous task of phasing out backward production capacities and alleviating storage pressure. The unlimited expansion of production capacity and the breaking of the weak supply-demand balance remain the industry's major risks.

When production capacity remains excessive and the textile and clothing industry grows slowly, it's still possible that the prices of some textile products will hit another record low and affect the profitability landscape of the chemical fiber industry.

Since the chemical fiber products in China are in homogeneous competitions, enterprises tend to win by expanding operations and increasing production. The technologies and added value levels are still limited. As the turning point of the demographic cycle approaches, the cost of capital and labor increases. As a result, the dominant advantage once enjoyed by China's coastal chemical fiber manufactures is unlikely to return. Instead, Southeast Asian countries have shown greater competitive advantages in such aspects as labor costs and raw materials mining and transport, posing a threat to Chinese enterprises. This pushes enterprises in China to find new profit models and look for new positions along the industrial chain.

The chemical fiber industry has long been troubled by excess capacity. Since private enterprises make up a relatively large proportion in the industry, its debt risks are aggravated. Due to low technical barriers and added value of products, the profitability of chemical fiber enterprises is subjected to greater influence of raw material prices and supply-demand conditions – hence greater fluctuations. In 2014, after massive expansion, the production of PTA reached its peak. Since then, no new capacity has been introduced; instead, more requirements on environmental protection were proposed and policies to close down outdated capacity were issued. Thus the supply-demand contradiction has been somewhat eased. Despite this, the industry still lacks core competitiveness, relies excessively on raw materials and requires extensive investment. The preliminary conclusion of this study is that the debt of the chemical fiber industry might have reached its turning point around 2014 when PTA production capacity reached a historical high.

5.5.2 Petrochemical Industry

1. **Industry status quo**

Data from this study group show that from 2000 to 2014, very few of the 30 major sectors saw their debt leverage increase. The petroleum and natural gas exploitation sector and the petroleum processing and coking sector were two of them, the former registering an annual increase of 1.08% in its debt leverage and the latter registering 0.78%.

Overinvestment, with local governments as the major driving force, is the main reason for the overcapacity in the petrochemical industry. Since the global financial crisis broke out in 2008, the world economy has slowed, and the demand for petrochemical products remains weak. These factors aggravate the overcapacity problem. According to authoritative estimates, around 60–70% of petrochemical products in China are coping with this issue.

Table 5.13 Asset-liability ratio of petrochemical industry

	Asset-liability ratio of petroleum and natural gas exploration sector	Asset-liability ratio of petroleum processing and coking sector
2000	40.0	59.5
2001	36.5	56.3
2002	35.6	56.4
2003	35.6	51.3
2004	37.1	54.0
2005	34.2	56.5
2006	37.1	57.0
2007	38.6	56.6
2008	39.1	61.9
2009	45.8	62.4
2010	43.7	60.9
2011	48.6	63.0
2012	46.9	65.0
2013	46.8	66.0
2014	46.5	66.3

The downward trend of the macroeconomy combined with low oil prices further stresses the petrochemical industry; this exacerbates the overcapacity. The capacity utilization in different sectors of the industry has fallen and remains at a low level. Currently, the capacity utilization in the oil refining, synthetic rubber, PTA and acrylic acid sectors is lower than 70% (Table 5.13).

Saddled with declining profits and expanding production, the asset-asset-liability ratio of the petrochemical industry continues to increase. The debt leverage of the petroleum processing and coking sector is higher than that of the upstream petroleum and natural gas exploration sector. As of 2014, the ratio reached 66.3%, approaching the warning line of 70%. In fact, ever since 2012, the debt-profit elasticity and debt-income elasticity have entered a downward track – dropping significantly and even going below zero. This implies that every unit of increase in the petrochemical industry's debt – instead of bringing in more profit or income – would lead to a decrease in profit/income. So the petrochemical industry is faces severe overcapacity as well as excess debt (Tables 5.14 and 5.15).

2. **Identification of the industry's debt turning point**

China's government work report and the draft proposal of the 13th Five-Year Plan shed light on the supply-side reform of the petrochemical industry and the institutional reform of oil and gas. Just as the chemical fiber industry, non-ferrous metal industry, iron and steel industry, coal industry and many other industries with excess capacity, the development of the petrochemical industry will be focused on de-capacity and destocking, especially in such sectors as oil refining, synthetic rubber, PTA and acrylic acid with severe overcapacity problems. Furthermore, by introducing private capital into the institutional reform of the oil and gas sector, the

Table 5.14 Income and profit elasticity of petrochemical industry's debt

	Debt-income elasticity of the petroleum processing and coking sector	Debt-income elasticity of the petroleum and natural gas exploration sector	Debt-profit elasticity of the petroleum processing and coking sector	Debt-profit elasticity of the petroleum and natural gas exploration sector
2001	−0.88	1.59	417.42	2.68
2002	−3.92	−0.46	359.05	−4.70
2003	−4.41	2.24	−21.20	2.74
2004	1.18	1.24	3.69	1.59
2005	1.03	11.20	−4.34	21.24
2006	1.39	0.86	8.99	0.76
2007	0.84	0.34	−7.37	−0.12
2008	0.72	0.98	−15.57	0.98
2009	−0.52	−0.79	−16.22	−1.62
2010	2.13	4.98	1.75	8.58
2011	1.10	0.84	−2.66	1.66
2012	0.39	0.97	−2.01	0.60
2013	0.32	−0.08	9.05	−1.30
2014	0.04	−0.23	−12.78	−2.39

Table 5.15 Capacity utilization of some petrochemical products

	Capacity (10,000 tons)	Output (10,000 tons)	Capacity utilization rate in 2014	Historical capacity utilization rate
Crude oil processing	74,628	50,277	67.40%	88.2% (2005)
Ethylene	1928	1697	88.00%	96.1% (2005)
PTA	4335	2655	61.20%	84.1% (2007)
Butadiene	381	250	65.70%	85.2% (2004)
Butadiene styrene rubber	168	97	57.80%	92.9% (2004)
Cis-polybutadiene	170	86	50.40%	94.8% (2004)
Acyclic acid	267	154	57.80%	73.6% (2009)

Source: Economic Analysis of China Petroleum and Chemical Industry, Research Institute of Haitong Securities.

vitality of non-public sectors of the economy will be stimulated in the petrochemical industry; by attracting private and social capital into the upstream oil and gas exploration sector, and reversing the situation of public sectors of the economy dominating oil and gas exploration, the role of market forces will be strengthened. This, in turn, will improve operational efficiency.

The reform blueprint promises bright prospects for the petrochemical industry. Nevertheless, it's essential that we are aware of potential risks. For one thing, the industrial reform and the de-capacity process may not go as well as expected. As the petrochemical industry is burdened with heavy debt, it may be unable to strike a balance between supply and demand and thus get rid of the development dilemma as soon as expected. For another, as the Chinese government attaches greater importance to production safety and environmental protection and keeps enhancing relevant requirements, the petrochemical enterprises – as some of the largest industrial polluters with huge emissions of waste water, waste gas (SO_2 and nitrogen oxide, etc.) and solid waste – are highly responsible for energy savings and environmental protections. Thus they may face greater obstacles in both business expansion and sustainable operations. Stricter standards of production safety and environmental protection have put forward higher requirements for the petrochemical enterprises' production techniques, working skills, management levels and equipment sophistication. For those sectors still trapped in overcapacity, the ensuing financial stress and production pressure will be tremendous. To be more specific, to introduce advanced equipment, techniques and talents, petrochemical enterprises may need the support of external financing. The external financing used for production and construction always becomes debt with interest. In the short term, the accumulating debt with interest will worsen the financial conditions of the industry. However, should this input be effective, there will be increasing returns to scale. In this sense, raising funds externally is of great benefit to the remarkable progress of the whole industry. If enterprises fail to accurately assess their production capacity and just blindly increases production, they may aggravate the deterioration of operational conditions. This could result in potential risks at the industry level. Therefore, rational choice is necessary.

In 2011, the debt-income and debt-profit elasticity of the petrochemical industry evidently deteriorated and began a downward trend. We believe that the turning point of the debt of the petrochemical industry might have appeared at that time, rather earlier than that of many other industries we studied.

5.6 Summary and Suggestions

In recent years, many enterprises – state-owned enterprises included – have been expanding, launching projects and vying for rankings. The operations goals often are only concerned with size rather than quality, bringing about the problems of overinvestment, overcapacity and repeated construction. For instance, the coal industry already reached the turning point of its debt in 2006. However, 3 years later, it was still taking on debts. We believe this just an example of the blundering mindset of development. At present, all industries should think strategically, understand the necessity and possibility of allocating economic resources globally, and endeavor to improve the efficiency of resource allocation. In one aspect, the fundamental role of the market in resource allocation should be strengthened; in another – with regard to the local failures of market regulation – the government must decisively intervene, set clear boundaries for market operations, and strengthen long-term and persistent macroregulation to tackle problems of spontaneity, blindness and hysteresis within market regulation.

Based on our analysis in this chapter, we believe that concerned departments should consider making strategic adjustments in several aspects:

1. **Understand the phenomenon of industrial overcapacity and improve enterprise competitiveness to solve the problems of overcapacity and obsolete structures.** Market standards should be used to assess the problems of industrial surplus and excess capacity, although many Chinese scholars claim these problems do not exist. In a market economy, any kind of excess is normal and marginal; the invisible hand is always regulating excess effectively, thus maintaining the balance between supply and demand. Therefore, it's too simple to assert that some industries have overcapacity just with a comparison of actual productivity and effective demand based on the logic of a planned economy. In China, the material crux of industrial surplus is not a structural one; it is the result of insufficient enterprise competitiveness. Because of a lack of market competitiveness, the quality of products supplied cannot meet the upgraded demand, hence the supply-demand deviation. To solve the problem of industrial surplus and excess capacity, the focus should not be on "de-capacity," but it should be on enhancing the capacity of the real economy and improving the competitiveness of enterprises and products.
2. **Take the disposal of "zombie enterprises" as a strategically important matter in industrial development, and vigorously tackle problems caused by these enterprises.** There are lessons to learn. After Japan's economic bubbles burst, instead of shutting down or reorganizing "zombie banks" and "zombie enterprises," Japan decided to maintain minimal operations. However, these entities did more to occupy social resources and obstruct economic recovery than contribute anything to economic growth. So China must seize the opportunity to reform state-owned enterprises by decisively disposing of "zombie enterprises" and low-productive and ineffective assets. It's also important to dispose of the enterprises' assets at fair market prices through legal transactions of securities and property rights in the capital market. The structure of stock debts should be safely optimized by lowering the debt leverage of some industries and taking on new debts rationally. In this way, the forms of state assets can be altered, and the risks of zombie enterprises can be mitigated. More capital will be guided into supporting industrial restructuring and upgrades which will help the development of the real economy.
3. **Draw upon the experience and lessons of deleveraging. In the history of China's economic development, deleveraging has been conducted more than once.** The deleveraging approaches adopted from 1997 to 2002 achieved remarkable results and are worth drawing on. During that period, the decrease in the rate of China's corporate debt was higher than that of the national economy. After some temporary economic pain, in 2003, relevant indicators started to recover and grow, yielding satisfactory results from deleveraging. It's important to learn

from experience, approaches and influence. Combining international and national economic conditions can steadily promote deleveraging and de-capacity. According to the marginal investment profit model we proposed, profit is a material factor resulting in debt leverage differences among major industries. Lowering the debt size while neglecting improvements in profitability would make it hard to fundamentally solve the manufacturing industry's debt problems. Therefore, greater importance should be attached to improving profitability, in an effort to radically advance healthy and sustained development of the entire industry.

4. **Adjust measures to local conditions for different industries and refrain from the practice of "one size fits all."** For example, the steel and iron industry is burdened with heavy debt and a high debt leverage. The short-term debt makes up too large a portion, hence the prominent liquidity risk (as illustrated by financial figures). However, if we simply demand steel and iron enterprises to stop reviewing new projects while increasing and accelerating repayments, it's possible that the industry can temporarily steer away from the risk of collapse. But this fails to promote the healthy development of the industry. Studies have shown that the steel and iron industry has a low concentration ratio, dispersed resources and low-tech products. The market has few high added-value products; for example, special steel accounts for a relatively smaller proportion among all products.

   Due to low working efficiency and difficulties with marketing and planning, many famous industrial giants are confronted with excess capacity and inventory pressure. The key to solving these problems lies in accelerating and strengthening the ownership reforms of state-owned large and medium-sized steel and iron enterprises, encouraging mergers and reorganizations that are beneficial to industrial growth, supporting the enterprises to introduce advanced techniques, new equipment and high-caliber workers, and improving day-to-day operations and management. If the governments see only one aspect of the problems and exercises strict control over new debts, the enterprises might run into development and innovation capital shortages due to a credit crunch and financing restrictions; they could lose opportunities for increasing added value of products and enhancing competitiveness. Similarly, to promote deleveraging in the coal industry, the governments should control debt and encourage coal enterprises to upgrade production technologies, develop deep processing of coal and improve profitability.

   In this analysis of debt in China, we found that it's possible that the same category of data calculated by different departments – or even within the same department – can have substantial variations. Without high-quality data, it will be impossible to conduct an objective analysis of China's debt as the whole – let alone provide a strong reference for policymaking and implementation. To learn about the actual debt size of China's economic sectors and to have a deep understanding of shadow banking, contingent liability, implicit guarantees, etc., we suggest further study on China's total debt size. A reasonable and effective method of collecting debt data should be constructed on this basis. A high-quality database will lay a foundation for debt monitoring and management.

Chapter 6
A Study of the Debt of Real Estate-Related Industries

This chapter focuses on the debt turning point of the upstream and downstream industries relative to the real estate industry. Considering the importance of real estate-related industries to the national economy, and the fact that the total output of these industries accounts for as much as 20% of the GDP, we selected six industries – coal, iron and steel, non-ferrous metals, building materials, household appliances and real estate – for analysis and turning point estimation. As in the study of China's debt as a whole, a linear regression model was adopted, with the profit of an industry's core businesses as the independent variable and the debt size and its square as the dependent variables. After working out the coefficient of regression, we can determine whether the industry has reached the turning point of its debt. With further calculations, we could determine the debt size and industry profit at the turning point. Then we also could identify the time when the industry reached (or will reach) its debt turning point. The results showed that **the coal industry reached its debt turning point in 2011; the iron and steel industry reached theirs in 2012; the non-ferrous metal industry and the real estate industry both reached theirs in 2013; and only the building materials industry has not reached its turning point**.

We also concluded that the debt of the real estate industry included household debt (mortgage) on the demand side and the real estate developers' debt on the supply side. **The debt problem of China's real estate industry lies on the supply side. The debt turning point of the real estate industrial chain moved from upstream industries to downstream ones. This was opposite of what occurs in typical economic cycles** where downstream consumption industries are more sensitive to economic fluctuations than upstream ones, which are mostly at the beginning of a transmission channel. This also explains why the upstream industries tend to take on excessive debts for business expansion and reach their turning points relatively soon.

In this study, we analyzed not only the official data, but the latest market events and on-field investigation results from Henan Province and Shanxi Province. In the

X. Zhu et al., *A Study of the Turning Point of China's Debt*,
https://doi.org/10.1007/978-981-13-1325-7_6

last section, the latest market situation and research results in 2016 were sorted for a comprehensive discussion about "de-capacity."

6.1 An Analysis of Debt in the Real Estate Industry

6.1.1 Status Quo of Debt in the Real Estate Industry

The real estate industry is very important to China's economy and to Chinese people's daily lives. In fact, the development of all major economies in the world is closely related to real estate because it involves a wide range of industries in the national economy, including resource-intensive industries like coal and cement; industries with overcapacity like iron and steel and non-ferrous metal; downstream consumer industries like household appliances, furniture manufacturing and home furnishings; and financial industries like leasing and credit. Hence it's fair to say that a slight move in the real estate industry may affect the overall economy. In the long run, the rise and fall of the real estate industry is intimately intertwined with the economic development of a country. Some in the industry believe that, in theory, the growth of the real estate industry will be in tandem with the growth of GDP and the per capita income of a country. The real estate market's temperature is determined by the fundamentals in a country's economy. Deviations usually are caused by demographics (such as the demographic dividend, aging, etc.). However, in the short run, the market trends in real estate are, in a way, a sort of "monetary phenomenon." If loose monetary policies are adopted and mortgage rates are lowered, extra money will flow into the real estate market and push for prosperity. Thus it can be concluded that the health of the real estate market may involve many aspects in society, such as GDP, monetary policies and demographics. Meanwhile, as the real estate industry has a relatively high leverage ratio, it is particularly important to study its debt burdens.

According to data released by the National Bureau of Statistics, the leverage ratio of China's real estate industry has fluctuated around 75%. Before the 2008 financial crisis, the ratio remained basically stable, fluctuating around 74%; after the crisis, it rose slightly from 72.30% to 77.00% in 2014. The leverage of the real estate industry in broad terms includes two parts, i.e. household leverage on the demand side and real estate developers' leverage on the supply side. We believe that, due to multiple factors, household leverage has maintained relatively rapid growth. Nevertheless, the level of growth has been lower than that in many developed economies. Meanwhile, the real estate developers' debt leverage has been increasing rapidly, the overall liquidity pressure on the industry has risen significantly and the funding structure has been irrational. As a result, there are concerns about the steady operation of financial systems as well as economic development. Therefore, we analyzed the status quo of debt on both the demand and supply sides in the real estate industry and probed deeper into the debt within the real estate industry chain.

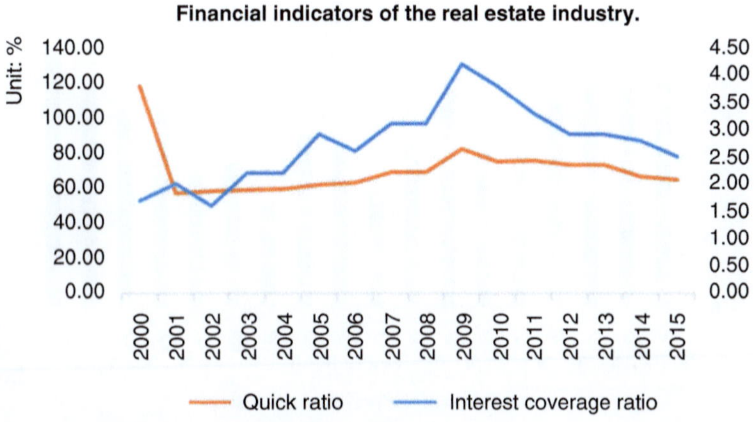

Fig. 6.1 Financial indicators of the real estate industry

We were not optimistic about debt on the supply side. A lot of listed real estate developers are practicing radical expansion strategies. Many buy land at high costs, and the debt ratio soars, which undermines enterprises' profits and creates worries for their financial future. Above all, the debt ratio of the real estate industry runs as high as 77%. Since there are bubbles in the real estate market – the risk exists at least in third- and fourth-tier cities and non-core second-tier cities – and the industrial assets risk deflation, the ratio might continue to climb. With excessively high leverage ratios, some less-competitive enterprises that expand too aggressively may become insolvent. Moreover, after analyzing the financial data of listed enterprises, we believe that the hidden trouble is real. In view of the high proportion of housing inventories (i.e., homes for sale) in real estate enterprises, we chose two indicators – quick ratio and interest coverage ratio – to measure the short- and long-term solvency of real estate enterprises. After 2011, the two indicators significantly declined, showing a weakening of the whole industry's short- and long-term solvency (Fig. 6.1).

After 2000, the real estate market in China picked up rapidly, and every round of price increases created quite a stir. In the wake of the financial crisis, domestic home prices went up many times. Particularly in first-tier cities like Beijing, Shanghai, Guangzhou and Shenzhen, the home prices continued to rise, despite regulatory policies. The leverage of the real estate industry is one key issue in the public debate. From the perspective of demand, the status quo of household leverage in the real estate industry is one factor to be analyzed. Households mainly have two motivations for buying houses – to have a place to live and/or to make value-added investments. A regional imbalance in economic development has been a long-standing problem in China. First-tier cities like Beijing, Shanghai and Shenzhen boast a lot of material, cultural, educational and medical resources. Considering the impact of China's family planning policy in combination with fluctuations in the stock market, the ways to wealth appreciation are limited. Meanwhile, the demand for asset value maintenance and appreciation remains, so investing in real estate has

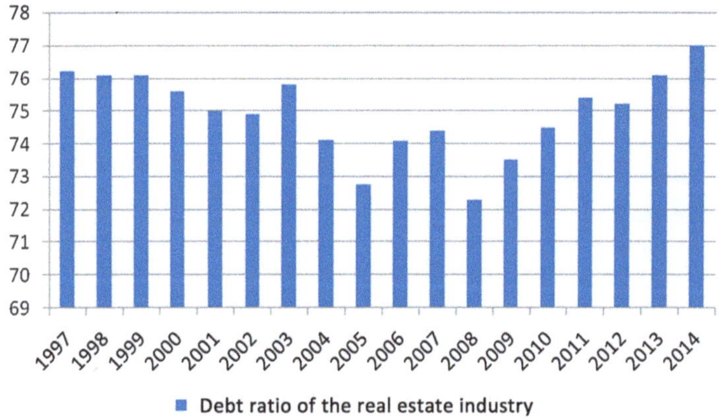

Fig. 6.2 Debt ratio of the real estate industry

become the best choice for Chinese people to allocate large household assets. In the short term, price volatility in the real estate industry is, in a way, a sort of "monetary phenomenon." In the easing cycle of monetary policies, lower mortgage rates and easing home purchase restrictions (e.g., by lowering down payments) facilitated the surge of individual housing loans in 2015. New individual housing loans amounted to RMB 2.67 trillion, accounting for 37% of the housing sales volume of the year. However, this number was still relatively small compared to those in major developed economies. Therefore, the leverage of housing loans remains low, and there is room for further increases. The major problem lies in that the debt ratio of real estate developers has climbed rapidly, hence heavy debt loads. Moreover, the developers are excessively dependent on bank credit financing.

Approximately 65% of funds in real estate developers come from the banking system, far exceeding the global average level of 40%. Once a debt crisis arises, the banking system will be the most affected. Therefore, the debt problem of the real estate industry involves the enormous real economy of real estate-related industries and affects the bank-dominated financial system (Fig. 6.2).

From the perspective of household leverage on the demand side, historically, every significant increase in household leverage was highly correlated with monetary policies and home pricing regulations. For example, the peak of the household leverage in 2015 was associated with local governments' lowering down payments for homebuyers. Nevertheless, despite the policy stimulus, China's household leverage remained at a low level, reporting a considerable gap between that of developed economies and presenting significant political periodicity. Hence, household leverage has had little effect on the surge in leverage within the real estate industry.

The debt ratio of domestic real estate developers has been trending upward. Though the data for 2016 have not been released yet, based on the preliminary data from major regions nationwide, we expected that the ratio would continue rising. This judgment was made for two reasons. First, as the macroeconomy soured, the profits of enterprises in the real economy remained unsatisfactory and the returns on the real economy ran low, the profit-seeking capital inevitably flowed into the real estate market. As with enterprises in many industries – especially those with overcapacity – that are suffering heavy losses, banks would consider infrastructure and real estate development as the best options for their loans. Compared with the four large, state-owned banks (i.e., the Industrial and Commercial Bank of China, the Agricultural Bank of China, the Bank of China and the China Construction Bank), small banks can hardly attract customers engaged in infrastructure development and rail transportation. Thus the real estate industry is the best choice for small- or medium-sized banks. However, as such banks usually have a more stringent and urgent demand for profits, they may take more radical measures on the review and approval of credit programs, thus driving up the debt ratio of the real estate enterprises. Second, the real estate market has been buzzing since 2016, with banks, developers and other market players seemingly pleased. Due to surging home prices and market optimism, real estate enterprises began leveraging. As part of our investigations in Henan Province, we found that some real estate developers in the capital, Zhengzhou, operated at high leverage ratios; some enterprises even attempted to pay deposits through financing.

In the short term, the debt ratio of the real estate industry may continue its upward trend. Yet in the long run, the leverage ratio in the industry may settle at a relatively high level, without further significant rises. We found two reasons for this:

First, in 2016, China's home prices did not increase across the board, presenting significant differentiation among regions and categories. In terms of regional differentiation, first-tier and core second-tier cities boasting developed economies, net inflows of population, and quality resources nearby, were much touted. For example, in cities like Xiamen, Zhengzhou and Nanjing – all which benefited from this round of home price surges – there was basically no housing inventory, hence no need for destocking. However, an oversupply of houses was severe in third- and fourth-tier cities, and it might take 3–4 years for them draw down the inventories. Meanwhile, they did not benefit from this round of home price surges, as the home prices remained dull and home sales appeared frustrating. In terms of category differentiation, although there was hardly any residential real estate inventory in core cities with a price rally, the sales of commodity real estate were not that satisfactory, hence excess commodity real estate inventories. Zhengzhou, for example, with an increase in its home prices, was free from the problem of residential real estate inventory. However, the commodity real estate near the Zhengzhou East Railway Station and the Longhu Financial Center had massive excess inventory. Due to the structural differentiation, the market would not blindly expect a continuous rise of home prices. The price rally in core cities might exert a limited impact on other cities. Meanwhile, local governments successively imposed restrictions on home purchases after October 2016. In the short run, these policies should help take steam out of the real estate market to some extent. Once the core cities are less motivated for further price surges, players in the real estate market will become less optimistic, which will dampen the sharp rise of the industry's leverage ratio.

Second, we found that, in some regions with only slight increases in home prices, local banks have tightened conditions for issuing loans to real estate enterprises. In

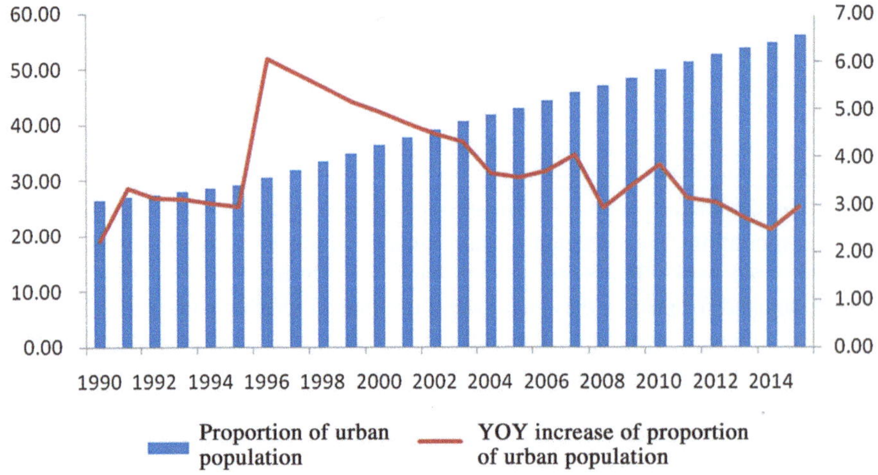

Fig. 6.3 Proportion and increase of urban population

2016, branches of state-owned banks in some prefecture-level cities halted credit extension to real estate enterprises. As stated in the previous section, most funds from real estate enterprises in China came from the banking system. By tightening credit, banks are tightening capital for real estate enterprises. The leverage ratio in the industry thus loses momentum for continued price increases.

As mentioned in the previous section, household leverage on the demand side has been relatively low, as the debt problem may lie more with real estate developers on the supply side. Since our study was concerned with the turning point of debt, we focused on real estate enterprises (instead of further studying household leverage).

6.1.2 Development Trends of Debt in the Real Estate Industry

The real estate industry, as a typical demand-driven industry, has reached the turning point of a long-term demand cycle. For one thing, economic growth moderates and urbanization has slowed; for another, China's baby boom (1983–1990) and the peak of new marriages and childbearing came to an end. Therefore, we expected that people's demand for homes will be gradually undermined, the growth rate of real estate investment would decline and the supply-demand relationship would continue deteriorating (Fig. 6.3).

There are both long-term and short-term cycles in the real estate industry. The long-term cycle is influenced by population and urbanization, while the short-term cycle is affected by financial policies and capital flow. Taking a macroeconomic view of the long-term cycle, we probed into the evolution and future development of the real estate industry. Cycles in the real estate industry are, to a great extent, part of the population cycle. That is mainly because the population cycle and population movement from rural to urban areas can boost the potential growth of the economy, increase households' disposable income, and facilitate consumption upgrades – all of which will stimulate the demand from first homebuyers and upgraders. The overall increase in the number of homebuyers directly leads to the rapid growth of property demands and investments, high rates of saving, continued expansion of the funds outstanding for foreign exchanges and excess liquidity. As a result, the prices of real estate assets are lifted as well.

It is generally believed that amid the recovery of the real estate industry, the rapid rise of home prices can bring in more capital, which will, in turn, drive up home prices and accelerate the formation of bubbles in the market. In contrast, amid a recession within the industry, falling home prices accelerate the outflow of investment funds into other large category assets, worsen the supply-demand pattern and further reduce home prices.

Again, due to the special nature of the real estate industry, it is inappropriate to include deposits received as debt in the leverage ratio calculation. However, even after excluding deposits received from debt and assets, there was still a continued rise in the leverage ratio in the real estate industry. The adjustment made to deposits received can only change the absolute value of the leverage ratio in the industry.

As the demographic dividend fades away and economic growth slows, the real estate industry is in a transition from high-speed growth to stable operations, from quantity expansion to quality improvement.

In recent years, many have argued about bubbles in the real estate industry in first-tier cities and in some second-tier cities. The differentiation among cities is becoming increasingly significant, while there are huge housing inventories in third- and fourth-tier cities. Some parts of smaller cities are uninhabited "ghost towns," while first-tier cities like Beijing, Shanghai and Guangzhou are experiencing over-heated property sales due to the continued net inflows of population and insufficient land supplies for permanent residents. However, the real estate markets in cities at different levels may affect one another. If there are big supply gluts and collapsing home prices in third- and fourth-tier cities, first- and second-tier cities will not escape the consequences. This will then influence the stability of banks and other institutions in the financial system and even result in social upheaval. For a long period to come, the real estate market will still focus on destocking which will closely impact whether the market can develop healthily.

Driven by policies including cutting interest rates, required reserve ratios and down payments, the performance figures of the real estate market in February 2016 were much better than expected. However, in view of the general cycle of the industry, the demographic turning point and the overall surging housing inventories, the industry is still exposed to risks of unsatisfactory sales and dramatic price swings due to policy changes.

An analysis of the debt problem in the real estate industry is usually more complicated compared to that in the iron and steel and coal industries, because it involves both household debt on the demand side (property demand) and the debt of real estate-related enterprises on the supply side (real estate development and land acquisition). In the long run, household debt on the demand side is affected by the overall demographic structure and population movement and will lead to the differentiation of property demands among different regions and categories. But in the short run, it is affected by monetary factors like real estate regulatory policies, monetary and interest-rate policies, and capital positions. In terms of real estate-related enterprises on the supply side, their leverage ratio keeps rising. Once the upward price momentum fails to reach market expectations, the tense capital chain of developers will affect the major source of funding, i.e. the banking system. Hence, it is truly an interconnected sector and may bring about bigger risks associated with the turning point of debt.

The era in which real estate enterprises could reap huge profits has ended. Cities, except some core ones, are seeing net inflows of population and huge housing inventories. Home prices have lost their momentum, and developers have not dissolved the existing stock of debt. Overall, debt in the real estate industry has reached its turning point. Since real estate is downstream from the iron and steel and coal industries – as well as a key industry to both the real economy and virtual economy – we posit that debt in the real estate industry will reach its turning point slightly later than debt in the steel and coal industries. For one thing, the turning point in the industrial chain of the real estate industry is "contagious" from upstream to downstream industries; for another, the real estate industry – as a major industry impacting the national economy – is significantly influenced by policies.

6.2 Debt in Real Estate-Related Industries

The real estate industry is related to many aspects of the national economy. Businesses in the real estate industry chain – closely linked in their development – rise and fall together. In 2015, the real estate industry chain contributed 16–19% to China's GDP. More specifically, the real estate industry accounted for six percentage points; construction and building materials accounted for five to six percentage points; household appliances, furniture manufacturing and home furnishing accounted for four to five percentage point; and real estate financing accounted for one or two percentage points. From 2015 to October 2016 when a series of regulatory policies were introduced, the performance of the real estate market may have further lifted the numbers. A conservative estimate would be that more than 20% of the GDP in 2016 could be attributed to the real estate industry chain. Hence the sector has had a significant impact on the national economy.

In view of the commonalities between organizations along an industry chain, we will not limit the study of real estate debt to only the real estate industry. Rather, we also will explore the upstream and downstream industries, combine the industries by developing a concept of "the real estate industry chain" and elaborate on the status quo of debt in the real estate industry.

The industries of coal, steel, non-ferrous metal, furniture manufacturing and household appliances are all upstream and midstream industries relative to the real estate industry. Faced with a huge gap between production and sales, all of them have suffered from heavy debts, rising leverage ratios and surging risks. While their debt burdens are soaring, their profits keep falling. As the macroeconomy weakened and demands became feeble after 2011, these industries' overcapacity problems were highlighted, and the imbalance between production and sales was increasingly prominent.

Thus this study will focus on debt size with these industries and analyze their turning points of debt.

6.2.1 Debt in the Coal Industry

The coal industry is an upstream industry in the national economy. It is a typical resource- and capital-intensive industry, with an extended industry chain. The industries of power, steel, building materials and chemicals are all direct downstream from the coal industry, and these industries consume up to 80% of the coal in China. Meanwhile, the coal industry is highly cyclical. Hence, when studying the outlook for the coal industry, we should consider the cyclical swings in the macroeconomy as well as analyze the midstream and downstream industries – such as iron and steel, power, building materials, chemicals and real estate – which can impact the performance of the coal industry.

The major products in China's coal industry can be divided into three categories: steam coal, charred coal and anthracite coal. Steam coal is mainly supplied to the industries of power and building materials; charred coal to the ferrous metal smelting industry, i.e. the iron and steel industry; and anthracite coal to the chemical industry. Meanwhile, the industries of building materials, iron and steel, and chemicals are all upstream from the real estate industry. Therefore, the coal industry is at the top of the real estate industry chain. Through the spillover effect along the industry chain, the climate of the real estate industry can determine the demand, price and profits of the coal industry.

Since the coal industry is at the top of the real estate industry chain, the turning point of its debt may appear later. The industry's recovery and recession are usually driven by the demands from midstream and downstream industries. There is often a time lag between sluggish downstream demands and falling profits of the coal industry. The demand cycles of the coal industry tend to lag the demand cycles downstream. For example, real estate sales – reflecting performance of the industry – fluctuate 1 year ahead of the prices of cement and steel; while in the iron and steel industry, an industry downstream from the coal industry and a midstream industry in the real estate industry chain, the performance indicator – steel price index – always changes 1–2 months ahead of the price of charred coal (Fig. 6.4).

Coal prices peaked in 2009 and then started to decline, with a short recovery in 2010 and a downtrend since 2011. Mining technologies and total costs have remained stable, but the fall of coal prices has directly undermined the profitability of the industry. This has crippled the industry's overall interests, drove up its leverage ratio and added to potential risks. According to data released by the Bureau

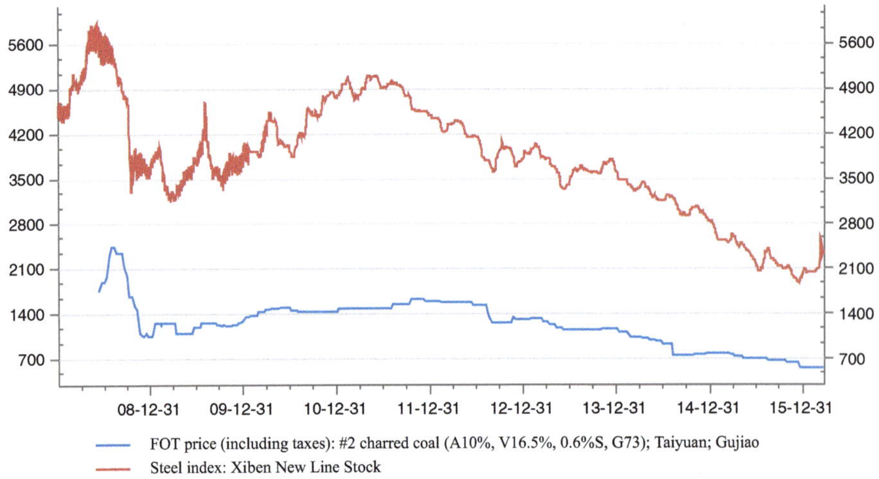

Fig. 6.4 Prices of coal and steel (unit: yuan/ton). (Source: Wind)

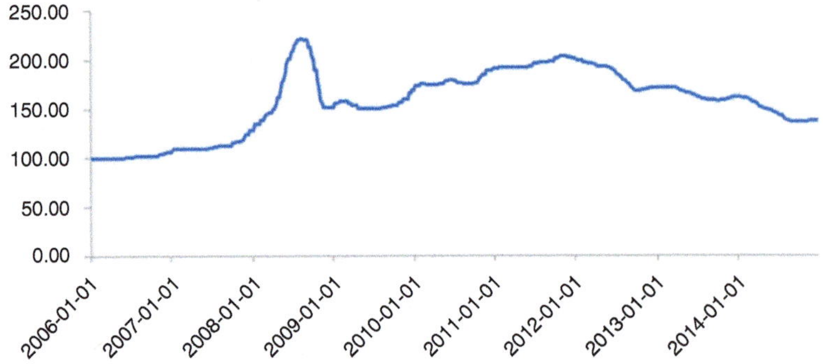

Fig. 6.5 China's coal price index. (Source: Wind)

of Economic Operations Adjustment under the National Development and Reform Commission, by July 2015, more than 70% of big and medium-sized coal enterprises suffered losses, and the losses amounted to RMB 48.41 billion (Fig. 6.5).

Coal enjoyed stable mining and transportation expenses. Therefore, its price changes have been mostly influenced by downstream demands. The coal industry is a typical high-beta industry, so its demands and profits have been significantly correlated with economic cycles.

A surging leverage ratio used to suggest capacity expansion and excessive growth. However, after carefully studying the data, we found that the practice of assuming debt for business expansion can no longer account for the leverage ratio surge in the coal industry in recent years. Industry profits have gradually become a more critical factor.

From 2006 to 2008, the coal industry expanded rapidly, and the investment growth increased year by year. The 2008 global financial crisis caused a slowdown in investment growth within the coal industry; in fact, investment "growth" was negative after 2009. Two years later, China introduced a series of policies and credit crunch measures, aiming to strictly control irrational expansion within the coal industry and to restrict banks' financial support for coal. Since the coal industry had excess capacity, its new investments were regulated in many ways. Meanwhile, coal has always been the most important nonrenewable energy source in China, so the central government adopted a considerable number of policies to regulate it. The country attempted to restrict capacity expansion, contain product supply, and thus tackle the existing overcapacity problem. This was accomplished with industrial policies and taxation measures – such as production limitation policies (including sweeping coal mines in violation of laws and regulations), curbing excess production and limiting imports – and financial support policies (including tightening credit and raising the financing threshold). However, the leverage ratio still grew at a relatively high rate, which was largely because of the rapid decline of net profits. After 2013, the net "profits" of the coal industry became negative. In 2014, its profitability was further undermined, pushing the leverage ratio to approach the warning line of 70%. We believe that the debt ratio of the coal industry probably has already exceeded 70%, but enterprises – constrained by the credit threshold – are motivated to bring it down on financial statements.

After 2012, the growth of interest-bearing debt in the coal industry maintained a downward trend and reached its lowest level in 2014. Industry profits have been increasingly unable to support the debt expansion. This was associated with both the debt stock and regulatory policies. It can be concluded that the incremental debt was no longer a core factor leading to risks. In fact, the problem lies in the excessive debt stock brought by blind capacity expansion in the past decade. We hold that the debt of the coal industry within China has peaked, and we don't expect it to rise much in the future. Therefore, too much emphasis on tightening credit for coal enterprises and strictly controlling the launches of new programs is not the best solution. Instead, we believe it is important to promote deep processing within the industry chain, increase value addition, improve management and operational efficiency, and restore the industry's profitability.

Based on these findings, we concluded that, with strong demand followed by continuously rising prices, the coal industry prospered from 2003 to 2008 with considerable profits. After the financial crisis, coal enterprises, driven by policies, increased their leverage ratios and expanded capacity. In 2012, the macroeconomy was sluggish, downstream demands were thin and high capacity was not arranged in an orderly manner. The oversupply of coal caused coal prices to decline sharply. Coal enterprises performed poorly, and the profitability of some large ones even turned negative. Businesses in the coal industry suffered tremendously. Due to the tight cash flow, the new proceeds were insufficient to cover the principal and interest of their debt; hence, they had to renew debt or issue more debt, so that old debts could be rolled over with new borrowing. As a direct result, the enterprises' debt loads piled up, the financing costs became increasingly high, and their financial figures became increasingly gloomy. In June 2016, Yangquan Coal Industry, one of the seven largest coal groups in Shanxi Province, had to suspend paychecks and cut wages, hoping to survive tough times and maintain its image in the capital market. The other coal enterprises all tried every means to pay their debt. Even though coal prices increased after the second half of 2016, it was far from enough to handle the huge debts accumulated over the years. Based on a qualitative analysis of the industry, we made an initial judgment that debt in the coal industry reached its turning point around 2011.

6.2.2 *Debt in the Iron and Steel Industry*

The real estate industry is downstream from iron and steel. The significant positive correlation between downstream demands and the macroeconomy causes the iron and steel industry to be highly cyclical. The real estate industry accounts for 17% of downstream demands, with infrastructure development accounting for 23%. In the real estate industry chain, the midstream iron and steel industry has bigger fluctuations in profits compared to upstream industries like coal. This is largely because midstream industries serve as a link connecting upstream and downstream industries; profitability is exposed to more diversified and complicated factors, and it is more sensitive to the economic climate and product prices.

Since 2011, the growth of net profits in the iron and steel industry turned negative, and the proportion of profitable steel mills has fluctuated with seasonal variations. This trend resembled that of the coal industry (Fig. 6.6).

After the RMB 4 trillion stimulus package was implemented in 2008, the steel industry had a serious overcapacity problem, with low capacity utilization rates.

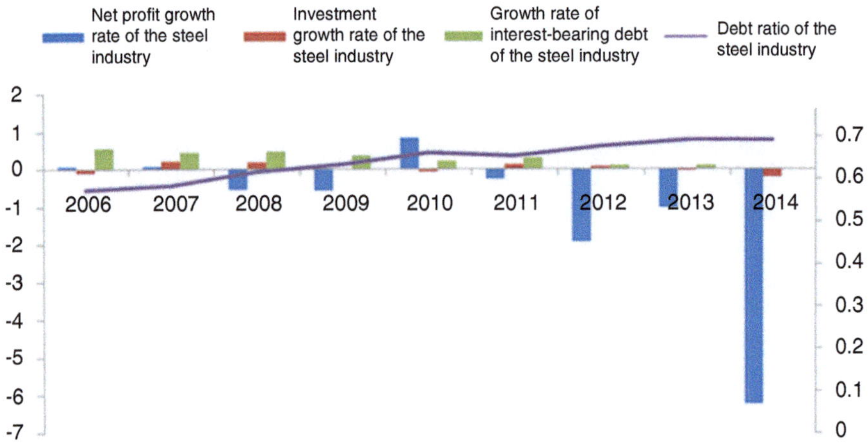

Fig. 6.6 Financial overview of the steel industry (unit: %). The right axis represents the debt ratio of the steel industry. (Source: Wind)

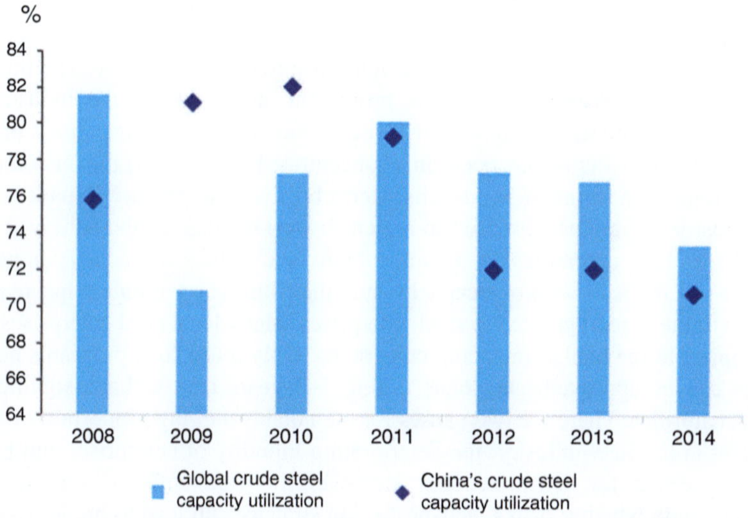

Fig. 6.7 Crude steel capacity utilization. (Source: Wind, GTJA Research Institute)

Since 2011, the profitability of the steel industry has picked up modestly, propelled by short-term booms. However, that was soon undermined by a quick release of supply, and the recovery of gross margins was difficult to sustain and stabilize. The capacity utilization of the steel industry was lower than the global average, and the steel price index maintained a downward trend (Fig. 6.7).

The success or failure of the steel industry depends largely on the real estate industry. The past decade saw a boom within the steel industry. During the post-financial crisis period between 2009 and 2010, the global economy was hit hard by the financial crisis; external demands softened, and steel capacity utilization fell to a record low of 70.83%. Despite all that, propelled by an RMB 4 trillion stimulus package and driven by real estate and infrastructure development, China's steel industry continued to prosper. In 2011, however, the excess capacity was yet to be released, and the incremental demands in the real estate industry were not enough to match the blind capacity expansion in the steel industry. As a result, steel prices continued to trend downward and even touched bottom, as there was an oversupply in the industry. From 2011 to 2014, the China steel price index fell as much as 45%.

After 2013, investments in fixed assets, real estate development and infrastructure construction all showed a clear downward trend; meanwhile, the floor space under construction, the floor space of newly started projects, and steel consumption also significantly decreased. Real estate's drag on the steel industry was particularly prominent. The profits of steel enterprises in 2013 and 2014 improved somewhat – despite the headwinds. Yet we found that the modest recovery in profits was largely enabled by positive changes in costs, instead of the rebounding demands in the downstream real estate industry. More specifically, it was due to a sharp decline in ironstone and coal prices.

The proportion of short-term debt in the steel industry continues to soar, which is likely to create risks. The short-term debt now makes up more than 60% of the industry's interest-bearing debt, and the figure is moving toward 70%. The liquidity problem for enterprises appears quite prominent, and many in the industry are "rolling over old debts with new borrowing." Once there is a huge shock of steel prices, corporate defaults may occur in a concentrated manner, and the outcome will be catastrophic. In terms of bonds, short-term bills are the primary issuance in the steel industry and are usually used to replenish working capital and address capital shortfalls in daily operations. In regard to bank credit, the steel industry is usually labeled as an industry with overcapacity, and the Chinese government has required banks to tighten credit granted to steel enterprises. Many local steel enterprises have been subject to the banks' financing constraints. Only a few loan programs beyond 3 years can be approved, and loans lasting 1–3 years tend to have significantly shorter maturities. There are two causes for the notably surging proportion of short-term debt in the steel industry: the deteriorating liquidity of enterprises and banks' tightening credit for self-protection. However, relevant authorities need to be concerned with whether banks' self-protection strategy will lead to bigger risks.

As with the coal industry, the status quo and development history of debt in the iron and steel industry are closely related to several factors, including an enterprises' capacity expansion through borrowing and the macroeconomic downturn. Directly downstream from the coal industry, the steel industry is closely linked to the coal industry, with each rising and falling together. Therefore, debt in the steel industry may have reached its turning point at a similar time to the coal industry. We came to an initial judgment that debt in the steel industry might have passed its turning point around 2012.

6.2.3 Debt of the Cement Industry

Cement – one of China's important basic resource products – is highly correlated with macroeconomic trends and fixed asset investments. As with the industries of coal, iron and steel, and nonferrous metal, the cement industry is confounded by the problem of severe overcapacity. The real estate industry constitutes an important part of the demand for cement. The cement industry is in the midstream of the real estate industrial chain. This year, even in the peak season of cement sales, the sales volume seemed to be weak.

In cement production, the cost of coal accounts for as much as 35%, so the fluctuation of coal prices is key in the analysis of cement prices and profit trends. Since 2011, continuous declining coal prices had, to some extent, mitigated the decline in cement prices. In 2015, the market generally assumed that the coal prices were yet to reach their lowest point – with some room remaining for a small drop. Thus a potentially lower cost provided some support to the profitability of the cement industry (Fig. 6.8).

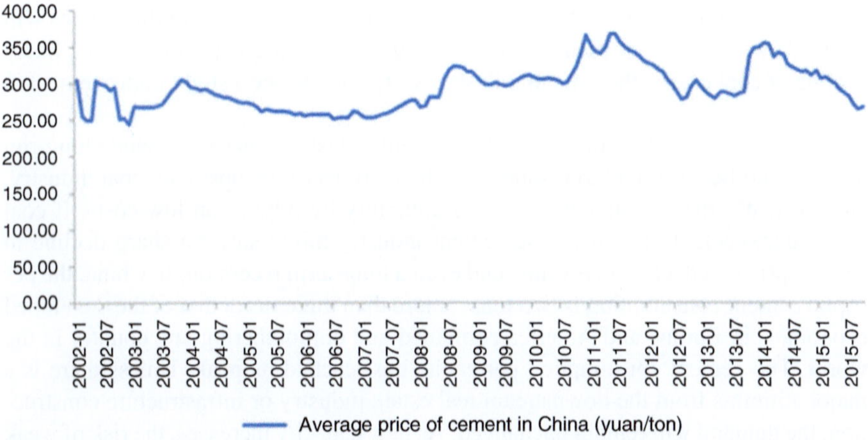

Fig. 6.8 Average price of cement in China

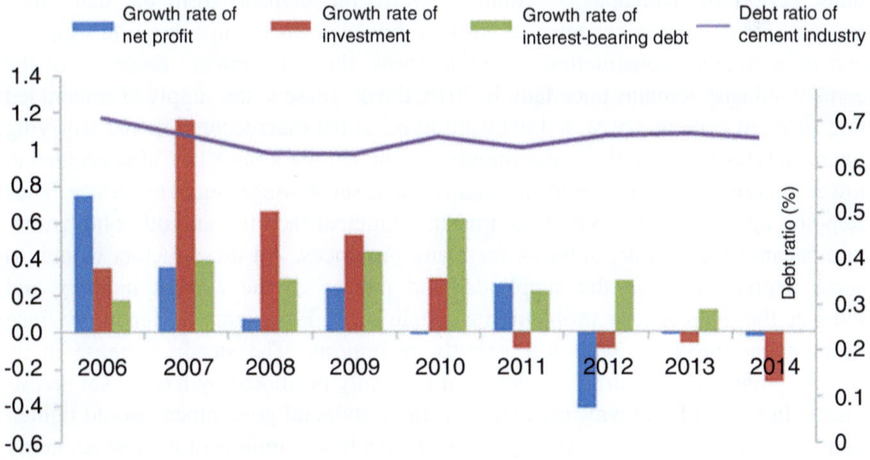

Fig. 6.9 Financial overview of the cement industry (unit: %). The right axis represents the debt ratio of the cement industry

Though the macroeconomy and industrial cycle entered a downward trend, the cement industry has managed to elude long-run losses. This may have been a result of the continued slump in upstream coal prices that squeezed the profits upstream and promised economic feasibility to new production lines and new capacity – even in times of declining profit (Fig. 6.9).

From the perspective of demand, real estate and infrastructure construction have taken up as much as 70% of cement consumption. Generally, the demand for cement, to be affected by decreasing real estate investment, will see a slower growth rate, and an equilibrium tends to sustain itself for a while. As the government sets more stringent requirements for environmentally-friendly production, a new supply of cement will be subjected to energy conservation policies, and product prices will remain low. Notably, as mentioned earlier, given its cost composition or the likely decline of coal prices, the cement industry is expected to see a slight improvement in profits.

As mentioned earlier, the reason the cement industry managed to elude long-run losses could be attributed to it squeezing the margins of the upstream coal industry. However, it's risky to maintain weak profitability by relying on low costs. If coal prices unexpectedly fluctuate, the cement industry might suffer a sharp decline in cement prices, a decline in revenue and even a long-term recession. In China, the per capita cement consumption is two tons – more than three times that of the developed economies in Europe and America combined and outnumbering any country in the world. The cement consumption per capita has reached its peak. Unless there is a major stimulus from the downstream real estate industry or infrastructure construction, the demand will remain unchanged. As new capacity increases, the risk of weak demand and excess capacity will inevitably increase.

With a weak balance of supply and demand, the cement industry weathered a bitter period of overcapacity. Going forward, the demand from the real estate industry for cement is expected to weaken; however, as the upside on the supply-end infrastructure construction begins to show, the development tendency of the cement industry remains uncertain. In 2016, the decrease in the supply of cement led to a surge in cement prices, a downward trend in the macroeconomy and worrying financial returns within the real economy. As the People's Bank of China decided to lower its economic leverage, the problem of an asset shortage began to surface. Thus stepping up the construction of rail transit, municipal facilities and other infrastructure became the primary solution for many provinces. All these factors would, to some degree, improve the supply-demand pattern of the cement industry and mitigate the overcapacity problem in a certain stage. For example, Henan Province is an inland province with few exports or imports. The steady increase in its consumption and economic development is mainly promoted by fixed asset investments. In times of a downward economy, the provincial government would tighten up its infrastructure construction, to offset the decline in returns of the real economy and boost economic growth. Therefore, during the special period of economic restructuring, the cement industry may still have some space to release new capacities; and it is still hard to tell whether the debt in this industry has reached its turning point.

6.2.4 Nonferrous Metal Industry

The nonferrous metal industry is one of the upstream industries with excess capacity and an evident cycle. In times of economic recession, the industry is sluggish. Among various industrial sectors, the overcapacity problem of the electrolytic aluminum sector was especially serious. In 2009, due to impacts of the global financial crisis and weak external demands, the prices of major nonferrous metals experienced a sharp decline. From late 2009 to 2010, driven by the downstream real estate and infrastructure construction industries, the number of nonferrous metal orders increased, and prices picked up. However, as the macroeconomy turned down and downstream industries remained sluggish, sales of nonferrous metals plummeted, resulting in difficulty in soaking up the excess capacity produced by the RMB 4 trillion stimulus package. Compared with such traditional competitors as Japan and Korea, China was disadvantaged in terms of technical content and processing skills, which further added to the country's woes.

Overcapacity in the nonferrous metal industry has been a problem for a long time – especially in the sectors of electrolytic aluminum and copper. The growth rate of the apparent consumption of aluminum in China has slowed since 2011; nevertheless, capacity expansion has become increasingly fierce. By the end of 2014, the aluminum production capacity in China had reached 4.4 million tons, while the production was only 23.684 tons, implying a capacity utilization rate of around 50%. Nowadays, there are more than one million tons of capacity input annually, and regions with energy resource advantages continue their capacity expansion. The production of electrolytic aluminum in China increases by 35,000 tons every year. However, the demand is decreasing instead of increasing, which puts pressure on prices and sales.

We found that there was a correlation between the industry's debt maturity structure and production costs. By improving production techniques, increasing the products' technical contents and added value, and lowering the relative production costs, the nonferrous metal industry is expected to optimize its debt structure to some degree.

The logic of this theory is clear: a higher proportion of production costs means a greater demand for capital in daily production and operation. Since short-term debt was the primary source of such capital, industries with higher proportions of production costs would be in demand for more short-term debts, to pay for necessary costs such as raw materials and labor. An analysis of the debt maturity structure figure of the five industries of coal, iron and steel, nonferrous metal, cement, and paper-making also showed that the coal industry had the lowest proportion of short-term debt, followed by the cement industry, the nonferrous metal industry, the paper-making industry and the iron and steel industry. Thus a correlation between the industry's debt maturity structure and production costs truly exists. That is, in the industry with the highest proportion of production costs in terms of sales income, its short-term debt tends to make up the largest share in the debt maturity structure (Figs. 6.10 and 6.11).

This theory can provide some guidance regarding restructuring and development within the nonferrous metal industry and the development of the iron and steel industry. If the iron and steel industry can enhance production techniques, intensify industrial concentration, and increase the proportion of special steel in its product mix, it will become more competitive in the market and able to alleviate its debt burden with better profitability.

Nowadays, the Chinese economy has entered a "new normal," featuring a steady slowing in the growth rate of GDP and base metal consumption. Hence, the

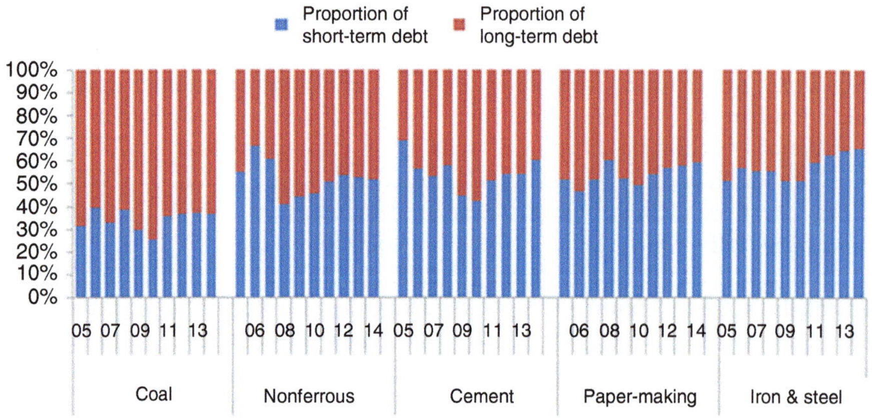

Fig. 6.10 Debt maturity structure of nonferrous metal industry

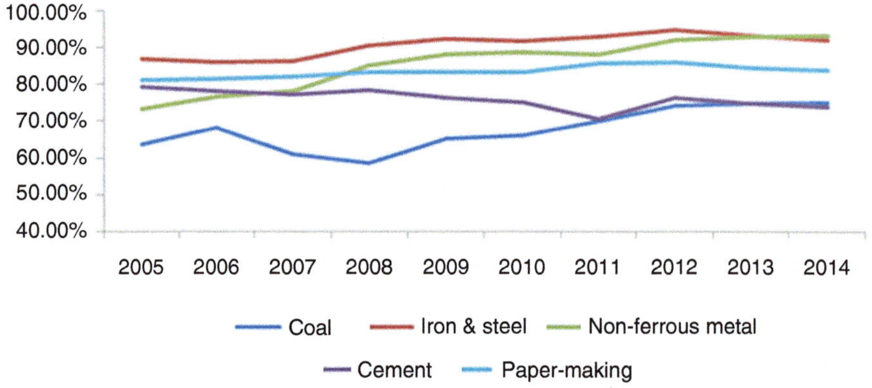

Fig. 6.11 Proportion of production costs in terms of revenue

overcapacity problem of the nonferrous metal industry should last for only a short period. Due to a relatively low level of production techniques, the industry is challenged by excess low-end products, with the production capacity of base metals exceeding 50% of the total. The industrial production capacity has reached a physical climax as well as the climax in its carrying capacity for resources and the environment. As the rapid expansion of electrolytic aluminum has wrapped up temporarily, there will be an inventory shortage of bauxite. The Belt and Road Initiative and some infrastructure programs promote the construction of rail transit, so demand for aluminum is likely to increase. This should decrease the pressure on the supply-end of the nonferrous metal industry. Still, a high growth rate of the base metal demand in the nonferrous metal industry and the new material industry is unlikely. This is because China, the largest consumer of base metals – with consumption of copper, aluminum and zinc accounting for more than 40% of worldwide consumption – has entered a stage of steadily slower growth within its national economy and its fixed asset investments. Thus it would be a major change for the nonferrous metal industry to restrict new capacity – especially in the electrolytic aluminum sector and others already with excess capacity. Restricting new capacity would include de-stocking and increases in exports. The aluminum sector has shown momentum toward exporting overcapacity. According to export data released by China's General Administration of Customs, from January to August 2015, the total exports of aluminum amounted to 2.84 million tons, registering an increase of 30.1% over the previous year.

Since the nonferrous metal industry is upstream from the industrial chain, in the analysis of its future profits, it's essential that the supply-demand conditions of nonferrous metals be highlighted. Once the demand from downstream industries increases, the prices of nonferrous metals will regain a competitive edge; otherwise, it is very likely that the prices will continue to run low. For now, the progress made with de-capacity has been less satisfactory. However, given the "pull effects" of the Belt and Road Initiative on nonferrous metal demand – and the benefits from favorable policies – the industry still has opportunities to recover from its losses. And the electrolytic aluminum sector also is likely to be alleviated from the serious overcapacity problem. Since the aluminum price has reached the average level of cash costs, production costs will provide some support for the prices.

Notably, the global financial situation will influence the prices of base metals such as aluminum and copper, as well as precious metals such as gold, and the Fed's rate hike and the oil price drop will impact those of nonferrous metals, causing fluctuations in market demand. In the aftermath, corporate and industrial profits will fluctuate. The Chinese economy has entered a "new normal" with slower economic growth. So a stimulus for demand downstream is unlikely to yield results. Adding the effects of alternative new energy materials, future development within the industry seems to be full of uncertainties.

The nonferrous metal industry is not a typical upstream or downstream industry along the real estate industrial chain. Thus in identifying the turning point of its debt, we made little reference to the real estate industry's conditions. Inside the industry, different sectors have different degrees of overcapacity. Electrolytic aluminum and copper have been restrained, while gold and silver remain safe assets for value preservation and appreciation. Therefore, it's difficult to calculate the turning point of the nonferrous metal industry's debt through qualitative analysis alone. Data shows that corporate profits of the nonferrous metal industry have dropped significantly since 2012, and several financial indicators of profits and debt solvency also weakened in 2012 and 2013. So we reached a preliminary conclusion that the nonferrous metal industry might have reached its debt turning point in 2012 or 2013.

6.2.5 Furniture Manufacturing and Household Appliance Industries

The furniture manufacturing and household appliances are both downstream along the real estate industrial chain. However, unlike the iron and steel, nonferrous metals and cement industries along the chain, the household appliance industry is more defensive. The rural-urban disparities in China have led to overcapacity in urban areas for the household appliance industry, with supply outweighing demand, but with a lower penetration rate in rural areas. Since such disparities are likely to last for a quite a while, the situation also will remain unchanged. In recent years, vying for a larger share in the gradually saturated urban market, the household appliances providers engaged in unscrupulous competitions, hyping concepts or hoarding for profiteering purposes. This resulted in a general decline in industrial profit growth and even bankruptcies in several enterprises, including Xiamen Overseas Chinese Electronic Co., Ltd. and Amoi Electronics Co., Ltd.

The household appliance industry differentiates itself from the coal industry and the iron and steel industry along the real estate industrial chain because it is more defensive; first-time homebuyers and upgraders typically increase the demand for furniture and household appliances. Such basic demands still apply to other urban residents who want a furniture and appliance upgrade.

The household appliance industry has benefited from the fall in raw material prices and has experienced slight increases in its profitability. This advantage is likely to continue. The recession of the nonferrous metal industry drives down the prices of copper, steel, aluminum and other raw materials. The significant price decline of steel, in turn, brought a "cost dividend" to the downstream household appliance industry. According to estimates, such a price fall can save around 5% of production costs for the industry. Hence, cost advantages can facilitate an overall improvement in the industry's profitability.

However, the cost-based profit increase cannot be sustained long term. Even in profitable times, the household appliance industry should not expand capacity and assume debt blindly, as was the case with the iron and steel industry. As the turning point of the real estate industry approaches, the demand for furniture and household appliances brought about by new houses will be cut significantly. If the industry fails to maintain its debt at a reasonable level, it's likely that the industrial profits will be weighed down.

There has already been a sign that the turning point of debt has been reached. Take the furniture manufacturing industry as an example. As Fig. 6.12 illustrates, in 2003, the slope of the blue line representing debt started to get notably higher than that of the red line representing profit, and the gap tended to widen. Nevertheless, after 2011, though the debt-profit elasticity of the iron and steel industry and the coal industry plunged below zero, that of the furniture manufacturing industry remained stable due to its defensiveness. In general, the debt-profit elasticity of the industry entered a downward trend. If there is no reasonable control on its debt size, the

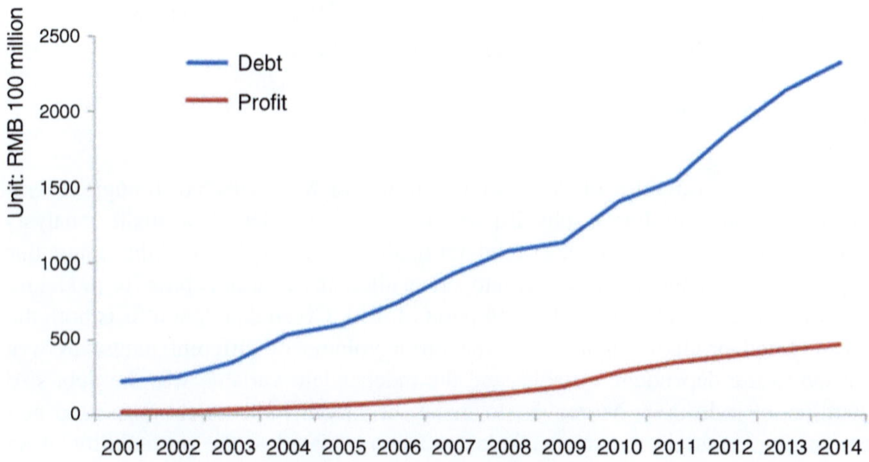

Fig. 6.12 Debt and profit of the furniture manufacturing industry

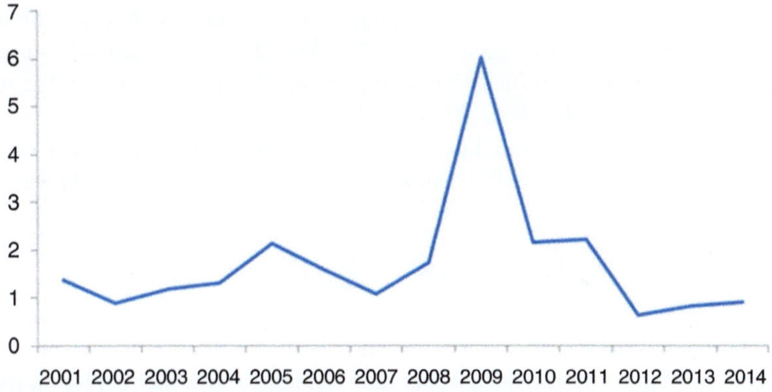

Fig. 6.13 Debt-profit elasticity of the furniture manufacturing industry

furniture manufacturing industry might repeat the tragedy of the iron and steel industry and the coal industry (Fig. 6.13).

Though the furniture manufacturing industry and the household appliance industry are faced with risks such as low-price competition, product homogeneity and investment expansion, neither industry has seen a clear sign of a turning point of debt from either industry or corporate data. Perhaps at the turn of a domestic consumption transformation and upgrade, the debt problems accumulated over time will emerge. Since the data available for the furniture manufacturing industry and household appliance industry are not as robust as the data for the coal industry and the iron and steel industry, there is less market research and fewer quantitative analyses we can use as references. Therefore, we will stay focused and attempt to conduct pressure tests, to predict the turning point of debt in this industry.

6.3 An Econometric Analysis of the Debt of Industries Along the Real Estate Industrial Chain

6.3.1 Econometric Model Design

The alternative variables of the econometric model were selected through several steps, including building a long list of alternative variables, data quality analysis (length and scarcity) and data trend rationality analysis. Meanwhile, using our experience-based judgment, we developed an alternative variable base for modeling that was closely related to the turning point of debt. Given that debt affects both the revenue and profit of an industry, the profit volume of different industries was chosen as the dependent variable, and the independent variable was the debt size of different industries. Moreover, to make the model more scientific, sound and convincing, multiple macro and industry factors related to the profitability of an industry were chosen to be exogenous variables: macro-level factors (e.g., GDP, total industrial added value and total fixed asset investment) and industry-level factors (e.g., new capacity and fixed asset investments).

Since there are many different industry classification systems in China, we adopted the industry classification standards released by the National Bureau of Statistics (NBS), to avoid difficulty in comparisons. Basic data used in the model were published by the NBS from 2000 to 2015.

The profit volume of various industries was selected as the dependent variable, and the debt size served as the independent variable. The model formula was:

$$Y_t = \alpha + \beta_{1t} X_{1t}^2 + \sum_{i=1}^{4} \beta_{it} X_{it} + \varepsilon_t \tag{6.1}$$

In the model, Y_t represented the profit volume of different industries; α was the constant term of the multiple linear regression model; β_{1t} was the regression parameter of the debt effect of different industries (which implied the existence of a turning point of debt effect in one industry if it were negative); X_{1t} represented the debt size of various industries; and ε was the stochastic term.

6.3.2 Calculations of the Turning Point of Debt for Different Industries

1. **Calculation of the turning point of debt for the coal industry**

We adopted a linear function and a quadratic function regression method to conduct a regression analysis of the debt and profit in the coal industry. The results showed that the goodness-of-fit (R-squared) of the quadratic function (Eq. 6.3) was 0.893 – notably better than that of the linear function (Eq. 6.2) of 0.285. Furthermore, the

Table 6.1 Analysis of the turning point of the debt of the coal industry

Model	Unstandardized coefficient		Standardized coefficient	t	Sig.
	B	Standard error	Trial version		
(Constant)	−1484.289	315.461		−4.330	.001
MT	0.47649058	0.052333085	3.283	8.529	.000
MT2	−1.11453E-05	1.47736E-06	−2.625	−6.818	.000
Goodness-of-fit (R-squared)	0.8934455				

regression results of Eq. 6.3 show that its linear term coefficient was positive, while the quadratic term coefficient was negative. This appears to prove the existence of a turning point. The calculated debt size when the coal industry reached its turning point was around RMB 2.14 trillion – lower than the debt volume (RMB 2.26 trillion) of the coal industry in 2011 and higher than that in 2010. Thus the estimate suggests that the turning point of debt in the coal industry was reached in 2011 (Table 6.1).

$$MTLR_t = 548.964 + 0.065^* MT_{1t} + \varepsilon_t \quad (6.2)$$

$$MTLR_t = -1484.289 - 1.115^* 10^{-5*} MT_{1t}^2 + 0.477^* MT_{1t} + \varepsilon_t \quad (6.3)$$

Definitions:

MLTR represented the profit volume of the coal industry.
MT represented the debt size of the coal industry.

Hence debt growth positively drove the growth of profit before 2011 when the overall debt level was reasonable. This may because it could guarantee the production and operation of businesses while providing financial support for the innovation R&D and investment and production expansion at the same time. Yet after 2011, the growth of debt no longer exerted a positive impact on profits. Debt grew faster than revenue, and the high debt level undermined the efficiency of capital allocation of businesses and thus posed a risk of bankruptcy.

Notably in 2011, coal prices plunged drastically and began a downward trend, after which the profitability of coal enterprises weakened substantially. Due to national regulation and a credit crunch, the year over year growth rate of industry debt remained relatively stable after 2011. But the year over year growth rate of core business revenue and the cumulative year over year growth rates of total profit and the profit margin of sales all fell (Fig. 6.14).

The debt of the coal industry was as much as RMB 3.46 trillion in 2014 – far higher than the calculated turning point at RMB 2.22 trillion. This means that the debt stock of this industry reached a rather dangerous level. There would be a lot of

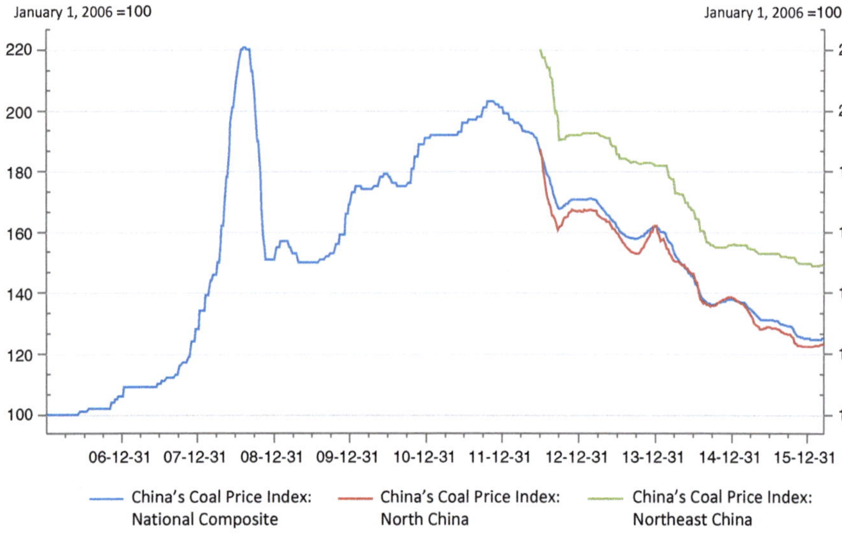

Fig. 6.14 Changes in coal prices. (Source: Wind)

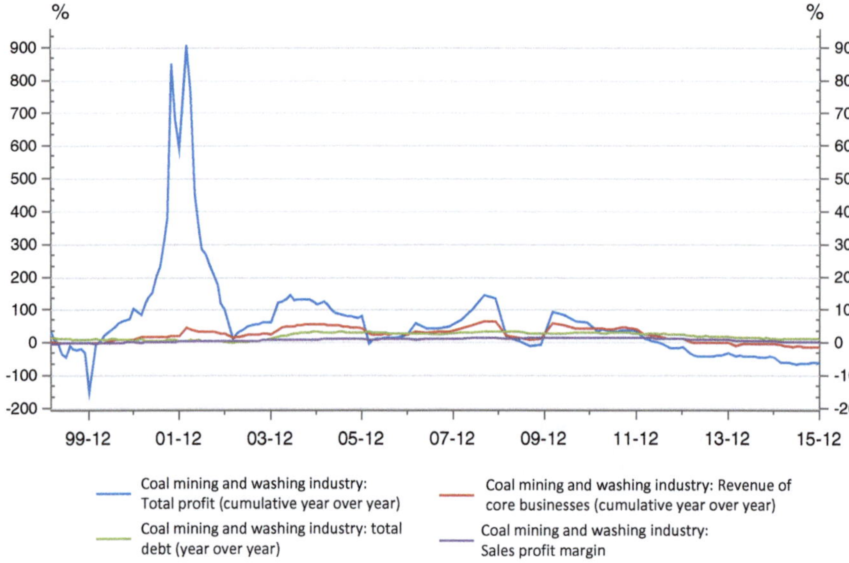

Fig. 6.15 Operations of the coal mining and washing industry. (Source: Wind)

room for de-leveraging in the future – around RMB 1.24 trillion, equivalent to the debt volume of the entire year of 2008 (RMB 1.15 trillion). The arduous task of de-leveraging can be seen from Fig. 6.15.

Table 6.2 Analysis of the turning point of debt of the iron and steel industry

Model	Unstandardized coefficient		Standardized coefficient	t	Sig.
	B	Standard error	Trial version		
(Constant)	−715.162	399.370		−1.791	.097
GT	0.199800547	.039	3.064	5.082	.000
GT*2	−2.77406E-06	.000	−2.354	−3.904	.002
Goodness-of-fit (R-squared)	0.805163				

2. **Calculation of the turning point of the debt of the iron and steel industry**

Using industry data, we employed a quadratic function model regression analysis of the debt (GT) and profit of the iron and steel industry (Eq. 6.4). The results show that the coefficient of the linear item of debt (GT) was positive, and the coefficient of the quadratic item (GT2) was negative. The goodness-of-fit was above 0.805, which implies the existence of a turning point of debt of the iron and steel industry. Based on our calculations, the iron and steel industry would reach its turning point when the debt reaches RMB 3.60 trillion – close to the debt size of RMB 3.88 trillion at the end of 2011. Therefore, it can be estimated that the turning point of the debt of the iron and steel industry was reached around 2012 (Table 6.2).

$$GTLR_t = -715.1616 - 2.774 * 10^{-6} * GT_{1t}^2 + 0.1998 * GT_{1t} + \varepsilon_t \qquad (6.4)$$

Definitions:

GTLR was the profit volume of the iron and steel industry.
GT was the debt size of the iron and steel industry.

Due to the macroeconomic shock, the prices of iron and steel products also plunged around 2011 as did coal prices. The value of the Myspic composite steel price index dropped by 16% in 2012 compared to the previous year. The number of loss-making businesses also skyrocketed. The RMB 4 trillion stimulus package created many "zombie businesses" with low operational efficiency and insufficient market competitiveness. These businesses were obscured by the boom in the real estate industry and downstream infrastructure construction. Once the economy started on a downward trend with sluggish demand from downstream industries, these businesses saw their products' prices plummet. The lack of scientific management led to blind expansion during the "boom," which caused considerable debt accumulation that squeezed shrinking profit margins (Figs. 6.16 and 6.17).

The debt of the iron and steel industry was already as high at RMB 4.88 trillion in 2014 – higher than the calculated turning point of RMB 4.21 trillion in the model.

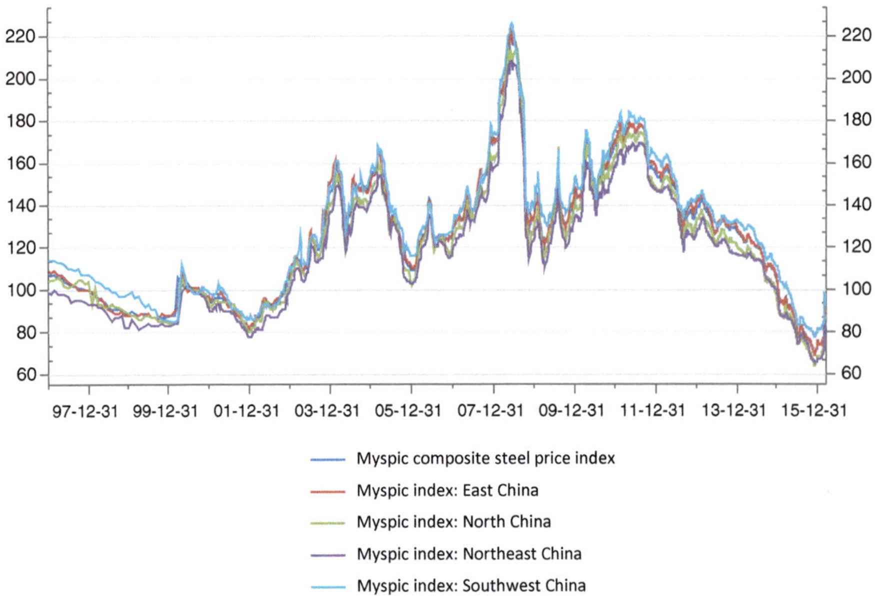

Fig. 6.16 Movement in China's steel prices. (Source: Wind)

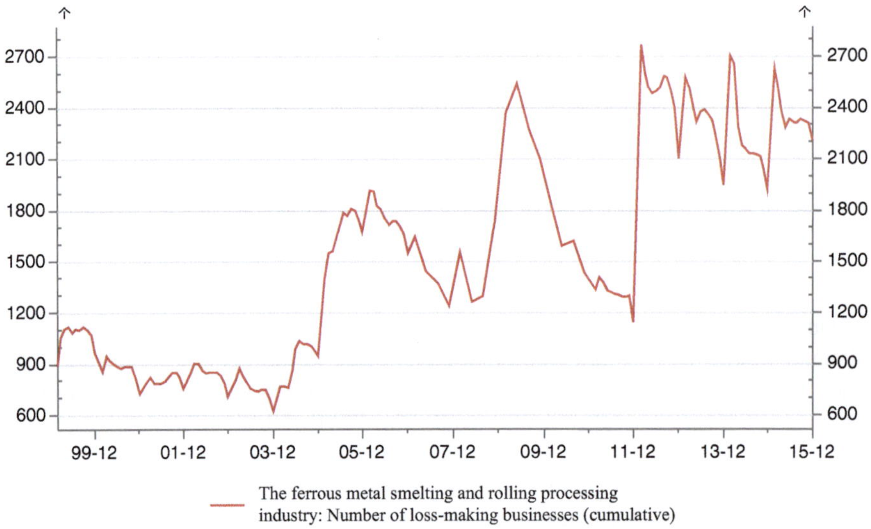

Fig. 6.17 Number of loss-making businesses within the iron and steel industry. (Source: Wind)

The room for de-leveraging is approximately RMB 0.67 trillion – lower than the target of RMB 1.15 trillion for the coal industry. This, according to estimates, might be related to the relationship between the upstream and downstream industries in the

Table 6.3 An analysis of the turning point of debt of the building material industry

Model	Unstandardized coefficient		Standardized coefficient	t	Sig.
	B	Standard error	Trial version		
(Constant)	−1808.396	248.740		−7.270	.000
JC	0.42813061	.042	2.016	10.190	.000
JC*2	−7.24592E-06	.000	−1.065	−5.385	.000
Goodness-of-fit (R-squared)	0.981695				

industrial chain, value added to products and profit margins. The iron and steel industry was downstream from the coal industry and had a higher added value, so its deterioration of debt was less severe than in the coal industry.

3. **Calculation of the turning point of debt of the building materials industry**

Based on data from the building materials industry, we conducted a quadratic function model regression analysis of the debt (JC) and profit. The results show that the coefficient of the linear item of debt (JC) was positive, while that of the quadratic item (JC2) was negative. The goodness-of-fit reached 0.982, which implies the existence of a turning point of debt in the building materials industry. Based on our estimates, the debt size will be RMB 2.95 trillion when the industry reaches its turning point. By the end of 2015, the debt size of China's building materials industry was RMB 2.76 trillion, lower than the value at the turning point. This means that the building materials industry had not reached its turning point of debt in 2015 (Table 6.3).

$$JCLR_t = -1808.3957 - 7.2459^* 10^{-6*} JC_{1t}^2 + 0.4281^* JC_{1t} + \varepsilon_t \tag{6.5}$$

Definitions:

JCLR represented the profit volume of the building material industry.
JC represented the debt size of the building material industry.

In the building materials industry, profits had been on the rise, and the industry had been fluctuating in a landscape of weak balance. However, sectors such as the cement and plate glass industries have overcapacity problems. Thus this industry is faced with slightly less pressure to cut overcapacity and debt compared with the iron and steel and coal industries. However, according to the regression results, if the coefficient of the quadratic item of debt were negative, it means there would be a turning point of debt. The current debt volume has not reached the turning point in theoretical terms, but the risk should not be overlooked.

Table 6.4 An analysis on the turning point of debt of the nonferrous metal industry

Model	Unstandardized coefficient		Standardized coefficient	t	Sig.
	B	Standard error	Trial version		
(Constant)	−623.031	173.402		−3.593	.003
YS	0.313568137	.034	2.844	9.255	.000
YS*2	−7.87091E-06	.000	−2.051	−6.674	.000
Goodness-of-fit (R-squared)	0.936577				

4. **Calculation of the turning point of debt of the non-ferrous metal industry**

Using data from the non-ferrous metal industry, we conducted a quadratic function model regression analysis of debt (YS) and profit. The results showed that the coefficient of the linear item of debt (YS) was positive, while that of the quadratic item (YS2) was negative. The goodness-of-fit reached 0.936, implying the existence of a turning point of debt in this industry. Based on estimates, the debt size will be RMB 1.99 trillion when the non-ferrous metal industry reaches its turning point. This is higher than the debt size of RMB 1.96 trillion at the end of 2012. Consequently, it can be estimated that the turning point of debt for this industry was reached around 2013 (Table 6.4).

$$YSLR_t = -623.0313 - 7.8709^{*}10^{-6*}YS_{1t}^{2} + 0.3136^{*}YS_{1t} + \varepsilon_t \tag{6.6}$$

Definitions:

YSLR was the profit volume of the nonferrous metal industry.
YS was the debt size of the nonferrous metal industry.

The turning point of debt within the coal industry was reached in 2011, while the iron and steel industry reached this point in 2012, and the non-ferrous metal industry reached it in 2013. These industries are resource-intensive with overcapacity. So why was the turning point of debt for the non-ferrous metal industry reached later than in the other industries? The initial model adopted in this study combined the non-ferrous metal mining and processing and non-ferrous metal smelting and rolling processing industries into the non-ferrous metal industry, whereas the electrolytic aluminum sector – the major sector with overcapacity – belongs to the nonferrous metal smelting and rolling processing industry. Thus we separated the two industries and conducted an econometric analysis of the statistics of the non-ferrous metal smelting and rolling processing industry. The results showed that the debt size at the turning point of debt of this industry was RMB 1.87 trillion – lower than the debt in 2013 (RMB 2.07 trillion) and higher than the debt in 2012 (RMB 1.77). We then estimated that the turning point of debt for the non-ferrous metal smelting and rolling

Table 6.5 An analysis on the turning point of the debt of the real estate industry

Model		Unstandardized coefficient		Standardized coefficient	t	Sig.
		B	Standard error	Trial version		
2	(Constant)	−1219.513	433.628		−2.812	.015
	FDC	5.46583E-06	.000	2.520	8.894	.000
	FDC*2	−8.68832E-16	.000	−1.703	−6.011	.000

processing industry was reached in 2013. The debt size of the non-ferrous metal industry was RMB 2.31 trillion in 2014 with room for de-leveraging at RMB 0.44 trillion.

5. **Calculation of the turning point of debt for the real estate industry**

Based on data from the real estate industry, we conducted a quadratic function model regression analysis of debt (FDC) and profit. The results showed that the coefficient of the linear item of debt (FDC) was positive, while the quadratic item (FDC2) was negative. The goodness-of-fit reached 0.936, implying the existence of a turning point of debt in the real estate industry. According to our calculations, the debt size would be RMB 31.46 trillion when the industry reaches its turning point – close to that of its debt of RMB 32.32 trillion in 2013. This means that the turning point of debt was most likely reached in 2013 – later than in the upstream iron and steel (2012) and coal (2011) industries (Table 6.5).

$$FDCLR_t = -1219.5128 - 8.6883 * 10^{-16} * FDC_{1t}^2 + 5.4658 * 10^{-6} * FDC_{1t} + \varepsilon_t \quad (6.7)$$

Definitions:

FDCLR was the profit volume of the real estate industry.
FDC was the debt size of the real estate industry.

In analyzing relevant data, we found two major reasons for the time difference in the turning points of debt for coal, iron and steel, and the real estate industries. First, the time difference was caused by the industries' locations on the industrial chain. The real estate industry is downstream with higher added value compared with raw materials industries further upstream. Thus it has higher product prices and bigger profit margins as well as higher coverage of debt stock for its core businesses.

And second, the real estate regulation policy launched in 2012 by the Chinese government was aimed at stimulating effective supply, yet only proposing to meet reasonable demands on the demand side. Specifically, the government proposed to accelerate the construction of ordinary commodity housing and increase the effective supply. As a result, Fig. 6.18 shows that from 2010 to 2012, the average sales price of commodity housing maintained an upward trend. In 2013 and 2014, the growth of prices obviously slowed. The average sales prices of both office buildings and

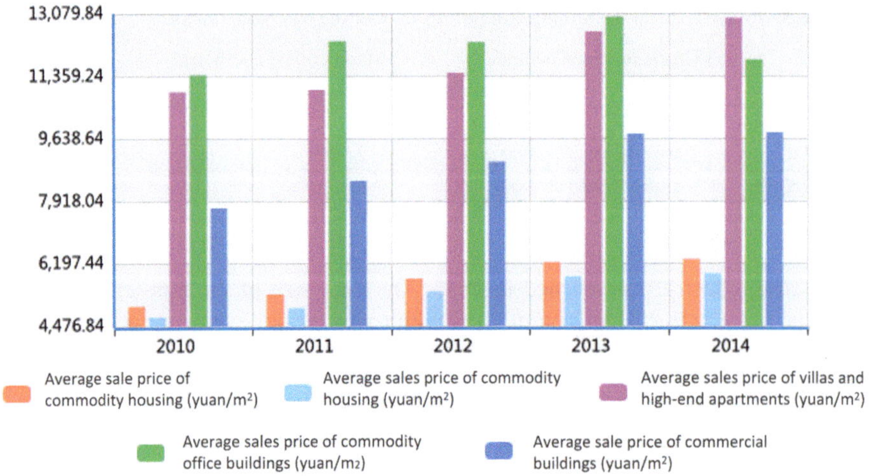

Fig. 6.18 Prices of various types of real estate businesses, 2010–2014. (Source: National Bureau of Statistics)

ordinary commodity housing – but not villas or high-end apartments – began to decline after 2013.

Therefore, debt for the real estate industry reached its turning point in 2013 when the debt size reached RMB 31.82 trillion. The debt of this industry in 2014 was RMB 38.41 trillion – slightly higher than the calculated RMB 31.82 trillion in the model. There is RMB 6.59 trillion in de-leveraging room.

6.3.3 Summary of the Econometric Analysis

We compared the actual values of debt in the coal, iron and steel, building materials, non-ferrous metal, non-ferrous metal smelting and rolling processing and real estate industries in 2014 and their calculated turning points (see Table 6.6).

With this comparison, it is easy to see that there are considerable disparities between different industries in terms of their turning points of debt and scale of de-leveraging. The scale and range of de-leveraging can reflect the difficulty in de-leveraging and reducing capacity for the industry. The larger the scale and the bigger the range, the more difficult the work will be.

The debt of the coal industry reached its turning point in 2011. Calculated with the 2014 price, the scale of de-leveraging was RMB 1.25 trillion, accounting for 36.13% of the debt size at the end of 2014.

The debt of the iron and steel industry reached its turning point in 2012. Calculated using the 2014 price, the scale of de-leveraging was RMB 0.67 trillion, accounting for 13.73% of the debt size at the end of 2014.

Table 6.6 Turning point estimates for debt in key industries to cut overcapacity and leverage

Year	Coal	Iron and steel	Building materials	Non-ferrous metal	Non-ferrous metal smelting and rolling processing	Real estate
2011	2.26	3.89	1.71	1.64	1.48	21.44
2012	2.72	4.36	2.06	1.97	1.77	26.46
2013	3.18	4.89	2.42	2.31	2.07	32.32
2014	3.46	4.88	2.67	2.58	2.31	38.40
Calculated turning point based on the 2014 price	2.22	4.21	3.27	2.06	1.87	31.82
Scale of de-leveraging	1.24	0.67		0.52	0.44	6.58
Time to reach the turning point	2011	2012	Not yet reached	2013	2013	2013

Based on data from 2014, the debt of the building materials industry had not reached its turning point. However, using the growth rate of debt at the end of 2014 and assuming the operational environment of the industry remained the same as that at the end of 2014, we can estimate that the debt size at the end of 2016 reached RMB 3.02 trillion – close to the debt size at its expected turning point.

The debt of the non-ferrous metal industry reached its turning point in 2013. Calculated with the 2014 price, the scale of de-leveraging was RMB 0.52 trillion, accounting for 20.16% of the debt size at the end of 2014. The scale of de-leveraging of the non-ferrous metal smelting and rolling processing was RMB 0.43 trillion, accounting for 18.61% of the debt size at the end of 2014.

The debt of the real estate industry reached its turning point in 2013. Calculated with the 2014 price, the scale of de-leveraging was RMB 6.58 trillion, accounting for 17.14% of the debt size at the end of 2014.

In sum, the industry with the largest de-leveraging scale was the real estate industry, and the industry with the biggest range of de-leveraging was the coal industry. Along the entire real estate industrial chain, the real estate industry had the biggest absolute debt size – even higher than the other four industries combined. Thus it is not surprising that the real estate industry has had the largest scale of de-leveraging. In general, the industry with the biggest range of de-leveraging was usually the one with the biggest debt pressure and the most prominent debt problems, often having reached the turning point of debt earlier than most of the other industries. According to previous analyses of the transmission mechanism of the turning point of debt in the real estate industrial chain, the coal industry – located upstream – was the first to reach its turning point. Its ability to resist risks was comparatively weak, so its debt pressure was higher, and it was exposed to more solvency risks.

6.4 Analysis on the Transmission of Turning Point of Debt Along the Real Estate Industrial Chain

6.4.1 The Debt Size of Major Industries Along the Real Estate Industrial Chain

From 2000 to 2014, the debt size of various industries – including coal, iron and steel, building materials (non-metallic mining, smelting and rolling presses) non-ferrous metal and real estate industries – substantially increased. Specifically, from 2008 to 2014, their debt sizes grew by 266.75%, 201.59%, 104.67%, 148.98% and 179.54%, respectively (Table 6.7).

Within this period, the debt sizes of the core industries along the real estate industrial chain were on a strong upward track. As the core of the industrial chain, the real estate industry had a notably bigger debt size than the other four industries, but they all maintained similar trends. Table 6.8 lists the growth rates of debt in the five industries from 2001 to 2014. In fact, 2014 witnessed the fastest debt growth of the five industries, which was the beginning of the boom of the real estate market and the iron and steel and coal industries. The debt growth rates in these industries had declined to rather low levels by 2014; debt growth rate of the iron and steel industry actually turned negative. The average annual debt growth rates of the real estate, coal, iron and steel, building materials and non-ferrous metal industries were 24.2%, 21%, 17.9%, 14% and 19.4%, respectively. The real estate industry had both the largest debt size and the highest debt growth rate. The average annual debt growth rates of the iron and steel industry and the coal and non-ferrous metal industry were roughly in the same range, and that of the building materials industry was much lower than the other four industries listed in Table 6.8. This corresponds with our analysis of core industries along the real estate industrial chain: the supply in the building materials industry (represented by the cement and glass sectors) was in a weak balance, and the turning point of debt may not have been reached.

Consequently, the debts of the five industries have been on a downward track that will most likely continue for several more years. Does this mean that their debt problems have been alleviated? We believe the answer is no, for three major reasons:

First, all five industries have high debt stock, and their debt growth rates, affected by the base effect, have not been very high in recent years and are expected to decline. Second, from the perspective of enterprises, their debt stock is already quite high with many in the coal and iron and steel industries having debt ratios above 80%. Given that the assets in industries like coal, iron and steel, and nonferrous metal mainly consist of factory buildings and production equipment that are of fairly low liquidity, the de facto debt burdens of these businesses are heavy. During the economic downturn, the problem of overcapacity in these cyclical industries became more prominent, and demand from downstream turned sluggish since there were few new projects demanding financing. Therefore, in order to avoid insolvency, it is wise for enterprises to refrain from increasing financing and focus on repaying the already heavy debt. Third, from the perspective of banks, the head offices of various banks

Table 6.7 Absolute debt sizes of various industries (unit: RMB 100 million)

	Real estate	Coal	Iron and steel	Building materials	Non-ferrous metal
2000	19,040.61	2527.16	5157.05	4392.61	2212.71
2001	21,425.11	2711.09	5132.32	4329.20	2376.52
2002	24,749.30	2742.24	5501.32	4568.53	2507.51
2003	30,688.76	3036.56	7225.06	5021.08	2990.19
2004	45,785.79	4281.81	9818.05	6058.84	3916.81
2005	52,520.73	5332.54	11,991.24	6594.92	4646.32
2006	65,477.54	6714.02	14,829.64	7285.49	6032.15
2007	82,642.18	8477.42	18,697.14	8421.76	7532.59
2008	104,714.70	1,1483.10	23,832.47	10,707.91	9215.13
2009	125,085.40	14,051.16	27,804.37	12,125.28	11,015.85
2010	167,228.00	17,418.53	33,199.55	14,770.19	13,807.54
2011	214,407.00	22,557.63	38,851.78	17,111.74	16,440.61
2012	264,597.70	27,205.07	43,578.52	20,642.11	19,688.73
2013	323,166.30	31,775.22	48,895.57	24,246.79	23,103.87
2014	384,037.40	34,631.81	48,777.71	26,661.03	25,759.91

Table 6.8 Growth rates of debt in five industries

	Real estate (%)	Coal (%)	Iron and steel (%)	Building materials (%)	Non-ferrous metal (%)
2001	12.5	7.3	−0.5	−1.4	7.4
2002	15.5	1.1	7.2	5.5	5.5
2003	24.0	10.7	31.3	9.9	19.2
2004	49.2	41.0	35.9	20.7	31.0
2005	14.7	24.5	22.1	8.8	18.6
2006	24.7	25.9	23.7	10.5	29.8
2007	26.2	26.3	26.1	15.6	24.9
2008	26.7	35.5	27.5	27.1	22.3
2009	19.5	22.4	16.7	13.2	19.5
2010	33.7	24.0	19.4	21.8	25.3
2011	28.2	29.5	17.0	15.9	19.1
2012	23.4	20.6	12.2	20.6	19.8
2013	22.1	16.8	12.2	17.5	17.3
2014	18.8	9.0	−0.2	10.0	11.5

have responded to the call of the Chinese government in recent years to cut overcapacity, de-leverage and tighten credit to the industries with excess capacity. Their branches and sub-branches need to follow the instructions of the head offices to tighten credit extension to industries such as coal, iron and steel, non-ferrous metal and real estate (mainly to the real estate enterprises in the third- and fourth-tier cities which may not significantly increase and bounce back in the future). As a result, even if enterprises in these five industries want to expand financing, banks will not

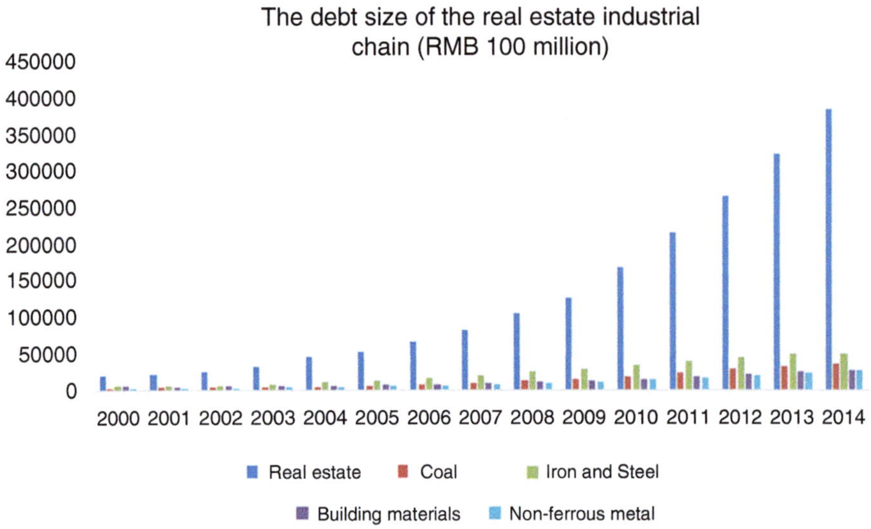

Fig. 6.19 The debt size of the real estate industrial chain

lend them money or offer them conveniences. To some extent, this is not good news for corporate debt because if indirect credit extension for financing is tightened, the qualifications for direct financing will be denied and the financial costs will be high. For example, it will be difficult for enterprises to get refunds and the stock debt cannot be sustained. This is likely to cause a solvency crisis in industries burdened with overcapacity.

Because of these three factors, core industries faced with debt problems in the real estate industrial chain have not alleviated their debt crisis, although their debt growth has slowed. This signals a worsening financing environment and increased possibility of a solvency crisis (Fig. 6.19).

6.4.2 The Transmission Effect of the Turning Point of Debt in the Industries Along the Real Estate Industrial Chain

When analyzing an enterprise or a company in an industrial chain, we typically pay attention to the transmission effect along the chain. Generally speaking, when an economic crisis breaks out, the recession is transmitted from consumer industries downstream to the raw materials and resources industries upstream. Meanwhile, the economic prosperity is transmitted from the downstream to the midstream and then the upstream. The cyclical loop of both recession and recovery starts downstream. So from a debt perspective, is there a transmission effect along the real estate industrial chain?

Our analysis of current industry data revealed that there is a transmission effect of the marginal utility of debt among industries in the industrial chain with the downstream real estate industry. Thus the real estate industry and its upstream industries reached their turning points of debt at different times, yet they presented a certain regularity. This reflected the impact of industrial chain factors to some extent. The data shows that the coal industry reached its turning point of debt in 2011, the iron and steel industry a year later, and the non-ferrous metal, non-ferrous metal smelting and rolling processing and real estate industries in 2013; however, the building materials industry has not reached its turning point. The debt turning point of the real estate industrial chain transits to downstream industries – the opposite of economic cycles.

There is a certain pattern in the transmission of the turning points of debt along the real estate industrial chain, from the upstream coal industry to the midstream iron and steel industry to the downstream real estate industry. But why is the transmission of the turning point of debt opposite to that of the economic cycle in the industrial chain? We think that this should be analyzed based on the nature of debt.

For economic cycles, the downstream industries are at the beginning of the transmission chain. This is mainly because downstream consumer industries are located at the "nerve ending" of the economy, and they are most sensitive to economic fluctuations. As a result, the logic of the transmission of the economic cycle is essentially different from that of the transmission of debt. According to the definition of corporate debt, there are three categories of debt sources for specific companies: the long-term debt raised to meet the demand for strategic development, the short-term debt borrowed due to fund shortages and the accounts payable generated by daily operations. During the boom, debt expansion is driven by the first category, which means that the industry is in a sound condition with many projects, so there is a need to raise long-term funds. But during a recession, the second category usually accounts for a larger share since the industry plummets and companies are faced with worrying operations with notably weakened solvency with a need for more short-term funds to ease the liquidity risk. When the economy remains stable, the shares of the first and second categories of debt drop while that of the third rises.

Consequently, corporate debt is highly correlated with the climate of the industry. The financing decisions of some enterprises might be affected by issues such as corporate governance and strategic plans. However, from the perspective of an entire industry, the debt expansion in an industry often takes place at the initial stage of the boom since enterprises expect a promising future and booming demand in the industry. Then they race to increase investment and capacity to meet the possibly ever-increasing demand. In contrast, an obvious increase in short-term debt in an industry usually appears during a recession when enterprises are under heavier solvency pressure and faced with tightened credit by banks which have greater difficulty in getting long-term loans approved.

Our detailed analysis of core industries in the real estate industrial chain showed that upstream industries were less sensitive to economic fluctuations than those further downstream. For example, the coal industry has been less sensitive to the economic climate than the iron and steel or real estate industries. Thus during economic recessions, their capacity and debt expansions could not be adjusted in a timely manner. In contrast, downstream industries have been more sensitive to economic conditions, so they have been better able to control production capacity according to relevant economic changes. Moreover, most upstream industries have been resource-intensive and have fewer types of products and lower added value compared to industries further downstream. Thus upstream industries have been less able to guard against risks and may be faced with more prominent debt problems. Therefore, these industries reached their turning point of debt earlier than those further downstream. So why did the non-ferrous metal and non-ferrous metal smelting and rolling processing industries both reach their turning point of debt in 2013? And why did the downstream real estate industry also reach its turning point in that same year? Researchers think there are two major reasons. First, the time points in the model were calculated on a yearly basis, so they may not show the differences of time within the same year. For another, the non-ferrous metal industry was not as strongly correlated with the real estate industry as the coal and iron and steel industries were. (This was mentioned in the industry analysis in the previous section.) Thus its transmission effect was weaker than that of the coal, iron and steel and real estate industries.

6.5 Summary and Suggestions

Industries along the real estate industry chain contribute as much as 20% to the GDP. It's fair to say that the healthy development of the real estate industry chain is of great importance for the entire national economy. Therefore, after analyzing the debt turning points and potential deleveraging of specific industries, we further probed the relationship between the real estate industry chain and economic growth. Available data revealed that the real estate industry chain has reached its turning point of its debt; however, some sectors – such as the building materials sector – have not reached their turning points of debt. Though reaching the turning point has not resulted in any noticeable effects, these sectors must confront their debt problems to different degrees. To prevent potential risks, they should be incorporated into key regulatory targets. Based on our detailed analyses, we suggest the following adjustments:

1. **Properly promote supply-side reform of the real estate market.**

To relieve the real economy of a heavy debt burden, China introduced supply-side reform. The reforms promote structural adjustments starting from the supply side, rectify irrational allocation of production factors, increase effective supply properly to meet public demands – all while shrinking (or even eliminating) inefficient supply. In view of the theory of market supply and demand, the supply-side reform has rules to follow. Some countries have already made attempts in this regard. For instance, in 1978, Japan issued the *Act on Temporary Measures for the*

Stabilization of Specified Depressed Industries and specified the iron and steel industry as a sluggish industry. Then, Japan worked to shrink its iron and steel supply by raising market access thresholds and subsidizing the scrapping of obsolete machineries. As a result, the growth of the industry shifted from high expansion to a downturn, with generally stable production and thus gradually improved prices. Since China implemented its supply-side reform, coal prices have witnessed a remarkable increase. So far, the progress is satisfactory. Though the supply-side reform cannot save the coal industry from a downturn, it can improve the industry's supply-demand pattern and encourage rational production.

We believe that the measures adopted for de-capacity and deleveraging in the coal industry can be applied to the real estate industry for its supply-side reform. Although different from the coal industry and others in the real economy, the supply-side reform of the real estate industry, with its intrinsic characteristics and significance to having a stable livelihood, should focus more on structural adjustments than on quantity reduction. It may even imply an expansion – rather than a contraction – of supply.

Capital is essentially profit-seeking, so the best tactic is to channel capital from the heavily-burdened and highly risky industries into the real economy. As discussed earlier, the debt problem of the real estate industry rests with real estate developers rather than with households, i.e. the supply side rather than the demand side. Generally speaking, when the real estate market is overheated and home prices rapidly rise, real estate developers expand their businesses and banks issue loans, which pushes up the debt size of the real estate industry. Hence the key to solving its debt problem is to control home prices and thus guard against a sudden surge or irrational exuberance. We analyzed problems from a market supply and demand perspective. Thus we propose that to control real estate market prices, there are two types of tools: those on the demand side and those on the supply side.

2. **Refine measures for the supply-side reform of the real estate market.**

Demand-side tools, as the name suggests, regulate the real estate market by regulating real estate demand. These tools are mostly administrative, usually manifesting themselves as purchase restrictions and credit limits when the market is overheated. For example, when home prices in Shenzhen, Hangzhou, Zhengzhou, Nanjing and other first-tier, quasi-first-tier and core second-tier cities soared in 2016, the local governments – under the guidance of the central government – successively adopted purchase restrictions and credit limit policies in September and October of that year. Beginning Sept. 19, 2016, Hangzhou started to restrict home purchases, halting home sales to residents without household registration of the municipality or who had one or more homes under certain conditions. Shenzhen, a "leader" of the country in regard to home price rises in 2016, also promulgated rather restrictive measures. So far, these measures have been effective in cooling the real estate market. Nevertheless, their exact influences can only be made clear with data from 2017, which has yet to be released. Aside from administrative restrictions, Chinese authorities can persuade banks to reduce residential mortgage loans through "window guidance," thus controlling the real estate market by regulating financing from banks.

Supply-side tools stabilize home prices by boosting the supply of homes. There are four ways to boost supply in the real estate market: (1) increase land supply for residential property development, (2) raise the ratio of ordinary commodity residential housing, (3) boost the supply of low-income housing and (4) accelerate the approval process. China implemented a system of state ownership of land. In this system, no individual has the right to land disposal; the enterprises can only acquire the right to land use by means of a bid invitation, auction or listing. The process and scale of land to be transferred is under the absolute control of government authorities. So in cases where the land supply is relatively abundant, real estate enterprises might find it easier and cheaper to acquire the right to land use, hence a lighter financing burden and lower home prices. But in cases where the government authorities intend to cut land supply, enterprises would have to weather fierce competition before they could take some parcel of land. In such cases, the land prices are inevitably higher, hence a piling up of corporate debt and an increase in home prices. So increasing the land supply for residential property development can regulate the property supply at its source. Adding the effects of the other three measures, the government can put an end to the home price upsurge and irrational exuberance resulting from such phenomena as "finding it hard to buy even one home" and "having several households scramble for one house." Notably, increasing property supply – especially the supply of low-income housing – is closely related with the national effort of cracking down on both "tigers" and "flies," i.e. fighting corruption and upholding integrity.

In fact, the importance of low-income housing to the stability of the real estate market has long been recognized, with local governments commencing the construction of low-income housing with a substantive input of labor and materials. Nevertheless, as the price of low-income housing is to some extent regulated by the administrative guidance of governments, the price and profit of low-income housing is relatively low compared with commercial housing in similar conditions. As a result, the construction of such homes – which are less attractive to real estate developers – is mostly undertaken by government-subordinate financing platforms or state-owned enterprises. The absence of social organizations and commercial entities notably aggravates rent-seeking behaviors in terms of low-income housing construction and allocation and even leads to corruption. Many government officials, taking advantage of their situation, secure wealth for friends and relatives in low-income housing, while turning down ordinary people in real demand for such homes. Therefore, the supply of low-income housing is correlated with the process, degree and effects of China's anti-corruption effort. The integrity of the government ultimately influences the efficiency of resource allocation.

In terms of real estate market regulations, demand-side and supply-side tools are important. China has made progress with demand-side tools in curbing the overly rapid growth of home prices in first-tier and some second-tier cities in 2016. However, these demand-side tools are imbued with administrative intentions and are dampening demand with such policies as household registration-based purchase restrictions. This has been detrimental to the reform of China's household registration system and the advancement of urban-rural integration and regional economic integration in the long run. The use of supply-side tools seems to be more critical. The stable real estate market in Chongqing can be attributed, to a large extent, to a relatively abundant supply of land and rich resources of low-income housing. Therefore, in regulating the real estate market, China can focus more on the supply side and adopt such measures as properly increasing land supply to avoid the emergence of "land kings," strengthening infrastructure construction to supply more low-income housing, and rectifying internal reviews for streamlined formalities and faster approval and implementation of quality programs. If home prices remain stable, the inflow of speculative capital will greatly decrease, and this will help prevent home prices from escalating and facilitate a virtuous cycle. It also will force real estate developers to de-leverage and adjust their debt structures.

3. **Implement supply-side reform for the real estate market in first-, second-, third- and fourth-tier cities.**

It's essential that different policies be adopted for different problems and that measures be adjusted for different local conditions, to ensure scientific decision-making in the process of policy implementation. We contend that as China has severe regional economic disparities and uneven population distribution, both resources and population tend to move to coastal areas and core cities, resulting in a net outflow of population from third- and fourth-tier cities. Hence, the local foundation in support of stable home prices in these cities is weak. So in implementing the supply-side reform of the real estate market of first-, second-, and third-tier cities, the government must adjust measures to local conditions and propose solutions in a targeted manner.

In first-tier cities, with robust and seemingly sustained demand for homes and a currently suppressed rigid demand due to household registration-based home purchase restrictions, the actual supply of homes is generally much lower than the real demand. However, since the first-tier cities have already enforced purchasing restrictions and credit limit policies, the room left for demand-side regulation seems small. Effective solutions must be found at the supply side, such as properly increasing land supply for first-tier cities, cracking down on rent seeking and corruption, and improving the efficiency of the low-income housing supply. Some may think that first-tier cities are already overcrowded. As the total amount of usable land is limited, and the population continues to grow, the increase of the land supply cannot meet the demands. In this regard, we posit that cities like Beijing have sent clear signals to control their population. This may bring a gradual slowing in population growth rates in these cities for a period to come – or at least put an end to explosive growth. Furthermore, as the first-tier cities boast the most abundant political, economic and human resources, there is no doubt that the transportation network becomes denser and the traffic more convenient, saving rural resident commuters from having to drive for 2 h as in other cities. With a developed system of subways, buses and urban light rail, an urban areas can be expanded to include adjacent rural areas and even nearby cities, thus forming a satellite city. A satellite city is conducive in alleviating population pressures; it's an effective option as well as an inevitable trend. Surprisingly, there still is much virgin land in rural areas and nearby cities.

Third- and fourth-tier cities have witnessed a net outflow of their populations in recent years and thus a dwindling demand for homes. There are huge housing inventories in these cities, some parts of which have become uninhabited "ghost towns." Nevertheless, as developed cities are capable of providing more job opportunities and educational resources, the trend of people flowing to first- and second-tier cities cannot be reversed in the short run. That is to say, in the near future, the demand for homes in third- and fourth-tier cities will remain sluggish. Hence it's especially important that the home supply be cut. As in industries with excess capacity, the adjustment of supply helps improve market demand and prices, profitability in third- and fourth-tier cities and the balance sheets of the industry.

Second-tier cities have conditions somewhere in between. Market players find it difficult to understand market supply and demand and tend to "play it by ear." For example, in cases where speculative money floods the market and drives up home prices, the governments would enforce purchase restrictions and credit limits to cool the property market. But when the growth of the economy is gloomy and resources from other cities declines, governments would loosen the restrictions and warm the market, thus striking a long-term balance of market supply and demand to some extent. We contend that less competitive second-tier cities such as Zhengzhou, Wuhan and Nanjing do not have problems with home inventories, yet they have much better demand conditions than third- and fourth-tier cities. So it's truly difficult to determine the supply-demand pattern. However, it's certainly not the best tactic to regulate in the aftermath of an imbalance. For one thing, with a time lag, the policies may fail to solve problems in a timely manner and even worsen existing contradictions. For another, if market sentiments and the ensuing property transactions fluctuate in a certain period, the changeable policies would harm social stability, local governance and long-term development. So it is suggested that the second-tier cities ensure pre-warning and precautions, instead of belated efforts, based on a detailed analysis of the supply-demand pattern.

4. **Implement home price regulation while considering the debt turning point of the real estate industry.**

"Houses are built to be inhabited, not for speculation." This statement from the central government demonstrates China's determination and confidence in controlling home prices, curbing speculation and preventing bubbles which can rapidly spread. The previous sections, therefore, shed light on controlling home prices and the regulation of supply and demand in the real estate market. But this section focuses on the issue of the debt turning point. We assert that the debt turning point has already passed. So how do the home prices and the supply-demand structure influence the debt turning point? In this section, various perspectives will be summarized.

Supply and demand governs the price of goods. Ultimately, home prices are determined by supply and demand within the real estate market. If supply outweighs demand, home prices will remain stable while facing downward pressure and the trading volume will be slight. If demand outweighs supply, the real estate market will be fiery, the trading volume will increase and home prices will surge. Supply and demand can result in an imbalance. For example, when the real estate market is faced with downward pressure, enterprises will suspend business expansion and banks will tighten credit granted to the industry. The two factors will result in a slowdown of the debt growth for the enterprises; the debt growth rate of some enterprises may even become negative. If the regulations are effective and adjusted to local conditions, the price of unsold homes will stabilize or even increase. This is also a great benefit to real estate developers: in one respect, their debt load will be reduced; but in another, the increase in profits will enable a lower debt ratio and help tackle the problem of high debt. It can be inferred that it's not feasible to solve the debt problem by bringing down home prices. Home prices need to be stabilized and even lifted; otherwise, the profits of real estate enterprises will fall significantly. In the case of declining profits, enterprises stop taking on new debts to avoid the dilemma of a high leverage ratio and ensuing insolvency. This is what makes it difficult for the real estate industry to de-leverage. We note that the key to lifting real estate enterprises out of this dilemma lies in the analysis of specific issues. According to the different characteristics of the real estate markets in first-, second-, third-, and fourth-tier cities, different policies should be adopted: expanding supply in first-tier cities; tracking supply and demand of the market and establishing policy pre-warning mechanisms in second-tier cities; controlling the launch of new real estate projects; and optimizing inventory in third- and fourth-tier cities. The government must guard against the ideology of "one size fits all" and the practice of enforcing administrative instructions inconsistent with market laws.

As we see it, the supply-side reform of the real estate market focuses more on structure and features clear targets, hierarchical measures and comprehensive consideration of local conditions. To promote reform in third- and fourth-tier cities, similar with that in the coal and steel industries with overcapacity, supply contraction is warranted. But first-tier cities are asked to release the proper amount of land and expand transferrable land resources by virtue of their naturally-endowed advantages and well-developed transportation networks. This will mitigate the increasingly prominent supply-demand contradictions. For second-tier cities with conditions somewhere in between, it might be better for them to act as the circumstances direct. Nevertheless, risk prevention and preparations must be stressed.

The regulation of the real estate market – a key process in macroeconomic regulation – is sure to affect the overall situation. As no theory or policy can best explain problems within the real estate market, our conclusions are based on an analysis of available data and summaries of field investigations. After some creative thinking, our suggestions are proposed for consideration. Hence, we call on all sectors of society to contribute useful opinions so that clever ideas can spring up for the development of a stable and healthy real estate economy.

Chapter 7
A Study of the Real Economy and the Virtual Economy

The economic growth of China has been slowing since 2015. In the third quarter of 2015, the growth rate of GDP fell drastically to less than 7% year over year. This represented a record low since the global sub-prime crisis in 2009. Recently, the State Council convened several conferences to reiterate the principle of guiding finances toward the real economy; the council stated that the relationship between the virtual economy and the real economy should be properly handled so that the former could better serve the latter. Economists agree that the virtual economy, within a reasonable range, can promote the development of the real economy, while over expansion might cause damage. However, so far, China has not set its standards and boundaries for the ratio of the real economy to the virtual economy.

The academic community and competent authorities often refer to the fact that the expansion of the virtual economy may give rise to financial turbulence and harm real economic development; however, few scholars have thoroughly explored how to identify the optimal ratio of the real economy to the virtual economy, the upper limits for the ratio, and the optimal size of China's virtual economy. Therefore, based on a systematic study of China's government, corporate and individual debts, we explored the coordinated development of the virtual and the real economies and their "golden ratio." We also searched for the upper limits for the ratio, which is of great significance to theoretical research and practical application.

This chapter proceeds from an analysis of the changes in the size of the virtual economy, taking total factor productivity (TFP) as the standard for calculation and then calculating the golden ratio of the real economy to the virtual economy. Furthermore, the results of filter analysis and the Granger causality test used to determine which entities in the virtual economy had the greatest influence on the real economy (industrial added value). The results showed that **the golden ratio of the virtual economy to the real economy was 16.7; meanwhile, this ratio in China has already fallen out of the reasonable range in 2009.** This is likely to have triggered excessive speculation and financial bubbles and thus dampened economic growth. Therefore, it is imperative to restructure the national economy.

X. Zhu et al., *A Study of the Turning Point of China's Debt*,
https://doi.org/10.1007/978-981-13-1325-7_7

Data also showed that the short-term fluctuations in the stock market and funds market can influence the short-term development of the real economy. And the long-term instability of the futures market, the commodity housing market and bond market can impact the real economy as well.

7.1 The State of the Real Economy and Virtual Economy

7.1.1 The Definition of the Real Economy and the Virtual Economy

Keynes defined the real economy as the sector existing in the form of goods and services. As the classical dichotomy in economics has evolved over time, the theoretical studies of the real economy and the virtual economy also were moving forward.

People may have different understandings of the definition of the virtual economy, but there are two ways to define it in China. The first school, represented by Cheng Siwei, argues that "the virtual economy refers to economic activities concerned with virtual capital circulation based on the financial system; simply put, it represents activities of making money from money." From this perspective, the virtual economy means activities in the financial sector. The other school, represented by Liu Junmin, states that theoretically, people should differentiate the real economy from the virtual economy based on "whether the activities are concerned with material production." Activities which are not concerned with material production fall under the category of the virtual economy, based on which they proposed the broad and narrow definitions of the virtual economy. By the definition in a broad sense, the virtual economy is not confined to the financial sector but exists in other service sectors as well.

Considering international practices, the U.S. Federal Reserve System has frequently used the term "real economy" in recent years, relating it to the part of the economy beyond the real estate market and financial market. The composition of the U.S. economic data shows that there are two systems in its national economic accounting: the first system is the Material Product System (MPS), which includes agriculture, industry and traditional service sectors and can be generalized into the "real economy." The second system is the System of National Accounts (SNA), which includes the financial industry, the real estate industry and the modern financial-services industry and can be considered the "virtual economy."

In view of China's economic structure, stages of economic development and financial markets, we defined the virtual economy as the part of economy dominated by the financial industry and real estate industry. It includes the transaction volumes in the stock, bond, securities, futures and commodity housing markets. Meanwhile, we assessed the real economy with industrial added value; in terms of the virtual economy, based on both domestic and foreign studies, we included the real estate market into the analysis and considered transaction volumes in the stock, bond, securities, futures and commodity housing markets.

The relationship between the real economy and the virtual economy has four dimensions. First, the virtual economy is built upon the real economy. Virtual capital is transformed from the surplus capital generated in the real economy; physical capital (or the real economy) is the foundation and revenue source of virtual capital. Second, the virtual economy is independent of the real economy and has its own unique regularity. Third, the long-term capital in the virtual economy may integrate with industrial capital in some ways and then exist in the form of the real economy. Therefore, the development of the virtual economy is a double-edged sword for the real economy. As the virtual economy develops, it can facilitate financing within the real economy, help optimize resource allocation and thus promote economic benefits and upgrade the industrial structure. However, the growth of the virtual economy tends to cause economic bubbles and increase the possibility of economic turmoil and crisis.

7.1.2 *The State of the Real Economy and the Virtual Economy*

The virtual economy, GDP and the industrial added value developed in tandem before 2006. After 2007, however, the growth of the virtual economy picked up, and its size far exceeded that of the real economy aggregate represented by industrial value added (Fig. 7.1).

In terms of the ratios between the virtual economy and the real economy, domestic and foreign scholars often look to the financial interrelations ratio (FIR). This important indicator refers to the relationship between total financial assets and

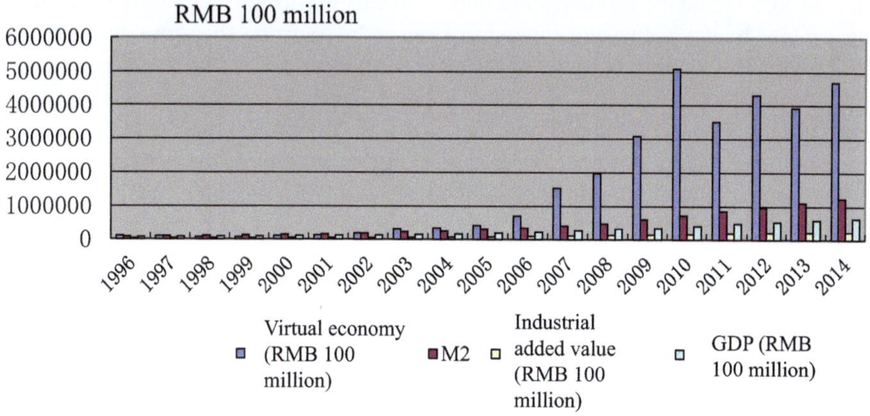

Fig. 7.1 The size of the real economy and the virtual economy. (Source: NBS website)

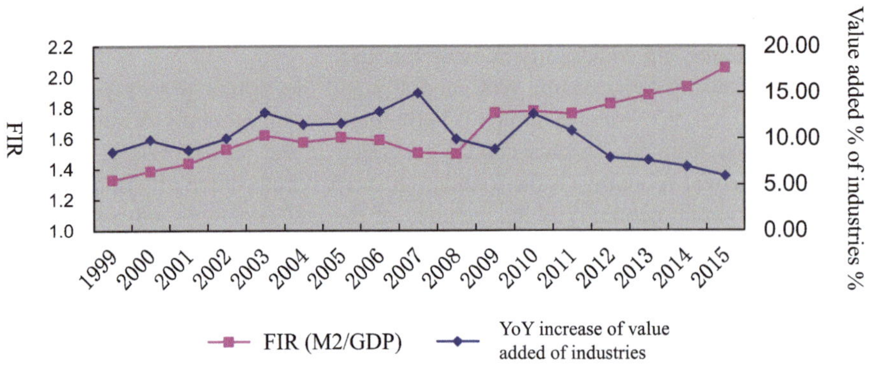

Fig. 7.2 FIRs of the real economy and the virtual economy

total physical assets, i.e. the ratio between the stock of financial assets and national wealth at some point in time. When the financial assets grow faster than the real economy, the FIR will increase – yet there are limits to its rise. According to foreign studies, the FIR may remain stable within the range of 1.0–1.5. Some Chinese scholars believe that the upper limit of China's FIR is around 2.5.

In real calculations, most domestic and foreign scholars consider M2/GDP as the FIR. Though the ratio is largely different from the FIR in its strict sense (the ratio of total financial assets to national wealth), it's still representative to some extent. In view of the movements of FIR and the industrial added value in China after 1999, the FIR remained relatively stable before 2009, and its trend was basically the same as that of industrial added value. After 2010, the FIR kept rising and the growth of industrial added value went on a downward spiral, so the two figures have presented a scissors gap since then (Fig. 7.2).

In fact, the virtual economy naturally emerges when the real economy reaches a certain stage of development. In one aspect, the sound operation of the real economy can provide solid support for the virtual economy; in another, the development of human society and the economy and improvements in social welfare were ultimately determined by the real wealth created and owned by humans. Therefore, the stability of the virtual economy is based on whether virtual capital can be transformed into real social wealth. If the real economy cannot deliver gains which are necessary for the virtual economy, a major crisis may arise. If the real economy and the virtual economy can maintain proper paces and sizes, the growth of the virtual economy will strongly promote the development of the real economy and boost a nation's economy. When the virtual economy lags the real economy, financial repression may take place, which will lead to the ineffective use of capital and market segmentation and even hamper the development of real the economy. But when the virtual economy develops faster than the real economy and becomes bloated, it may result in speculative excesses and financial bubbles.

7.2 The Golden Ratio of the Real Economy and the Virtual Economy

We used total factor productivity as the standard to calculate the golden ratio of the real economy and the virtual economy.

7.2.1 Calculating Total Factor Productivity

Productivity reflects the influence of technical progress on economic growth in a comprehensive way. From the perspective of economic growth, productivity, similar to the input of labor, capital and other production factors, serves to promote economic growth. From the perspective of efficiency, productivity equals the ratio of a country's overall economic output to the total input of all kinds of resource factors. By its nature, productivity demonstrates the production capacity and effort levels that an economy displays in a certain period as it strives for economic growth. The neoclassical growth theory endorsed by Solow (1957) and other scholars posits that economic growth can be accomplished in two ways: increasing input of production factors or increasing production efficiency per unit of input. Nevertheless, as the marginal returns on capital gradually diminish in the long run, this first kind of economic growth cannot be sustained. Therefore, the sustainable development of an economy relies on technical advancement and thus improved productivity.

In assessing technical levels, the total factor productivity (TFP) is more suitable than the single factor productivity (SFP). TFP is composed of improved efficiency, technical progress and scale effects. In calculation, it is the residual which accounts for effects on total output not caused by the input of labor, capital and land. But there have been changes in TFP in China and its contributions to China's economic growth.

Model hypothesis: The production function of the Chinese economy follows the Cobb-Douglas production function model:

$$Y_t = A_0 e^{t\alpha} K^{\alpha_K} L^{\alpha_L}$$

In this equation, A_0, α_K, and α_L represented the output elasticity of capital K and labor L. If the returns to scale remain unchanged, $\alpha_K + \alpha_L = 1$, which means the productivity would not increase with scale expansion. And it's only by improving techniques that the economic efficiency can be enhanced.

With the natural logarithm processing of the above equation:

$$\ln Y_t/L_t = \ln A_0 + t\alpha + \alpha_K \ln K_t/L_t \qquad \text{(Model7.1)}$$

For Model 7.1, we used GDP data from 1991 to 2015 (RMB 100 million) as an indicator of the total output of the Chinese economy and the number of laborers in

Table 7.1 TFP regression results (part 1)

Model		Unstandardized coefficients		Standardized coefficients			Collinearity	
		B	Standard error	Trial version	t	Sig.	Tolerance	VIF
1	(Constant)	−1.121	0.015		−75.581	0.000		
	Year	0.088	0.001	0.998	82.738	0.000	1.000	1.000
2	(Constant)	−1.090	0.020		−53.772	0.000		
	Year	0.079	0.004	0.896	18.249	0.000	0.052	19.123
	lnk/l	0.064	0.030	0.105	2.129	0.045	0.052	19.123

Dependent variable: lny/l

Table 7.2 TFP regression results (part 2)

Model		Unstandardized coefficients		Standardized coefficients			Collinearity	
		B	Standard error	Trial version	t	Sig.	Tolerance	VIF
1	(Constant)	−0.777	0.042		−18.297	0.000		
	lnk/l	0.594	0.027	0.977	22.144	0.000	1.000	1.000

Dependent variable: lny/l

the society each year as an indicator of labor input. The amount of capital stock (RMB 100 million) was an indicator of capital input. These figures were calculated based on total fixed asset investments and depreciated 10 years on average, with the residual value standing at 0. The regressions from Model 7.1 are illustrated in Table 7.1.

As shown in Table 7.1, there was collinearity among independent variables and the coefficient of $\ln K_t/L_t$ was not reasonable. So we phased out the time variable t and changed the regression model:

$$\ln Y_t/L_t = \ln A_0 + \alpha_K \ln K_t/L_t \qquad \text{(Model7.2)}$$

The regression calculation results of Model 7.2 are shown in Table 7.2.

We can be infer from Table 7.2 that the coefficient of lnKt/Lt was relatively reasonable. In order to illustrate the impact of time on TFP, we replaced the time variable t with a dummy variable and updated Model 7.1:

$$\ln Y_t/L_t = \ln A_0 + \alpha D_1 + \alpha_K \ln K_t/L_t \qquad \text{(Model7.3)}$$

D_1 (2000–2008) served as a dummy variable. Due to the lag effects, the dividends of China's reforms were not released until 2000–2008, which promoted a significant increase in the total output of the national economy. (China started its economic reform in 1978, its industrial reform focusing on the double-track price system in

Table 7.3 TFP regression results (part 3, model summary)

Model	R	R^2	Adjusted R^2	Standard error of estimate	Durbin-Watson
1	0.977[a]	0.955	0.953	0.139776885517297	
2	0.990[b]	0.980	0.978	0.095914124091899	0.445

[a]Predictor variable: (constant), lnk/l
[b]Predictor variable: (constant), lnk/l, D2 (2000–2008)

Table 7.4 TFP regression results, (part 3, model coefficients)

Model		Unstandardized coefficients		Standardized coefficients		
		B	Standard error	Trial version	t	Sig.
1	(Constant)	−.777	.042		−18.297	.000
	lnk/l	.594	.027	.977	22.144	.000
2	(Constant)	−.861	.033		−25.815	.000
	lnk/l	.602	.018	.990	32.586	.000
	D2(2000–2008)	.208	.040	.157	5.181	.000

Dependent variable: lny/l

Table 7.5 The calculation of total factor probability

Year	TFP	Growth rate	Time (year)	TFP	Growth rate
1991	0.319247	–	**2004**	0.527183	−1.205%
1992	0.362087	13.419%	**2005**	0.517078	−1.917%
1993	0.395325	9.179%	**2006**	0.515891	−0.230%
1994	0.422660	6.915%	**2007**	0.518802	0.564%
1995	0.435773	3.102%	**2008**	0.498868	−3.842%
1996	0.451748	3.666%	**2009**	0.468243	−6.139%
1997	0.469521	3.934%	**2010**	0.457842	−2.221%
1998	0.478294	1.869%	**2011**	0.440908	−3.699%
1999	0.495921	3.685%	**2012**	0.424646	−3.688%
2000	0.519057	4.665%	**2013**	0.405239	−4.570%
2001	0.522373	0.639%	**2014**	0.393236	−2.962%
2002	0.531110	1.673%	**2015**	0.384045	−2.337%
2003	0.533614	0.471%			

1984, and its housing reform in the 1990s. China became a member of the WTO in 2001). Data concerning the GDP growth rate from 1991 to 2015 also implied that the growth continued from 2000 to 2008.

The regression from Model 7.3 had better performance, which provides further evidence of the significant economic growth from 2000 to 2008 (Tables 7.3 and 7.4).

Based on the above results, we calculated $\alpha_K = 0.602$, and $\alpha_L = 0.398$.

Thus TFP can be calculated as $TFP_t = Y_t / K^{\alpha_K} L^{\alpha_L}$, and the results are shown in Table 7.5.

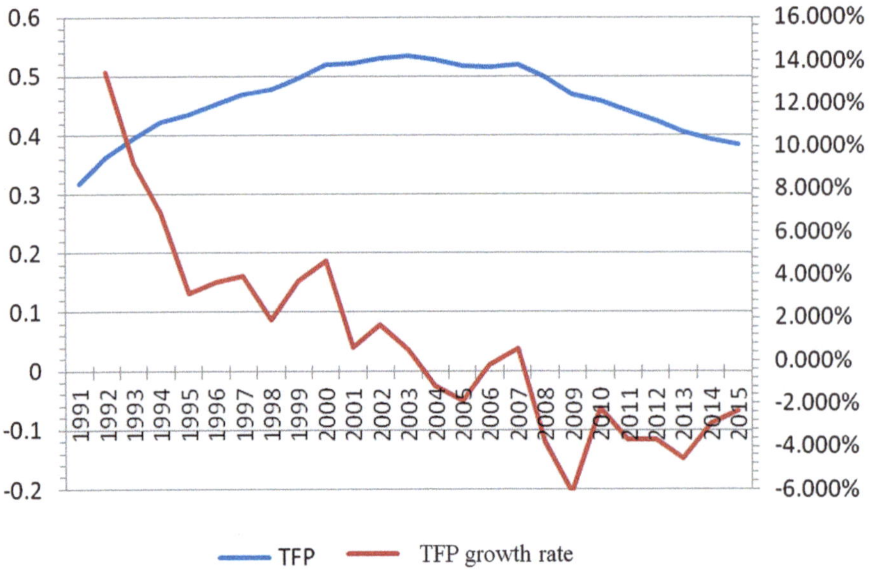

Fig. 7.3 Trends of TFP and TFP growth rate

7.2.2 *Trend of Total Factor Productivity*

We also looked at the changes of TFP and its growth rate over time. In the years prior to 2003, TFP was continuously rising. After 2004, the value declined (except for a slight rebound in 2007). Though gradually decreasing in the years before 2003, the TFP growth rate remained positive, whereas after 2004, the figure turned negative (Fig. 7.3).

From the changes of TFP, the following characteristics can be identified:

First, the returns on capital input were higher than the returns on labor input. This suggests that the role of labor has yet to be sufficiently leveraged to promote China's economic growth.

Second, since 2004, TFP began to decline, and its growth rate turned negative, showing that the output efficiency brought by the input of factors of production were gradually reduced. In this period, China adopted the typical input-based growth pattern and relied more on the input of capital, labor and other factors than on technical advancement to boost efficiency and then economic growth.

Third, the dividends of China's reforms, including the economic reform that began in 1978, the industrial reform characterized by the double-track price system in 1984, the housing reform in the 1990s and China's accession to the World Trade Organization, were gradually released from 2000 to 2008, exerting positive impacts on the Chinese economy.

Fourth, after 2008, as the dividend effects of these reforms started to wane and the massive economic stimulus programs resulted in redundant construction in

Table 7.6 The contributions of TFP to economic growth

	1996–2015	In stages 1996–1999	2000–2003	2004–2008	2009–2015
TFP growth rate	−7.80%	4.78%	1.39%	−2.72%	−9.44%
Output growth rate	134.53%	12.66%	14.36%	25.88%	26.84%
Contribution of TFP growth to output growth	−5.80%	37.73%	9.70%	−10.52%	−35.15%

Table 7.7 A model summary and estimates of parameters

Dependent variable: TFP									
	Model summary					Estimates of parameters			
Equation	R^2	F	df1	df2	Sig.	Constant	b1	b2	b3
Linear	.373	10.110	1	17	.005	.515	−.003		
Logarithmic	.285	6.792	1	17	.018	.531	−.024		
Quadratic	.378	4.870	2	16	.022	.519	−.004	4.596E-5	
Cubic	.611	7.855	3	15	.002	.453	.022	−.002	3.985E-5
Power-law	.290	6.941	1	17	.017	.533	−.053		
Exponential	.371	10.008	1	17	.006	.515	−.006		

The independent variable was the virtual economy aggregate/industrial added value

industries with overcapacity, technical progress, organizational innovation, professional operation and production innovation were crowded out, bringing down TFP.

We further analyzed the relationship between TFP and economic growth and arrived at three findings. First, from 1996 to 2015, the TFP of the Chinese economy generally rose and then fell, with an average annual TFP growth rate of −7.8%. In this period, the average annual growth rate of economic output was 134.53%, meaning that the contribution of TFP growth to output growth was roughly −5.8%. In general, instead of boosting output, productivity dampened economic growth from 1996 to 2015.

Second, from 1996 to 1999, the contribution of TFP growth to output growth was roughly 37.73%, and from 2000 to 2003, the contribution was nearly 9.7%. Therefore, the period of 1999–2003 was a golden period of TFP growth. Though its value appeared low, TFP contributed substantively to the increase of economic output, which also fully evidenced the effectiveness of a series of reforms China initiated in its transition from a planned economy to a market economy.

Third, from 2004 to 2015, TFP fell, and its growth rate was negative. From 2004 to 2008, the contribution of TFP growth to output growth was −10.52%, and from 2009 to 2015, the figure was −35.15% – a manifestation that the negative growth of TFP obstructed economic growth and that resource allocation at that time was unreasonable (Tables 7.6 and 7.7).

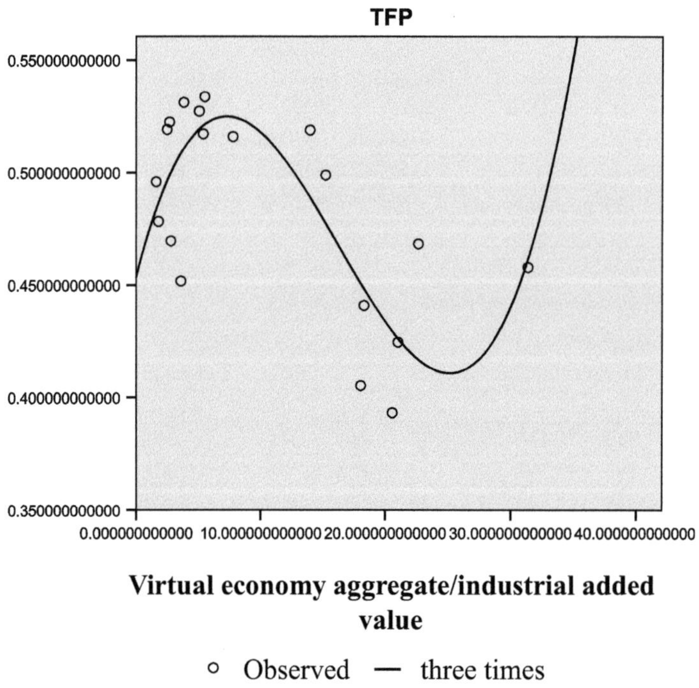

Fig. 7.4 Golden ratio of the virtual economy and the real economy

The regression equation was:

$$y_t = 0.00004X_t^3 - 0.002^* X_t^2 + 0.021 * X_t + 0.453 + \varepsilon_t$$

Based on the above equation, it can thus be inferred that the golden ratio of the virtual economy and the real economy that boosted TFP was X = 16.7. The data simulation is shown in (Fig 7.4).

Based on the data above, we found that when the aggregate of the virtual economy were 16.7 times that of the industrial added value, the two grew at a reasonable speed and scale and exerted a positive impact on TFP. The development of the virtual economy is a boost to the real economy and a country's economic growth. Figure 7.5 shows the changing trend of the ratios of the virtual economy aggregate to industrial added value. In 2008, the ratio reached 15.2; from 2009 to 2014, it far exceeded the golden ratio and peaked at 31.3 in 2010. This proves that the ratio of the virtual economy and the real economy have gone beyond a reasonable range since 2009. In other words, the virtual economy diverged away from the real economy, threatening to incur speculative excess and financial bubbles and undermine economic growth. Therefore, it is imperative to enforce economic structural reform.

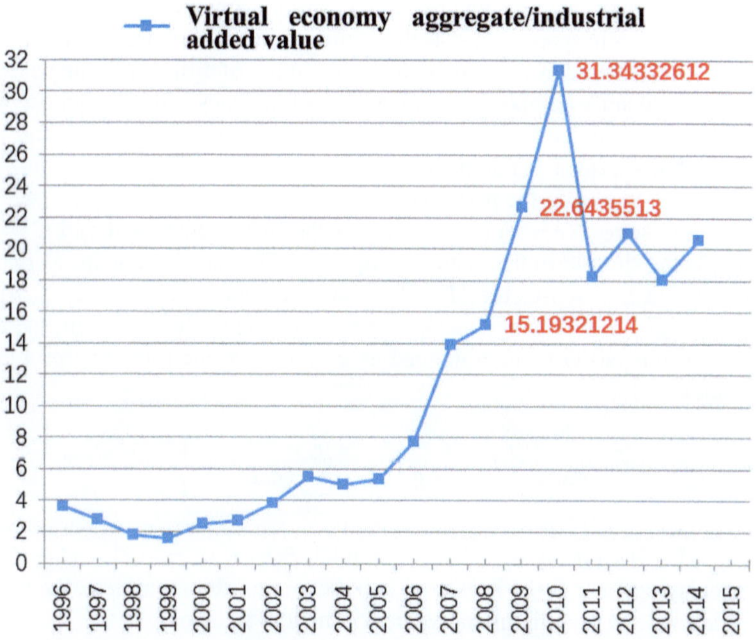

Fig. 7.5 The actual ratio of the virtual economy and the real economy

7.3 The Granger Causality Test of the Real Economy and the Virtual Economy

7.3.1 Filter Analysis of the Real Economy and the Virtual Economy

The development of the real economy and the virtual economy was influenced by both short-term fluctuations and long-term trends. China's real economy, its virtual economy and the major macroeconomic variables (such as GDP and economic value added) all cyclically fluctuated around their inherent deterministic trends. In addition, from the perspective of the micro-virtual economic sectors (such as the real estate, securities, funds, bonds and futures markets), though the trade volumes fluctuate to some extent, the fluctuations demonstrate certain trends. Therefore, no matter if it is observing macroeconomic fluctuations or analyzing trading changes of the virtual economic sectors from the microeconomic level, it's essential to understand the trend component of variables as well as their cyclical fluctuations. The filter method thus is very important; it can isolate the trends and cyclical fluctuations in a dynamic time series.

Currently, the most commonly used filter method was first proposed by the economists Robert J. Hodrick and Edward C. Prescott in their analysis of the economic climate of the U.S. The method – known as the HP filter method – has been widely applied in analysis and research of macroeconomic trends. The HP filter analyzes time series in spaces – just as the minimization of variance vitality in which time series is considered as a component superposition of different frequencies. The filter is used to identify components with a higher frequency and isolate those with a lower frequency. This is done to remove long-term trend components and study those of short-term, random fluctuations.

The HP filter works on the principle that supposes that $Y = \{y_1, y_2, \ldots, y_n\}$ is an economic time series, $G = \{g_1, g_2, \ldots, g_n\}$ is the trend component and $C = \{c_1, c_2, \ldots, c_n\}$ is the short-term fluctuation component. The sample contains as many as "n" subjects. In this sense, the HP filter can decompose $y_t(t = 1, 2, \ldots, n)$ into $y_t = g_t + c_t$, with g_t and c_t being unobservable values. Generally, in the time series Y, the unobservable part G is often defined as a solution to the following problem of minimization:

$$\min\left\{\sum_{t=1}^{n}(y_t - g_t)^2 + \lambda\sum_{t=1}^{n}(B(L)g_t)^2\right\}$$

Here, B (L) was a delay operator polynomial: $B(L) = (L^{-1} - 1) - (1 - L)$.

If the delay operator B (L) is entered into the minimization problem, the focus of the HP filter will be on minimizing values of the loss function:

$$\min\left\{\sum_{t=1}^{n}(y_t - g_t)^2 + \lambda\sum_{t=1}^{n}((g_{t+1} - g_t) - (g_t - g_{t-1}))^2\right\}$$

Next, we conduct the first derivative of $y_1, y_2, \ldots, y_n$ in the function above and use 0 as the derivative, which results in a trend time series y_n. After processing the HP filter, the sum of the short-term fluctuations equals $0 : \sum_{t=1}^{n} c_t = 0$. Regarding the minimization problem, $\lambda\sum_{t=1}^{n}(B(L)g_t)^2$ is used to adjust changes within the trend, and the value of $\lambda\sum_{t=1}^{n}(B(L)g_t)^2$ increases with λ. The value of λ determines the random fluctuations as well as the degree of variations. When $\lambda = 0$, $g_t = y_t$, the solution to the minimization problem lies in time series Y. As the value of λ increases, i.e. $\lambda \to \infty$, the estimated trend will fluctuate in a less volatile manner. When $\lambda \to \infty$, the estimated trend will be closer to a linear function. At this point, the HP filter can be replaced by the method of least squares.

Decomposed through the HP filter method, the trend components and fluctuation components of each variable will be identified. The trend component of industrial added value can be viewed as the potential growth rate of China's real economy, demonstrating the growth potential and movement direction of China's real economy in the long run. As the changes are relatively smooth, the adjustment to its direction of movement can also be regarded as the embodiment of an economic cycle. The difference between actual growth rates and potential growth rates reflected through cyclical fluctuation components, i.e. the so-called short-term fluctuations, reveals short-term fluctuations of real economic growth caused by both internal and external environmental changes in the macroeconomy. It can reflect the information in a timely manner, and the change in its direction of movement can be considered as the adjustment to the small cycles in the real economy. Correspondingly, after the variables of the virtual economy, industrial added value and stock exchanges with the HR filter are decomposed, their trend and fluctuation components will be available, representing the virtual economy aggregate, TFP, as well as the long-term trend and short-term fluctuations of all the virtual economic sectors.

For the virtual economic sectors, the trend component can better demonstrate the construction of market mechanisms and the trend of development scale. But the fluctuation component reveals more about investments and speculation behaviors of the market in the short run.

With the HP filter decomposition, the trend components and short-term fluctuation components of all variables' time series data can be put in order. For example, the growth rate of industrial added value is composed of a trend component T_GY and a short-term fluctuation component C_GY, with T representing the trend component and C representing the short-term fluctuation component.

As all data collected are time series data, and a dynamic time series model should be used as the analysis basis, before deeper model-based analysis, it's essential that every variable be tested for smoothness, the existence of a unit root or same order integration. The results of the ADF test of all the trend variables and short-term fluctuation variables are shown in Table 7.8.

7.3.2 *Co-integration Analysis of Long-Term Trends and Short-Term Fluctuations*

We examined the relationship between the changing trends of industrial added value and the virtual economy. Then, using the above-mentioned theory and data analysis, we conducted a co-integration analysis of the trend components of all variables. If the longest time lag among all variables were 1, the test results of the Johansen test for co-integration were viable (Table 7.9).

Next, we studied the relationship between the short-term fluctuations of industrial added value and the virtual economic sectors. Then, with the above-mentioned theory and data analysis, we conducted a co-integration analysis of the fluctuation components of all variables. If the longest time lag among all variables were 1, the test results of the Johansen test for co-integration were viable (Table 7.10).

Table 7.8 Unit root test results

Variable		Equation	ADF value	Value %
Industrial added value	T_GY	(0,0,1)	−1.734424	90
	C_GY	(1,1,1)	−3.850451	99
TFP	T_TFP	(0,0,3)	−4.779547	95
	C_TFP	(0,0,0)	−2.307865	95
Virtual economy aggregate	T_XN	(1,1,1)	−1.054487	–
	Δ(T_XN)	(0,0,1)	−3.833167	95
	C_XN	(0,0,0)	−4.731076	95
Bond transactions	T_SPF	(0,0,1)	0.551812	–
	Δ(T_SPF)	(1,1,1)	−16.99257	99
	C_ZZ	(0,0,0)	−3.367211	95
Commercial housing	T_SPF	(0,0,1)	−5.852230	99
	C_ SPF	(0,0,2)	−3.759439	95
Future transactions	T_ QH	(1,1,1)	−3.430519	99
	C_ QH	(0,0,1)	−3.330019	95
Fund transactions	T_ JJ	(0,0,1)	−2.474125	95
	C_ JJ	(0,0,0)	−2.474125	95
Stock exchanges	T_ GP	(1,1,1)	−3.324769	99
	C_ GP	(0,0,0)	−4.792459	99

Note: Δ represents the first-order difference of variables; the three parameters in the equation represent the constant c, time trend t and lag order of the unit root test equation. The appearance of 0 means no c or t. And the inclusion of the lag order is to prevent residual terms from becoming white noise

Table 7.9 Test results of the co-integrating relationship between trend variables of industrial added value and six virtual economic sectors

Industrial added value	Hypothesized no. of CE(s)	Eigenvalue	Trace statistic	0.05 critical value	Prob.
With real economy	None	0.84838	50.21999	15.49471	1.53E-07
With real estate	None	0.987286	90.15775	15.49471	2.86E-06
With bond	None	0.998635	107.8645	15.49471	0.0001
With stock	None	0.954531	73.27511	12.3209	9.08E-06
With fund	None	0.971289	77.63794	15.49471	7.98E-08
With future	None	0.88992	44.84686	15.49471	6.87E-07

Table 7.10 Test results of the co-integrating relationship between fluctuation variables of industrial added value and six virtual economic sectors

Industrial added value	Hypothesized no. of CE(s)	Eigenvalue	Trace statistic	0.05 critical value	Prob.
With the real economy	None	0.454485	17.53104	15.49471	0.024350
With real estate	None	0.612791	15.6333	15.49471	0.047671
With bonds	None	0.895797	43.57517	15.49471	1.03E-06
With stocks	At most 1	0.414743	9.106962	3.841466	0.002546
With funds	None	0.706202	24.66595	15.49471	0.001589
With futures	At most 1	0.370955	7.880395	3.841466	0.005000

Table 7.11 The results of the Granger causality test of trend variables of industrial added value and virtual economic sectors

H0	F-statistic	Prob.	Conclusion
XNZZ_TREND does not Granger Cause GYZJZZZ_TREND	6.25701	0.01376	Null hypothesis rejected
GYZJZZZ_TREND does not Granger Cause XNZZ_TREND	3.81684	0.05213	Null hypothesis accepted

7.3.3 The Results of the Granger Causality Test of Long-Term Trends

The null hypothesis for the Granger causality test is that every current value of every variable can be explained by a lagged value of other variables. Notably, the variables capable of explaining are always borne out of variables with values to be explained.

The results of the Granger causality test demonstrated that in the long-term development trends of the virtual economy and the real economy, the development of the virtual economy as a whole had stable impacts on the real economy. Also, the development of the real economy (industrial added value) exerted little influence on that of the virtual economy. (Therefore, it's fair to say that virtual economic development can promote real economic growth, whereas real economic growth cannot account for the development features of the virtual economy, i.e. has only minimal influences.) In addition, there was a Granger causality relationship between the real economy and commodity housing, stocks, bonds and funds. And though the future development of the futures market can explain the development trend of the real economy, the latter cannot account for the former. The Granger causality relationship here was a one-way relationship (Tables 7.11 and 7.12).

Table 7.12 The results of the Granger causality test of development trend of industrial added value and virtual economic sectors

	Null hypothesis:	F-statistic	Prob.	Conclusion
Virtual economic sectors and the real economy	JJZZ_TREND does not Granger Cause GYZJZZZ_TREND	27.61371	0.000144328	Null hypothesis rejected
	QHZZ_TREND does not Granger Cause GYZJZZZ_TREND	20.60578	0.000131538	Null hypothesis rejected
	SPFZZ_TREND does not Granger Cause GYZJZZZ_TREND	73.41447	2.01E-05	Null hypothesis rejected
	ZQZZ_TREND does not Granger Cause GYZJZZZ_TREND	26.09087	0.000107569	Null Hypothesis rejected
	GPZZ_TREND does not Granger Cause GYZJZZZ_TREND	21.41368	0.000109927	Null hypothesis rejected
The real economy and virtual economic sectors	GYZJZZZ_TREND does not Granger Cause JJZZ_TREND	90.45124	1.10E-06	Null hypothesis rejected
	GYZJZZZ_TREND does not Granger Cause QHZZ_TREND	0.08902	0.91542943	Null hypothesis accepted
	GYZJZZZ_TREND does not Granger Cause SPFZZ_TREND	4.78308	0.04904182	Null hypothesis rejected
	GYZJZZZ_TREND does not Granger Cause ZQZZ_TREND	173.19784	1.74E-08	Null hypothesis rejected
	GYZJZZZ_TREND does not Granger Cause GPZZ_TREND	62.28029	4.60E-07	Null hypothesis rejected

7.3.4 The Results of the Granger Causality Test of Short-Term Fluctuations in the Virtual Economy and the Real Economy

As can be inferred from the results of the Granger causality test of short-term fluctuation statistics, at a significance level of below 5%, both the virtual economy and the real economy accepted the null hypothesis, showing that there was no Granger causality relationship between them (Table 7.13).

The Granger causality test of the short-term fluctuation statistics of the real economy and the virtual economic sectors (such as the stock, funds, commodity housing, bonds and futures markets) showed that when the significance level were 5%, the null hypothesis was rejected, i.e. the short-term fluctuations of the stock market and the funds markets experienced a Granger causality with those of the real

Table 7.13 The results of the Granger causality test of short-term fluctuations of industrial added value and virtual economic sectors

Null hypothesis:	F-statistic	Prob.	Conclusion
XNZZ_CC does not Granger Cause GYZJZZZ_CC	1.924326	0.188423	Null hypothesis accepted
GYZJZZZ_CC does not Granger Cause XNZZ_CC	0.453501	0.645855	Null hypothesis accepted

Table 7.14 The results of the Granger causality test of fluctuations of industrial added value and virtual economic sectors

	Null hypothesis:	F-statistic	Prob.	Conclusion
Virtual economic sectors and the real economy	GPZZ_CC does not Granger Cause GYZJZZZ_CC	5.313863	0.022245	Null hypothesis rejected
	JJZZ_CC does not Granger Cause GYZJZZZ_CC	5.973219	0.022341	Null hypothesis rejected
	QHZZ_CC does not Granger Cause GYZJZZZ_CC	0.211196	0.812561	Null hypothesis accepted
	SPFZZ_CC does not Granger Cause GYZJZZZ_CC	3.169271	0.104704	Null hypothesis accepted
	ZQZZ_CC does not Granger Cause GYZJZZZ_CC	0.661781	0.537137	Null hypothesis accepted
The real economy and virtual economic sectors	GYZJZZZ_CC does not Granger Cause GPZZ_CC	0.511444	0.61213	Null hypothesis accepted
	GYZJZZZ_CC does not Granger Cause JJZZ_CC	1.259649	0.329363	Null hypothesis accepted
	GYZJZZZ_CC does not Granger Cause QHZZ_CC	0.96491	0.408709	Null hypothesis accepted
	GYZJZZZ_CC does not Granger Cause SPFZZ_CC	1.277288	0.336592	Null hypothesis accepted
	GYZJZZZ_CC does not Granger Cause ZQZZ_CC	2.694697	0.115849	Null hypothesis accepted

economy. However, in case of the other markets, the null hypothesis was accepted, implying that there was no Granger causality between the short-term fluctuations of the real economy and the futures market, the commercial housing market or the bond market (Table 7.14).

Ultimately, the Granger causality between the real economy and various virtual economic sectors was evident. This means that the long-term healthy and sound development of the virtual economy was conducive to real economic growth, and the sound development of the real economy also promoted the growth of virtual markets. What's more, the short-term fluctuations of the stock market and the bond market can impact the short-term development of the real economy. Thus in the development of these two markets, long-term institutional analysis, trend analysis and risk control should be prioritized, and short-term fluctuations of the real economy should be highlighted. However, the short-term fluctuations of the futures market, the commodity housing market and the bond market have limited influence on the real economy. So in the development of these three markets, it's more important to enforce sustainable and standardized management that focus on mechanisms, regularities and trends.

7.4 Summary and Suggestions

In this chapter, we calculated the golden ratio of the real economy to the virtual economy. The calculations suggested that capital input contributed a decreasing amount to TFP; labor played a bigger role in production compared to capital; and the growth of TFP turned negative. This reveals that the current composition of factors of production was not sound. After conducting a regression analysis of the ratio between the real economy and the virtual economy and TFP, we discovered that when the size of the virtual economy were 16.7 times that of industrial added value in the real economy, both the virtual and the real economy were maintaining proper development paces and sizes. In this context, they can exert a positive impact on TFP, and the development of the virtual economy can effectively promote real economic and national economic growth. However, the data concerning China's economy showed that since 2009, the ratio between the virtual economy and the real economy has slipped out of the reasonable range: the virtual economy developed faster than the real economy and became bloated. This is likely to cause speculative excesses and financial bubbles and have a negative impact on economic growth. As a result, economic structural reform must be carried out. Based on our analyses, we recommend that future work should be conducted with an emphasis on improving and adjusting the following aspects:

1. **Comprehensive adjustments should be made to the industrial structure**. In light of the current TFP, it is quite necessary to carry out an industrial structural reform. In terms of the input of the factors of production, the government should focus more on the input of labor. For other factors of production which are related to industrial development and economic transformation, we should especially concentrate on structural and fundamental issues such as the coordinated development of the real economy and the virtual economy and consumption and saving ratios.
2. **Regulation and restrictions on the virtual economy should be strengthened.** The data showed that the ratio of the real economy to the virtual economy has fallen out of the optimal range. The development of the virtual economy is based

more on speculative psychology and the independent regularity of virtual capital than on the real economy. As a result, the prices of financial assets and real estate rise faster than the growth of productivity, thus presenting a bogus economic boom. The U.S. subprime crisis showed that once economic bubbles burst, it may have an adverse impact on every section in social reproduction and then harm the real economy. Therefore, in order to safeguard the healthy development of the real economy, competent authorities must restrict the growth of the bubble economy, and supervise and control various speculative activities which may facilitate the growth of bubbles.

3. **The access thresholds for financial institutions and capital market should be raised.** The virtual economy must develop in tandem with the real economy, to avoid excess liquidity and precisely and effectively channel funds to the real economy. First, we should raise the thresholds for financial institution establishment and capital market access; regulate the development order of the financial markets; strengthen policy requirements for market access in terms of product design, risk control, capital discipline, professional experience and technical application; and strengthen market access thresholds by regulating licenses when necessary. Second, we must be deeply aware of the essence of financial innovation, meet the essential requirements of financial innovation to see whether the practices can increase the efficiency of financial services in supporting the real economy and reduce financial and systematic risks, and govern and regulate the channel-type, replicated financial innovations like P2P and crowdfunding in a timely and proper manner. Third, for banking institutions which are equipped with sound risk management systems, we should shift from a business-oriented regulation to a capital-oriented one and intensify capital regulation. We also should encourage commercial banks to optimize their asset structure under capital disciplines, improve the efficiency and refinement of asset allocation, and facilitate the transformation of banking institutions to a model of low capital consumption.
4. **The construction of market economy should be deepened, and a two-way mechanism for promoting the real economy and the virtual economy should be established.** In the long run, there is a significant Granger causality between the real economy and various virtual economic sectors. This suggests that the healthy and stable development of the virtual economy in the long term can promote the growth of the real economy. Meanwhile, the sound development of the real economy can facilitate the growth of various market entities in the virtual economy. During the construction of the market economy and transformation, the coordination of policies introduced by different authorities has yet to be improved. As a result, policies in different markets are disconnected, and the exchanges, coordination, or mutual promotion remain insufficient. This is one reason why the virtual economy diverges from the real economy. For example,

many problems arise in the development of the real economy, such as resource exhaustion, environmental pollution, trade frictions, comparative advantage decline, and awkward economic structures; the virtual economy is also troubled by such issues as immoderate speculation and disproportions. Hence, in developing the real economy, we should focus on upgrading of economic structures and enhancing technology. In this way, it will provide the capital base for the healthy development of the virtual economy. But only when the virtual economy develops healthily and properly can it provide profound support for the real economy.

Chapter 8
Summary

8.1 Research Value

Debt is an organic component of the macroeconomy, and the sound development of the macroeconomy cannot be achieved without proper debt leverages. Nevertheless, the macroeconomy may be jeopardized when the total debt volume becomes too large. Among previous studies, there are few on the quantitative relationship between debt and economic growth. Hence arguments concerning debt lack necessary underpinnings, and debt-related policies lack theoretical basis. For this reason, we focused our study on debt problems in China and attempted to reveal the relationship between debt and economic growth by analyzing systematic and complete debt data.

Our research highlighted the problem of China's overall debt, the debt of various entities, the debt of various industries, and the ratio of the real economy to the virtual economy in China. Our work was comprised of three orientations:

First, the study was theory-oriented. Using certain theories, we focused on the relationship between debt and economic growth, which is a classical problem in macroeconomics. Yet so far, many theoretical and quantitative studies at the frontiers of economics at home and abroad have aimed at analyzing the problem of government debt, with no one systematically exploring the total debt of a country. Thus the classical economic theories we used for our innovative study were of great value. Meanwhile, the model construction and analysis of our study relied on theoretical models, calculations and metrological analysis methods in the form prior economic studies. Hence our conclusions are of theoretical value.

Second, our study was data-oriented. After theoretically elaborating on the relationship between debt and economic growth, we used a quantitative research paradigm to shift our focus to the analysis of debt data, especially the metrological analysis of debt and economic growth. However, we encountered challenges due to the limited accessibility of public debt data. In order to tackle this problem, our study creatively established several measurements for different variables when designing

X. Zhu et al., *A Study of the Turning Point of China's Debt*,
https://doi.org/10.1007/978-981-13-1325-7_8

specific research subjects and variables for the study of total debt. Also, in each chapter, we used theoretical arguments as a foundation for our data analysis. Therefore, this study also provided a model that other macroeconomic quantitative studies can follow.

Third, this study was policy-oriented. China's debt problems are not just an economic issue, but – more importantly – they present significant practical problems as well. The total debt in China remains at a very high level. How does debt influence economic growth? How can we properly adjust, regulate and manage debt from various entities, sectors and industries? These questions require sufficient theoretical and empirical evidence. The arguments and conclusions from our research can help answer these questions, which makes our study valuable in policymaking.

8.2 Research Summary

Using available data, we specified the measurements for China's total debt and the debt of various entities, and we elaborated on their current state and distribution characteristics. The curvilinear relationship between the total debt volume and economic growth was illustrated with a linear regression model. We found that the increase of total debt boosted GDP at the beginning; however, as the total debts reached a turning point, the GDP tended to decline. China's current total debt has already exceeded its turning point, which means that debt is now adversely influencing GDP. Therefore, it is urgent to promptly curb the debt size, improve economic structure and enhance sound economic development in China. We reached a similar conclusion based on our study of the debt of various entities.

In light of the influence of government debt on economic growth, it can be concluded that central government debt is still positively related to economic growth, while local government debt has already been damaging economic growth after exceeding its turning point years ago. In other words, further increases in local government debt would pose a more significant, negative impact on GDP performance. Therefore, at the current stage and for a rather long period to come, it is essential that China prioritize the absorption of local government debt in policymaking. Further, improvements are needed in financial transparency to promote economic restructuring and industrial adjustment and to propel the healthy and sound development of domestic economic activities.

Our study of the banking sector revealed that there also was a turning point for bank debt. The estimated turning point of bank debt suggested that the influence of the size of China's bank debt on GDP has reached (or is about to reach) the "critical point" of the descent stage. Hence, the banking sector needs to be cautious about the absolute size of debt, take appropriate measures to reduce bank debt, construct an assessment oriented to capital returns rather than rules and regulations, and promote commercial banks to transform from "scale banks" into "value banks."

The analysis of debt in various real economic sectors showed that although the debts of various industries were on the rise, their debt leverages have varied. Industry profitability is the main cause for the differentiation between trends within debt leverage in different industries. We also conducted an analysis of the turning point of debt in the chemical fiber manufacturing industry and petrochemical industry – two typical industries with overcapacity. The conclusions suggest that the debt of the chemical fiber manufacturing industry might have reached its turning point around 2014 when PTA capacity peaked, while the debt in the petrochemical industry might have crossed its turning point around 2011.

Our study of real estate-related industries revealed that they reached their debt turning points at different times. The coal industry reached its debt turning point in 2011; the iron and steel industry reached it the following year; and the non-ferrous metal industry and real estate industry reached it in 2013. However, the building materials industry has not reached its turning point of debt. Our study also suggests that the debt of the real estate industry includes two parts, i.e. household leverage (housing loans) on the demand side and real estate developers' leverage on the supply side. The debt problem within China's real estate industry primarily lies on the supply side. Unlike economic cycles, the debt turning point of the real estate industrial chain transits from upstream industries to downstream ones.

We also conducted theoretical and quantitative studies of the relationship between the real economy and the virtual economy. We calculated the golden ratio of the real economy to the virtual economy; we concluded that the real economy and the virtual economy can exert positive impacts on total factor productivity when the golden ratio is realized. Yet in China, this ratio fell out of the reasonable range in 2009. This means that the virtual economy developed faster than the real economy and became bloated; this caused speculative excesses and financial bubbles and negatively impacted economic growth. As a result, structural economic reform is needed.

8.3 Policy Suggestions

Based on the conclusions of the study, we make the following policy suggestions:

1. **Prioritize debt control in macroeconomic restructuring for integral control of China's total debt.**

The data showed that China's total debt is close to – or has reached – its turning point. In other words, credit or debt-driven GDP growth is hard to sustain. Further expansion of debt will exert a negative impact on economic growth. This to some extent verifies Reinhart's and Rogoff's "threshold theory." The awareness of reasonably using debt leverage should be raised across the whole society and the task of controlling debt size in macroeconomic restructuring should be prioritized. Admittedly, the leverage brought by constant expansion of debt can accelerate capital circulation and even drive economic development, but too much reliance on debt expansion is likely to harm the structure of economic development and even threaten the macroeconomic security of the entire society. Given the current total of debt in

China, various debt entities have been adept in using debt leverage to acquire funds for development and even instinctively turn to debt issuance once trapped in a financial dilemma.

The abusive use of debt, however, has dampened economic development. And given that China's overall debt is approaching – or has reached – its turning point, adjusting debt size has become a more pressing task. Relevant authorities should take multiple measures to adjust the overall debt level in China, to make it converge and stay at the optimum level in the long run. This means that China's overall debt size should correspond with economic growth, and the growth rate of the debt balance should be coordinated with the changing pace of macroeconomic figures. In terms of the debt of various entities, government debt and corporate debt are at extremely high levels, which has generated potential risks that might negatively impact macroeconomic operations. Thus auditing and supervision of debt should be enhanced, and debt expansion should be curbed with immediate measures. As for incurred debt, repayment pressure should be gradually relieved by slowly addressing the problem until the crisis subsides.

2. **Properly define the function and role of government in economic growth and strengthen regulation of government debt.**

China also faces a grim external development environment. The domestic consumption market, the private investment market and the labor market are all under pressure. Thus it is even more important to fully understand the functions and positions of governments. China's government debt indicates that local government debt has already negatively impacted economic growth. Though this is not the case with central government debt, we cannot afford to neglect its absolute volume. To effectively control government debt – especially local government debt – it is critical to strengthen the legal supervision system for government bonds. This will involve stipulating issuer qualifications, fund usage, targeted areas, debt repayment, information disclosure, crisis responses and disciplinary actions, and providing a basis for local government debt management and risk control. China also should work to improve its fiscal transparency and raise the efficiency of the use of government funds. Fiscal transparency constitutes the foundation of governmental macro-policies – especially fiscal policies – and provides basic conditions for the analysis of government balance sheets and the management of government debt. In managing government debt, increased fiscal transparency should be emphasized. We should actively draw on the experiences of foreign governments in improving fiscal transparency and gradually work to narrow the gap between China's fiscal transparency and international standards. Improvement in this regard can force the government to formulate more reasonable fiscal policies and thus avoid excessive debt.

3. **Accelerate comprehensive adjustments to the industrial structure to release more space for the real economy.**

The Chinese the real economy is confronted with a situation which requires adjustments to be made for various aspects of its industrial structure. First, it's important to fully understand industrial overcapacity and work to address the deep-rooted problems of excess capacity and obsolete structure in an effort to boost enterprises' competitiveness. The state of Chinese industrial overcapacity reveals that the material crux was insufficient enterprise competitiveness (rather than structural problems). As a result, the quality of products supplied cannot meet the upgraded demands, hence the supply-demand deviations. Therefore, to solve the problem of industrial surplus and excess capacity, the focus should not be on "de-capacity" but on enhancing the capacity of the real economy and improving the competitiveness of enterprises and products. Second, the government should take the disposal of "zombie enterprises" as a strategically important matter in industrial development, and vigorously tackle problems caused by these enterprises. China must seize the opportunity of the reform of state-owned enterprises to decisively dispose of "zombie enterprises" with low productivity and ineffective assets. It's important to dispose of the enterprises' assets at fair market prices through legal transactions of securities and property rights in the capital market. The structure of stock debts also must be safely optimized by lowering the debt leverage of some industries and taking on new debts rationally. In this way, the forms of state assets can be altered, and the risks of zombie enterprises can be mitigated. More capital will be guided into supporting industrial restructuring, upgrades and the development of the real economy. Third, China should adjust measures to local conditions for different industries and refrain from the practice of "one size fits all." It's essential to accelerate and strengthen the ownership reforms of state-owned large- and medium-sized iron and steel enterprises; encourage mergers and reorganizations that are beneficial to industrial growth; support the enterprises to introduce advanced techniques, new equipment and high-caliber workers; and improve day-to-day operations and management.

4. **Improve the competitiveness of banking sector through proactive "value management."**

We assert that value management is the future of commercial banks. "Value banks" are not a vacuous concept, but a construction built upon the concrete features of banks. Five things are especially important for Chinese banks. The first is to implement a strategy of developing "capital-light" businesses. As capital regulations become tighter, it is increasingly difficult and costly to raise exogenous capital. As a result, capital will be the most prominent constraint on banks' development. Banks need to focus on tapping internal potential and establishing a strategy of developing "capital-light" businesses by actively adjusting the business structure. The second is to strengthen intensive approaches of capital replenishment and maintain limited expansion. Banks need to continue improving profitability, enhancing internal capital accumulation and achieving intensive development. Meanwhile, they must proactively study and explore the application of innovative capital instruments and seek to replace high-level capital with low-level capital. They still have to optimize the structure of risky assets, prioritize the development of capital-light businesses like consumer loans and decrease the demands for capital replenishment. The third is to establish stable expectations for the return on investments. Banks should work to develop clear, sustainable dividend policies, achieve sufficient information disclosure, increase investors' earnings estimates in real terms and protect consumers' interests. And banks must keep equity refinancing to a minimum and avoid diluting the existing shareholders' equity. The fourth is to optimize the shareholding structure and facilitate capital flows. To meet the inherent requirement of increasing the value of banks, we need to build a moderately dispersed shareholding structure. A reasonable shareholding structure can help establish a sound governance structure: it should prevent excessive interventions of the majority shareholder in banks' operations and handle the insider control problem when shareholdings are too dispersed. The fifth is to work to achieve greater development of the banks by replacing scale-oriented drivers with technology-oriented ones. Banks adapt to industry trends and new, diversified customer demands by innovating various financial products and non-financial services. Sustainable growth relies on innovation rather than capital input.

5. **Push forward with "supply-side" reform in real estate market through various policy tools.**

The reform of the real estate industry relies on two important tools: demand-side tools and supply-side tools. Demand-side tools regulate the real estate market by regulating real estate demand. At the current stage, such tools are mostly administrative, usually manifesting themselves as purchase restrictions and credit limits when the market is overheated. Aside from administrative restrictions, Chinese authorities can persuade banks to reduce residential mortgage loans through "window guidance," thus controlling the real estate market by regulating financing from banks. Supply-side tools stabilize home prices by boosting the supply of homes. With such measures as increasing land supply for residential property development, raising the ratio of ordinary commodity residential housing, boosting the supply of low-income housing and accelerating the approval process, the government can put an end to the home price upsurge and irrational exuberance that is common in China's housing markets. Furthermore, as China has severe regional economic disparities and an uneven population distribution, workers and other resources tend to move to coastal areas and core cities, resulting in the net outflow of population from third- and fourth-tier cities. Hence the local foundation in support of stable home prices in these cities is weak. So in implementing supply-side reform of the real estate market in first-, second- and third-tier cities, the government must adjust measures to local conditions and propose solutions in a targeted manner. To promote reform in third- and fourth-tier cities, similar with that in the coal and steel industries with overcapacity, supply contraction may be warranted. Thus the first-tier cities are asked to release a proper amount of land and expand transferrable land resources with their naturally-endowed advantages and well-developed transportation networks to mitigate the increasingly prominent supply-demand contradiction.

6. **Strengthen supervision and control of virtual economy and impose harsher access control for financial institutions and capital markets.**

The data showed that the ratio of the real economy to the virtual economy has fallen out of the optimal range. The development of the virtual economy is based more on speculative psychology and the independent regularity of virtual capital than on the real economy. As a result, the prices of financial assets and real estate rise faster than the growth of productivity, thus presenting a bogus boom within the economy. The U.S. subprime crisis showed that once an economic bubble bursts, it may have an adverse impact on every economic sector which can harm the real economy. Therefore, in order to safeguard the healthy development of the real economy, competent authorities must restrict the growth of the bubble economy and supervise and control various speculative activities which may facilitate the growth of bubbles. First, we should (1) raise the thresholds for financial institution establishment and capital market access, (2) regulate the development order of the financial market, (3) strengthen policy requirements for market access in terms of product design, risk control, capital discipline, professional experience and technical application and (4) strengthen market access thresholds by regulating licenses when necessary. Second, we must be deeply aware of the essence of financial innovation. This means we must meet the essential requirements of financial innovation to see whether the practices can increase the efficiency of financial services in supporting the real economy and reduce financial and systematic risks. Governance and regulations should be replicated for financial innovations like P2P and crowdfunding in a timely and proper manner. Third, for banking institutions which are equipped with sound risk management systems, we should shift from business-oriented to capital-oriented regulations. Thus we should intensify capital regulations, press and encourage commercial banks to optimize their asset structure under capital disciplines, improve the efficiency and refinement of asset allocation, and facilitate the transformation of banking institutions to a model of low capital consumption.

Postscript

Debt is among the major macroeconomic factors shaping China's development. And the leverage ratio has always been of special importance to economists.

China's total debt now far exceeds its annual GDP. It's fair to say that the Chinese economy is faced with the grave challenge of structural adjustment issues, such as whether to expand scale or enhance value, and whether to increase or decrease leverage ratios. If the debt problem cannot be understood and analyzed from a macroeconomic perspective, and no rational and empirical judgment is made on the relationship between debt and the macroeconomy, it will be hard to realize comprehensive, realistic policies for development.

Based on such theories and practical predictions, we took great interest in studying various aspects of China's debt problem. We spent 3 years researching, discussing and writing this book. Hence this book is a culmination of our efforts.

The researchers (and authors) of this book include Xiaohuang Zhu, chairman of the Supervisory Board of CITIC Group Corporation and chairman of the Financial and Legal Behavior Research Society under the China Behavior Law Association; Song Lin, professor of the Business School of the Central University of Finance and Economics; Lin Wang, business manager of the risk management department of China Construction Bank; Wenqi Wu, senior analyst of China Asset Management Company; and Quanli Qin, PhD at the School of International Studies of Renmin University of China.

As the team leader, Prof. Xiaohuang Zhu set the theoretical objective of identifying debt turning points and clarified the direction, basic paths, data system and content framework of the study. Song Lin, who compiled this book, organized the scholars to select specific theoretical perspectives and methods; he also constructed calculation models with *massive* amounts of data.

The preface and Chap. 1 of this book were written by Xiaohuang Zhuang and Song Lin; Chaps. 2, 3, and 8 by Song Lin; Chap. 4 by Lin Wang; Chap. 5 by Wenqi Wu; Chap. 6 by Wenqi Wu and Lin Wang; and Chap. 7 by Quanli Qin and Lin Wang. Meanwhile, we have tremendous gratitude for the experts and scholars who actively participated in study discussions and offered their valuable opinions. Due to

X. Zhu et al., *A Study of the Turning Point of China's Debt*,
https://doi.org/10.1007/978-981-13-1325-7

the limited length of this postscript, the names of these experts and scholars shall not be listed here.

Since the field is always changing, we might have inadvertently made certain omissions in this academic study in regard to new ideas and econometric techniques. **Thus your criticism and opinions are most welcome**. We believe that with the support and insights of our readers, our study of China's debt problems will be more profound, thus providing ample reference for socioeconomic research and practice.

The authors
June 2018

References

Abbas A E. Decomposing the Cross Derivatives of a Maldistributed Utility Function into Risk Attitude and Value.[J]. Decision Analysis, 2011, 8(2):103–116.

Aizenman J, Lee J. International Reserves: Precautionary Versus Mercantilist Views, Theory and Evidence[J]. Open Economies Review, 2007, 18(2):191–214.

Alesina A, Perotti R. The Political Economy of Budget Deficits[J]. IMF Economic Review, 1995, 94(1):1–31.

Auerbach A J, Lee R. Welfare and Generational Equity in Sustainable Unfunded Pension Systems.[J]. Journal of Public Economics, 2011, 95(1–2):16–27.

Baldacci E, Kumar M. Fiscal Deficits, Public Debt, and Sovereign Bond Yields[J]. Social Science Electronic Publishing, 2010(8).

Barro R J. Money and the Price Level under the Gold Standard[J]. Economic Journal, 1979, 89 (353):13–33.

Burnside C. Currency crises and contingent liabilities[J]. Journal of International Economics, 2004, 62(1):25–52.

Feng Wencheng, Liu Ying. Interest Rate and Government Debt [J]. Research on Financial and Economic Issues, 1993(3):45–48.

Financial Bureau, Ministry of Finance. Debt Management Report 2016[R], Japan, 2016:164–170.

Folkerts-Landau D, Garber P, Lane T. Payment system reform in formerly centrally planned economics[J]. Journal of Banking & Finance, 1993, 17(5):849–868.

Furceri D, Zdzienickadurand A. The Consequences of Banking Crises on Public Debt[C],Groupe analyses et de Theory Economies (GATE), Centre national de la recherché identified (CNRS), University Lyon 2, Ecole Normal Supergenre, 2010:289–307.

Gao Haihong, Yu Yongding. Connotations and Conditions of RMB Internationalization [J]. International Economic Review, 2010(1):46–64.

Geys B. Explaining voter turnout: A review of aggregate-level research[J]. Electoral Studies, 2006, 25(4):637–663.

Greenspan A. Activism[J]. International Finance, 2011, 14(1):165–182.

Guo Lin, Chen Chunguang. On the Four Major Causes of China's Local Government Debt Risk [J]. Journal of Shandong University (Philosophy and Social Sciences), 2002(1):121–126.

Hildreth W B, Miller G J. Debt and the Local Economy: Problems in Benchmarking Local Government Debt Affordability[J]. Public Budgeting & Finance, 2002, 22(4):99–113.

Hu Wenjun. Some Thoughts on Local Government Debt Issuance in China [J]. New Technology & New Products of China, 2010(15):222–223.

Institute O S, Hogye M. Local government budgeting[J]. Popular Government, 2002.

X. Zhu et al., *A Study of the Turning Point of China's Debt*,
https://doi.org/10.1007/978-981-13-1325-7

Levine H. The Impact of Debt Management Policies on Borrowing Costs Incurred by U.S. State Governments[J]. Public Finance & Management, 2011, 11.

Lin Guoqing. A Study of the Local Government Debt Problem of Fujian Province. [J]. Development Research, 2002(11):26–28.

Lin Sheng. Preventing and Defusing Local Government Debt Risk [J]. Development Research, 2005(12):55–56.

Lu Xiaoming. Sustainability and Influences of U.S. Government Debt [J]. Studies of International Finance, 2011(8):27–33.

Mcdermott C J, Wescott R F. An Empirical Analysis of Fiscal Adjustments[J]. IMF Economic Review, 1996, 43(4):725–753.

Mello M. Estimates of the Marginal Product of Capital, 1970–2000 [J]. B.e.journal of Macroeconomics, 2009, 9(1).

Miao Lianying, Cheng Xueyang. On Deepening Reforms of the Tax System, Local Government Debt, and the Central-Local Fiscal Relations: From the Perspective of Constitutionalism [J]. Journal of Henan University of Economics and Law, 2009, 24(4):24–30.

Mikesell J L, Mullins D R. Reforms for Improved Efficiency in Public Budgeting and Finance: Improvements, Disappointments, and Work-in-Progress[J]. Public Budgeting & Finance, 2011, 31(4):1–30.

Plekhanov A, Singh R. How Should Subnational Government Borrowing Be Regulated? Some Cross-Country Empirical Evidence[J]. Imf Staff Papers, 2006, 53(54):4–4.

Reinhart C M, Rogoff K S. Growth in a Time of Debt[J]. American Economic Review, 2010, 100 (2):573–78.

Rui Guijie. Thoughts on Preventing and Defusing Local Government Debt Risks [J]. Review of Economics Research, 2003(90):36–40.

Saint-Paul G. Technological choice, financial markets and economic development[J]. European Economic Review, 1992, 36(4):763–781.

Sargent T J, Wallace N. Some Unpleasant Monetary Arithmetic[J]. Quarterly Review, 1981, 5.

Solow R M. Technical Progress and the Aggregate Production Function. Review of Economics & Statistics, 1957, 39(70):312–320.

The Securities Industry and Financial Markets Association (SIFMA), U.S. bond Market[Z], available at http://www.sifma.org/legal/, 2015.

Tian Huimin, Tian. A Study of Improving National Development Investment Efficiency Under the Background of Supply-side Structural Reform [J]. China Market, 2016(26):49–54.

Yin Shouxiang. A Study of the Theoretical Basis and Practical Significance of Issuing Local Government Bonds [J]. Economic Research Guide, 2009(18):11–12.

Zhang Ming. The Impact of Sub-prime Crisis on the Current International Monetary System [J]. World Economics and Politics, 2009(6):74–80.

Zhang Qiang, Chen Jiyu. On the Debt Risk and Investment and Financing Mechanism of Local Governments [J]. The Theory and Practice of Finance and Economics, 1995(5):22–25.